The Principles of Comedy Improv

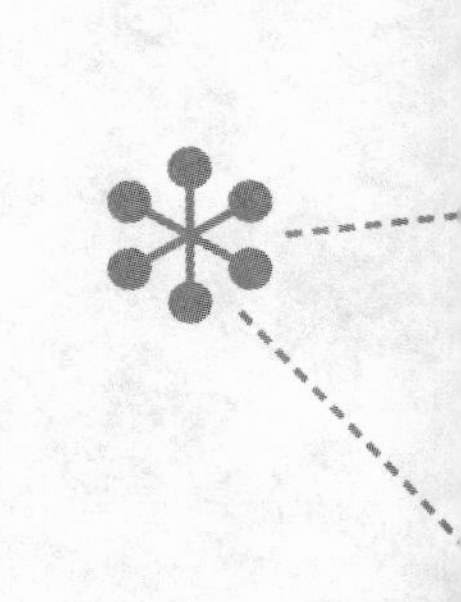

THE PRINCIPLES OF

Comedy Improv

Truths, Tales, and How to Improvise

Tom Blank

FOREWORD BY JENNIFER COOLIDGE

University of Iowa Press
Iowa City

University of Iowa Press, Iowa City 52242

uipress.uiowa.edu

ISBN 978-1-60938-885-0 (pbk)
ISBN 978-1-60938-886-7 (ebk)

Printed in the United States of America

Design by April Leidig

Printed on acid-free paper

Cataloging-in-Publication data is on file with the Library of Congress.

Contents

Foreword

BY JENNIFER COOLIDGE

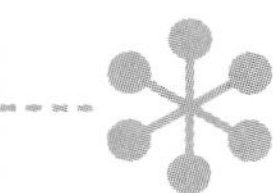

When I look back at the jobs I have been given over the years, there are four Christopher Guest films where all the dialogue is improvised. It is only in retrospect that I realize how valuable and beneficial improv has been in my life and work. It is the reason I am happy to write this foreword.

I got my first taste of improvisation at the Groundlings Theatre & School in Los Angeles, where I studied sketch writing and improv. When I started, I was far more interested in writing and putting on stage scenes that drew from my humiliating jobs or relationships.

Writing was about control. Improv is about discovery and flying without a net.

In improv, I was in awe of how quick others were—because I wasn't. Improv was a mystery to me. While my fellow classmates would kill to improvise in front of everyone, I would hide! Doing improv at first felt like standing in a puddle of my own sweat. It was humiliating, and nothing I said ever made sense. It was like one long anxiety attack. Somehow, I stuck with it, absorbed the spirit enough to get up there and trust that my brain would deliver some interesting factoid or realization or truth or emotion or random thing that made sense—but not in the way I could ever plan.

I've always been a sucker for a great improvisor. When somebody is really skilled and is confident treading in the unknown, it's like seeing inside someone's brain. It's surprising, entertaining, and irresistible.

Improv is the key to you. Everything in improv comes from you—words, actions, emotions. They come from some deep place in response to what others are doing. It's unedited. It's genuine. And it's always being seen for the first time. If you get good at it and can be honest, you'll be surprised at how seductive it is.

While at the Groundlings, I developed skills and made friends that I would have for life. Those skills opened new opportunities and changed how I interacted with the world. Things started to happen.

I was fortunate enough to get work in film, television, and theatre. It wasn't until much later that I realized how essential improv was to my creativity and career. It was the most important thing I had. It was always there to improve my situation—on the stage or in life.

Whether you're an actor or not, I think deep down we all want a reliable method to access whatever makes us unique, our innate abilities, so that when we reach down to pull something out of a hat, something is there.

I have shelves of acting books by big names like Meisner, Stanislavski, Chekhov, Adler, and Hagen, but I didn't know of any book that really captured this intimidating and beguiling art form. It has been so important to me, both personally and professionally. I don't know of any book that succeeds at breaking down improv as clearly as Tom's does, while making it so accessible. Of course, it makes sense that Tom would be the person to write the important improv book. He is a brilliant improvisor and instructor because he has an engineer's brain. Tom can explain how one can decipher the code to getting your thoughts said before your brain has a chance to critique them (the most important trick of all). Tom demystifies the intimidating aspects of improvisation while giving the future improvisor, you, the key to opening a world of possibilities that will make you forever grateful.

I appreciate improv now more than ever. It is a pure art form.

I'm excited for anyone who has access to this book. Read it and see where it takes you. I hope you wind up some place you never knew you always wanted to go.

PREFACE

Is This You?

Improvisation attracts people from a variety of backgrounds. Everyone holds different ideas about what improv is, how it's done, and what it creates. On this deep journey into comedy improv, we will discover truths that redefine those ideas, unlocking rich opportunities for you. But before we begin, let's look at you. This book will help four types of readers. Which of the following describes you?

1. **This book is for anyone who wonders if they should try improv, is learning improv, or is a seasoned improvisor looking for a new angle.** I hope this book inspires you to pursue your interests, supercharges your already pretty awesome skills, or provokes you to fling it across the room in disgusted disagreement. However it spurs you, let's call it mission accomplished.
2. **This book is for anyone who creates things, or who wishes they were the type of person who creates things.** Improvisation is the central, conscious, creative act. It is a skill that threads a lot of human activity and applies to our everyday life, whether creating a brunch, a book, or a conversation about a book over brunch. In improv we deal in real time with behaviors and beliefs that block us from creating spontaneously.
3. **This book is for anyone who works collaboratively with others.** With more than seven billion humans on the planet, you're likely to bump into a few at home, work, or play. Improvisational skills help those encounters, unleashing the power of multiple minds to create an experience beyond that conceived by an individual. Collaboration requires full communication through ideas, actions, and emotions to craft a shared reality. This is the sport of improvisors.

4. **This book is for everyone who likes brownies, zombies, dogs, cats, supercolliders, lumberjacks, Charles Darwin, sailing, Greek history, extraterrestrial life, mysteries of the pyramids, or super easy math tests.** This book contains all of that, and much more. If you have no interest in any of those things, this book is for you since you can skip those parts and finish reading before everyone else.

Whether your interest in improv is casual or deep, this book holds treasures. Improv—specifically comedy improv—fiddles with the mechanisms buried deep inside us that we use to navigate our lives. Exposing improv's secrets will empower you to change every moment of your life.

"Improv" is not just a quick way to say "improvisation." It refers to a simple setting that maximizes freedom: modest venues, small groups, and live interaction. It allows us to indulge any idea to its logical conclusion, making it an ideal laboratory for comedy. In this stripped-down environment we isolate a fundamental life skill, maybe *the* fundamental life skill: our ability to make something from whatever is available.

This is work that entertains and recharges us, but it also sharpens the tools we need to maneuver in a challenging world, one where technology, culture, and media ceaselessly strive to influence our lives and minds. It's no wonder that improv has gained in popularity as our world has gained in daunting complexity. Improv is an antidote.

This is a nonfiction work that contains a lot of fiction. I use stories to implant concepts before going into more technical discussions that are followed by pithy summaries. If this approach seems like a longer route, that's because it is. For our topic, the quickest way to understanding is the longer route. To get the spirit of our subject in our bones we must spend time with it. Short of hours and hours in workshops, this is the best way.

Fortunately, the longer route is a pleasure to travel. Consider it a scenic highway. You are getting a full tour and every stop on the itinerary has been well considered. Note that we will not stop to look at improv drills, which are better suited for in-person settings and described in detail by many other resources.

I am your guide on this scenic highway. This book is the concentration of my experiences as a student, performer, and instructor over the past twenty years. It informally began as I struggled to reconcile what I studied at each of the brand-name improv schools (Groundlings, UCB, Second City, iO) as well as various boutique theatres and gurus in Los Angeles. It took more shape as I helped create and run one of those boutique schools, and by teaching for the past decade at the Groundlings Theatre where I am a senior instructor. The book has been influenced by working with corporate clients such as Netflix, Saatchi and Saatchi, and Keck Medicine of USC, as well as by teaching tomorrow's artists through the National High School Institute at Northwestern University. Those experiences were viewed through, and built upon, my formal education in engineering (University of Notre Dame), business (Seattle University), and art (Art Institute of Seattle).

The stories in this book are from my extensive research and personal recollection and have been reviewed by academics who certify both are highly unreliable. But let's not be bothered by facts when we are dealing with truths.

Now, let's get to it.

PART ONE

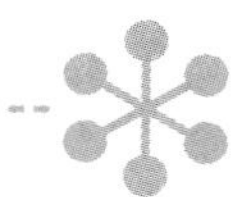

The Necessary Conditions

Details are dangerous. If we plunge in unprepared, we drown in information. So before we get to the detailed work, let's make sure the conditions are right. Because without the necessary conditions all is lost. I learned that the hard way. Here's my story.

I lived in an old walk-up apartment in Seattle that had one critical feature for the newly unemployed: a view of the water. I watched life skim across the surface of Lake Union through a window I propped open with a book. With each viewing I became more fascinated by sailing. But my rising interest wasn't innocent; it floated on a bubble of resentment. My anger swelled toward those sailors who grew up in sailing families with sailboats. I envied them, bitter that I didn't grow up near water. I moaned that I never had the time or opportunity. I stewed until one night I realized to myself—*wait, now I do live near the water, and I do have time, and the opportunity.* I could be a sailor. I just had to act.

The very next morning, I went to the south end of the lake to sign up for sailing lessons at the Wooden Boat Center. At the registration desk I knew the universe had given me a sign that I was on the right path. There was availability the following day for a lesson with Conner Swift—a retiree of the Coast Guard, the one-time youngest member of the U.S. Olympic sailing team competing in 6.9m Star-class keelboats, and a man who successfully soloed the Atlantic on his third attempt. It was extraordinary luck. But one thing I needed more than luck was patience. I couldn't wait twenty-four hours to start my destiny. Instead, a guy named Ernie was available in five minutes. Ernie was my man.

I found Ernie sitting on the back stairs of the Wooden Boat Center, chewing the last of his lunch, which appeared to be black licorice from a brown paper bag. He had no interest in my name, the waivers I had signed, or the fistful of cash I was to pay him.

"Bud, I don't worry about those things," he said. He crumpled up his bag and stuffed it into the pocket of his fleece vest. "I only sail." He examined a wet wad of licorice he had picked from his back teeth. "If you want to sail, follow me."

Ernie walked past me, down the walkway, beyond the docked boats, and onto the open beach.

I wanted to sail, so I followed.

From the shoreline, Ernie surveyed the water and the sky. He faced me, then cleared his throat. "Bud," he grinned, "to learn, you must do." He stared at me, holding his grin. He blinked. He blinked again. And again.

"I guess . . . I'll do?" I said.

"Yes," Ernie nodded slowly, "you will do." He gave me a thumbs up and laughed, "Let's sail, bud!"

I stood and watched as he marched into the lake fully clothed. The water rose above the knee patches on his Carhartt overalls as he continued farther into the lake until the water line settled just above his rope belt. He waited for me to join. "Bud," he shouted, "to learn you must do." I made my way in. We stood silently in the lake, looking at each other for what seemed like an hour. "How do you like sailing?" he asked, breaking the silence.

"I don't know. We're just standing in water."

Ernie shook his head and confessed, "This is not sailing."

He trudged out of the water and marched down the shore, following it as it curved to form a slender sand spit extending far out into the lake. He stood at its tip and raised his finger to the sky. He smiled, then marched into the water again. He waved for me to join him. I did.

Our new location was exposed to gusty winds and had waves that crested with white caps. We were out far enough that I had to struggle on my tiptoes to keep my mouth above the waterline. My ears grew numb. Ernie shivered and said, "Bud, this is wind. You can't sail without wind. Wind is the invisible force that moves you. Sometimes it's strong and sometimes it's weak. There are clues to find it: a whitecap, your hair, the sound in your ears. But you must always find the wind." I nodded. And waited.

I suffered the wet and cold and wind as long as I could, then through blue lips I pressed, "Hey Ernie, this doesn't seem . . ."

Ernie thrust his hand over my mouth. "Shhhh," he whispered. "How do you like sailing?"

"I hate it," I whispered back. "We're still standing in water but now there is a lot of wind."

Ernie splashed my face, "Of course, bud, because this is not sailing!"

He bounded out of the lake and disappeared into a small shed on the shore. He returned, giggling, holding a roll of canvas over his head. He handed one corner to me. We stood in the lake, with our hands above our heads, each gripping a corner of the canvas.

"Bud!" Ernie yelled into the heavy wind. "This is a sail! You can't sail without a sail! The sail is what makes the power of the wind real!" Sure enough, the wind flapped the sail that alternated between violently slapping the water and violently slapping my face. Ernie shouted, "How do you like sailing?!"

"This isn't sailing!" I yelled back. "We're idiots standing in water, making noise!"

Ernie looked shocked, then let go of his corner of the sail. It danced in a gust until coming to rest wrapped around my face, pinned in place by the wind. I heard Ernie's voice muffled through the wet canvas, "Exactly, bud! This is not sailing!"

I wanted to flip him off. I tried to toss off the sail, but the canvas was too heavy. I struggled to find air to breathe. I cursed at Ernie. I waded back toward shore, or what I thought was the direction of the shore but was farther into open water. The lake bottom dropped from beneath me. My anger turned to concern.

I thrashed my legs to stay afloat, but boots and jeans were horrible swimwear. My arms reached out to swim but the heavy sail weighed them down. I opened my eyes only to see the yellow of the canvas engulfing my head. Concern quickly turned to fear.

I coughed for air but choked in lake water. My lungs began to burn. Fear turned to panic.

I punched and kicked, desperate to find something solid that did not exist. Small stars began wandering across the blackness of my tightly closed eyes. Things had gone terribly wrong, terribly quickly, but I struggled to figure out what exactly I should be doing. So, I stopped doing anything. I remembered I left the window of my apartment propped open with a book.

I worried that rain would get in this winter. Then, I got sleepy. And for the first time all afternoon, I felt warm.

My quiet drift into sleep was interrupted by a muted voice, "Bud, drowning isn't sailing!" And in an instant, the warm darkness evaporated, replaced by cold gray sky and whipping winds and slapping waves. I gasped for air, coughing up lake water in fits. Standing above me in a sailing dinghy, clutching the waterlogged sail that had smothered me, was Ernie.

"Bud, you almost died!" Ernie shook his head, "Don't die, bud!" He hauled me aboard and I collapsed into the bottom of the boat. Ernie threw me a rolled-up wool blanket. He whistled while he struggled to rig the wet sail. I unrolled the blanket. At its center was a brown glass bottle, half-filled with liquid, labeled "XXX." I wrapped myself in the blanket. It smelled like wet dog. Ernie finished rigging.

He beamed at his work then shouted at the horizon, "Bud, you can't sail without a boat." He gave a one-two punch to the mast. "The boat controls the sail. It turns the wind power into motionnnnn!" He pushed the boom and the sail filled with wind. The boat turned and started to move.

And with that, Ernie began to sail around Lake Union while I shivered under the blanket. He sang a song that had a single verse: "Always remember you can't go sailing without a wind, a sail, and a boat!" It was a uniquely terrible song.

Ernie was oblivious to my reality. I was drenched and frozen and had just narrowly escaped a senseless death. "Hey," I snapped, "you could have just *told* me that."

Ernie's smile faded. He steered into the wind, the sail lost its fullness, and we stopped moving. The dinghy rocked gently. He stared at a buoy that was rolling back and forth in the bottom of the boat. The waves lapped the hull. "I'm not a good teller," Ernie revealed, "but I am a good shower. This is how I show. A boat makes sense after you know about a sail. A sail makes sense after you know about wind. Wind makes sense after you know about no wind." He shrugged. "So, I start there."

"You left out the cold, wet, dying bit," I said.

"Yeah, bud, learning can be uncomfortable." Ernie grinned and raised his left hand for a high five. He was missing two fingers. I slapped his hand hesitantly.

"Well, I guess now I know how to sail," I mumbled.

"No, bud, no!" Ernie laughed so hard he fell backward out of the boat. As he clambered back in he explained, "Now you know the first lesson. You know what you need every time you go out: a wind, a sail, and a boat. You can't sail without them. But they aren't sailing. If that's all you have, you'll struggle, and occasionally die. So, if you want to go places and party with your friends but not die, you need technique. Then you can sail with anybody you want, anywhere you want. But bud, even with technique, never go sailing without a wind, a sail, and a boat."

It was the most cogent thing he had said all afternoon. He pushed the boom. The sail filled with the evening breeze. The boat began to move.

Ernie was silent for the rest of our time together. As the daylight faded, we glided up to the dock. He dropped the sail, hopped on the deck, and secured the boat. I stepped out and turned to shake Ernie's hand. His grip was like a vise, a desperate vise. He reached out with his left hand and clutched my ascot. He drew me close. His breath reeked of black licorice. His eyes welled with tears.

"Bud," he pleaded, "please, please, please remember—no matter how much experience you get—before you go out always make sure you have a wind, a sail, and a boat. Every. Time." He began to weep. Then he fell to his knees, thrust out his fist, and pulled back his sleeve to reveal a tattoo on his forearm.

It was a simple graphic that looked like it was designed by a child and inked by a slightly older child. It was a wind, blowing on a sail, attached to a boat.

He broke down. I knelt beside him, unsure what to do. I asked why he was crying.

"Because," he looked up and, through spit and tears, sobbed, "this anecdote needs a dramatic end."

Ernie collapsed on the dock, rolled into the water, and wriggled off into its depths. His trail of bubbles traced a path far off into the lake, only to be swallowed by the encroaching night.

I never saw Ernie again.

The following week I returned for lessons and met Conner Swift, the retiree who sailed solo across the Atlantic. I asked about Ernie. "That man is a menace," he said, and then looking at the horizon, "and the best damned improv instructor you'll ever meet."

Ernie demonstrated the most important lessons about sailing, those things one can never set sail without. But at the same time, he revealed the most important lessons of improv.

A wind. A sail. And a boat.

Each means something to an improvisor. Each must be present to improvise. These are the most important lessons. That is why they are first.

1

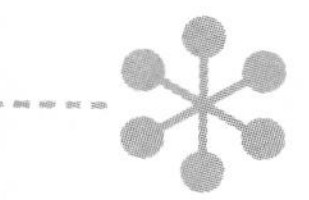

The Wind: Indulge

Never go sailing without a wind, a sail, and a boat. In improv the wind is our ability to indulge. We cannot improvise without it; it powers our motion. To see how it works, we must indulge in a little math.

The Problem

This math quiz assesses your aptitude for improv. Do not screw it up, your future depends on it. Ready, set, go!

From the selections, choose the correct answer to the equation $X + Y = 4$.

$$0 + 4 = 4$$
$$1 + 3 = 4$$
$$2 + 2 = 4$$
$$3 + 1 = 4$$
$$4 + 0 = 4$$

Time's up! Pencils down. Pass your papers to the aisle.

Congratulations, you got an A+. I won't check your answer because it doesn't matter. What matters is the process. If you noticed that each choice is a valid solution to the problem, good for you! They are. It makes grading easy.

If you hesitated when you tried to pick the correct answer, then good for you! You recognized the difficulty of trying to figure out the most valid answer from a list of equally valid answers.

If you clenched your butt cheeks and gave up as soon as you read "math quiz," then good for you! There are no more math quizzes in this book.

The Problem with That Problem

That math problem is indeterminate, it has more than one valid solution. We had five valid answers to choose from, but if we had included fractional or negative numbers the list of answers would be infinite, your decision more difficult, and this chapter much longer.

Life is loaded with indeterminate problems. They are not limited to the evils of math. They occur everywhere, big and small, such as:

- Side salad or fries?
- Should we get married?
- What do I write on a coworker's birthday card?

Some people find it difficult to choose from many valid options, others find it paralyzing. To resolve indeterminate problems in everyday life we rely on practicalities such as time, money, physics, and social conventions. We restrict choices further with personal codes or habits. If more help is needed, we have the eager assistance of family, government, media, or religion—all which help whittle our options down to "the correct answer"—what we could refer to as "helpers."

The problem is amplified in improv. A fictional world is absolutely filled with indeterminate problems, but our decision helpers are less relevant, maybe entirely irrelevant. And without these helpers, choosing the correct answer becomes maddeningly vaporous.

This is why making a choice, any choice, can be a monumental obstacle in improv. Your everyday strategy to be correct will destroy you. You need a new strategy, unless you want to be destroyed.

The Solution Is the Wind

Let's take the quiz again, after we redefine what it means to choose the correct answer. Instead of relying on external standards, use an internal one. I don't care what you use; it's whatever strikes you, just do it quickly. I assume you are like me and too lazy to turn back to the quiz, so here it is again.

From the selections, please choose the correct answer to the equation $X + Y = 4$.

$$0 + 4 = 4$$

$$1 + 3 = 4$$

$$2 + 2 = 4$$

3 + 1 = 4

4 + 0 = 4

How did you choose your answer? The first? The prettiest? The most symmetrical? I find even numbers friendly, odd numbers mean, and the talent of zero wasted when adding, so my choice is 2 + 2 = 4.

What you chose is not as important as how you chose. If you felt that process, then whoopee! You felt the wind!

To respond to an indeterminate problem, to be pushed in one of many equally valid directions, you must indulge some part of yourself. Just as the wind moves a boat when sailing, our ability to indulge moves us when improvising.

Indulge

To indulge is to allow yourself to enjoy a sensation. Usually the sensation is pleasurable. That may conjure images of couch naps, morning sex, bubble baths, rough sex, chocolate pudding, tired sex, and lotto tickets. That is a lovely Saturday, but all indulgences are not so decadent. Tater tots are indulgent, both to eat and to say. You may disagree. That's okay. Pleasure is different for everyone.

Indulging takes time. To rush through a candlelit bubble bath defeats the purpose of a candlelit bubble bath. Rushing kills pleasure because you focus on something other than the indulgent experience, such as whatever is rushing you. We must therefore carve out time to indulge, whether it's bubble baths or improv.

Indulgence requires that attention falls on someone. That someone will sometimes be you. It's not always comfortable to let others watch you indulge, like when you soak in a candlelit bubble bath. Fortunately, indulgences are not so revealing in improv. You must allow yourself to receive attention. You may be surprised how much people want to give it to you.

For our work, all sensations are not equal. We seek to indulge one thing.

Indulge Fun

We indulge fun. Fun is the prime mover for improv. Fun is characterized by buoyancy, possibility, novelty, irreverence, and joy. The spontaneity of improv and the flexibility of fun are perfect complements.

Of course, you could indulge in things other than fun such as terror, melancholy, or frenzy. What you indulge is rarely pure. It is a mix that defines your taste and changes what you create. Keep fun at the top of your list.

The word "indulge" is superior to "have." If you could will yourself into having fun, humanity would have never invented roller rinks. But we did because we know fun is a byproduct of doing something.

Through the activity of improvising, we find opportunities to indulge fun—but the goal is not to "have fun." That would invoke the pleasure paradox, which warns that the more directly one seeks pleasure the more elusive it is. What a horrible way to design a human. But that's what we got. So avoid making fun the goal or else it will scamper away.

Even if fun sits in front of you wagging its tail, you may not recognize it. You can reach adulthood being a stranger to fun because survival does not require the pursuit of it. Ironically, the point of survival might.

In your role in life, you may have had to suppress fun. Roles are often thrust upon us or adopted unconsciously: caretaker, overachiever, authoritarian, people pleaser, and so on. If we ignore fun for long enough, we can forget what it looks like, or worse, forget it even exists.

Luckily, fun never forgets us. It might be lounging in your brain with lips caked in cheese-puff dust, but it is dying to hit the gym. It wants to exercise. You just have to ask. Note that even after working out, getting ripped, and spraying on a tan your fun might speak softly. Listen close.

I had the opportunity to run an improv class for thirty fourth-graders. It was both enlightening and traumatic. They were connoisseurs of fun but wickedly fickle. Any time the "fun meter" dipped, they would announce impatiently with folded arms, "This is boring!" Then they would pursue their own brand of fun like running out of the gym screaming, wandering into storage closets, or crawling into odd crevices of the school. I felt the day was a success, mainly because I ended with same number of kids I started with. But just as importantly I realized that a fourth-grade fun connoisseur lives inside every adult. We just need to listen and always give that kid something to do.

Imposters of Fun

Do not confuse fun with one of its flashy imposters. Beware these three frauds.

IMPOSTER 1: FUNNY

Fun and funny may look alike, but they have their differences. That's not opinion, it's scientific fact.

The University of Southern California (USC) conducted a study that examined brain activity when people create and interpret funny things, published under the catchy title "The Neural Correlates of Humor Creativity." Test subjects were stuffed into a magnetic resonance imaging machine—researchers called an MRI, but I called a claustrophobic deafening tube—which recorded our brain activity while thinking of captions for cartoons and rating how funny each was. Other subjects were jammed into the MRI noise pipe and their brains were examined as they rated the funniness of comics that already had captions. This is what the mad USC scientists found:

1. When we create something we ultimately think is funny, the pleasure center of our brain fires first, followed by the linguistic and logic centers.
2. When we experience something we think is funny, the linguistic and logic centers fire first, followed by the pleasure centers.

I argue fun is closer to phenomenon #1. It is the pleasurable feeling you get from doing that precedes anything being interpreted as funny, even by you. That's why pondering "What would be funny?" is a creative dead end. Fun prefers less executive control and critical thought, which explains a lot of accidents. However if you can indulge funny and it is consistently fruitful, my hat is off to you. Also, you are a freak of science. USC says so.

IMPOSTER 2: CLEVER

Clever is the cousin of funny who drinks espresso in an apartment in Manhattan. Clever is not necessarily fun. Clever is not necessarily funny. Clever is simply . . . clever. It is mental athleticism. It is possible to achieve the trifecta of fun, funny, and clever—but clever is not the key. Be especially wary if you are one of those smart word talking people types. You know who you are.

IMPOSTER 3: FAMILIAR

The most cunning imposter of fun is familiarity.

Nine times out of nine, if you let familiarity be your guide you will end up in a place that is familiar, because that's the only destination familiarity knows. That sentence was so obvious it was hard to write. But it needs to be said.

Familiarity results when any activity, thought, or feeling has become routine, be it conscious or unconscious, beneficial or damaging. Whether it's a child demanding the same storybook or an adult arriving late to work yet again, familiarity is oblivious to its impact. Familiarity only craves the security of knowing what will happen, so it holds our hand as we mosey along the deep valleys of well-worn neural pathways. Mmmm, that sounds pleasant. And it is.

But it is not necessarily fun.

Fun and Fear Are Friends

Improvising may provoke fear, and that's okay. Fun and fear belong to the pantheon of celebrated contrasts: sweet and salty, pleasure and pain, peanut butter and banana. You know some of their collaborations: suspense movies, roller coasters, and skydiving.

A manageable amount of fear in an improvisor is not only expected but a sign of mental health. What is manageable? If you vomit, but keep it off the carpet, that is manageable.

There is no use denying fear, your physiology doesn't lie. You can't stop your adrenal glands from oozing rocket fuel, but it's up to you to determine if those signs point to a true threat. Pro tip: in improv they usually don't, you're just doing something different.

However, fear can signal when the natural enemy of fun does arrive: when things become unsafe.

Fun Needs Safety

It was 45,000 BC when Grog the Pointy Stick Maker first lamented "It all fun and game until Grog lose eye," but his wisdom applies to improv today just as it did in Upper Paleolithic times. While pioneering fun, Neanderthals discovered injury could mean death or, worse, bed rest in a cave thousands of years before the invention of the window.

A Neanderthal's concern also extended to others, as they cared for ailing members of their clans for years. Their tender hearts and massive brow ridges seduced more than a few articulate *Homo sapiens*.

Their love children were taught the need for both physical and emotional safety when indulging fun. Petroglyphs show that before daily improv class, each hairy child scratched out *safety is when no thing that matters is in jeopardy.* Their ancient definition deserves a closer look.

- Things that matter include whoever is participating in an event, both performers and audience, and extends to whomever (or whatever) those people care about.
- Jeopardy occurs when the probability of harm feels like it exceeds a threshold. The threshold is relative, and it is often noted by "Ooh, that's too far."
- The harm can be emotional or physical and must only be believed, even if it is scientifically improbable. No one feels safe in a hotel they believe is haunted, even though science has proven that ghosts are friendly.
- We must also believe the harm exists in everyday reality, not just a fictional reality. If we thought Godzilla crushed actual cities, it wouldn't be fun to watch Godzilla crush cities.
- People may have an exceptional class of things that is so dear they can never be jeopardized in any reality, such as cute babies, cute puppies, and cultural or religious figures who may or may not be cute.

When we feel unsafe, our DNA compels us to protect ourselves and others. We have crossed a boundary. The fun ends. The wind has died.

That boundary depends on the situation and is different for each performer and audience member. An improvisor gets a feel for the collective boundary of the group. That boundary is not fixed. It can be pushed and probed from moment to moment. Sensitivity to it allows you to toy with what can be said and not said, what can be done and not done. Occasionally you may misjudge and "cross the line," which is how you learn where the line is.

It's Not All About You

We have focused on your experience, your indulgence, your fun. You, you, you! So selfish!

We did that for a reason.

The ability to indulge your fun prepares you to indulge another's. If you played along with my math quiz (without eye-rolling) you already have a sense for indulging others. You may have supernatural faith that another person's fun may take you to some unexpected place that you find fun. That is super, and natural, and true.

After that, it's a tiny stretch for "another" to include many others, which you might call "the audience." You are wonderful, but remember it is not just about you.

- ❊ Indulge yourself.
- ❊ Indulge another.
- ❊ Indulge the audience.

Wrap It Up

It's tempting to conclude "Improv is all about fun! Wheeeeee, I can finally be wacky meeeeeee!"

Please, don't.

Remember—a wind, a sail, and a boat are required to sail, but they are not sailing. Letting the wind toss you around is not sailing. Indulging fun blindly is not improvising. Indulging fun is a necessary—but not sufficient—condition to create.

In improv, indulging fun moves you toward the correct choice when faced with innumerable correct choices.

Now, go have fun! (You know what I mean.)

2

The Sail: Share

A sail manifests the power of the wind. In improv, the sail is our ability to share. But what do we share?

Sharing

Everyone should have mastered sharing before graduating childhood. The following exercise determines if you deserved that diploma.

In the table, draw a line from an item you like in column A to an item you like in column B, then draw a line from your chosen item in column B to one item in column C . . . and so on until you have a line connecting one item from each column. Make the line as expressive as you like. Style counts.

A	B	C	D	E	F
My mind	is like	a Neanderthal	who enjoys	heated debate	!
My true self	would prefer	a dog	skilled at	filing state taxes	.
My soul mate	will be	a robot	who opposes	deep eye contact	?
My boss	wants to be	an outlaw	who weeps at	painting figurines	. . .

Now, using your hand like a sock puppet (naked of the sock), in your best hand voice have your hand recite the sentence formed by the connected items.

If you completed that exercise, thank you for sharing. If you skipped that exercise, thank you for sharing your reluctance to share. Either way, I validate your childhood diploma.

We don't care about the sentence; we care about what happened during its creation. To create and bring that riveting work to life you shared three different things, each in a different way, and all are demanded by improv.

- ✻ You shared the focus.
- ✻ You shared the work.
- ✻ You shared yourself.

Share the Focus

An improvisor shares the focus. The focus is what has attention. Whatever has focus becomes the raw material we use to make a reality, including a fictional reality. For people to have a common experience, like an improvised event, everyone must attend to the same elements. Thus, the focus for a group must always be clear. Competition for attention is counterproductive.

The exercise you completed serves as an example. A random person lucky enough to read our sentence would alternate between the words I wrote and the connections you drew. Their focus would bounce between your brilliant work and my brilliant work. By alternating, you and I share the reader's focus—a little for you, a little for me. We are so polite!

However, our sentence is simple. As more elements compete for attention, we must be more aware of the focus and how we influence it. For example, when looking at a photograph, our attention will drift from elements that are blurry toward elements that are clear. A fancy photographer purposefully influences the viewer's perceptual focus with use of optical focus.

A movie has many more elements competing for attention. At each moment in a film the focus could be on any part of the moving image on the screen or the sound blasting from the speakers or the person sitting next to you in the theatre munching popcorn. A director influences the viewer's focus by using artsy devices such as camera movement, editing, sound effects, and scoring.

Improvising on a small stage in front of a live audience (a common but not exclusive venue for improv), can have even more in competition for attention. There is less control over the environment, what a viewer hears, and where a viewer looks. An improvisor can still influence attention by using improv devices (which we'll examine in later chapters). However, not only are those devices less precise, but multiple improvisors influence the focus at the same time. In this wildness of less control and more improvisors, it is critical to share focus to form a common experience.

Sharing in this sense means to use in turns: give attention to whatever demands it, when demanded, and avoid pulling attention away prematurely. Sometimes what demands attention will be you, or someone else, or the audience, or an air-conditioning unit that is annoyingly loud. Focus lands on something for an appropriate time and then moves on. That appropriate time is longer than too short, and shorter than too long. It is a feeling. Let experience be your guide.

What gets focus is usually that which is different. It is what person A says after person B has spoken, what moves when all else is still, what is still when all else moves; what is noisy when there is silence, what is silent when all is noisy; who enters the room we are in, who is in the room we enter; the happy reaction to sad news, or the sad reaction to happy news. It all depends.

What it depends on is complicated, but don't sweat those details. Everyday life has wired you to focus on what is different. Obey your wiring.

There is always a focus if there is an observer. If it seems like nothing has the focus, if you swear nothing grabs your attention, then nothingness has your attention. Similarly, if everything competes for the focus, the resulting chaos commands attention. The focus can be the emptiness of a blank page, the ambiguity of a blurred photo, the inscrutability of white noise.

RULES FOR SHARING THE FOCUS

Sharing the focus is just like a playing with a ball, except the focus never goes flat. You should already know how to do this, but for those who got distracted by the library on the way to the playground, here are eight rules for playing with a ball.

1. **Keep your eye on the ball.** Always know where it is even if you aren't staring at it.
2. **If you don't have the ball, be open.** You are always playing, even without the ball. Stay open.
3. **If you haven't had the ball, get it.** It's easy to whisper "maybe next time," as recess winds down, but that only earns you a tinier cell in Procrastination Hell. Get involved.
4. **If someone won't share the ball, take it.** The game where one person bounced a ball for sixty minutes was called Dribbleball,

and it never caught on. If someone briefly loses their mind and hogs the ball, assert yourself. They want you to.

5. **If you have the ball, enjoy it.** You may want to rush, fearing someone will take the ball from you. Don't.
6. **If someone has not had the ball, give it to them.** If you lack this instinct, my words may not fix what is broken in you. But I'll try: everybody needs a hand once and a while.
7. **If you are done with the ball, let it go.** It's the old "if you love something, set it free" nonsense. But it's not nonsense. It must go to return.
8. **If the ball rolls into that puddle with an oil sheen and dead worms, grab it and wipe it off.** Each time with the ball is not always awesomeness. Do what needs to be done.

Share the Work

When we constructed our sentence at the beginning of this chapter, I tried to split the work between the two of us. Whether the sentence we made was really awesome or really, really awesome doesn't matter. We found that creating is easier when sharing the effort. Sharing in this sense means to participate jointly.

Sharing the work will be difficult if you are the responsible type who is the last to leave the office when the big project is due. In improv it is responsible to not be too responsible. Share the work so everyone owns the result. Even if it's crap, it's *our* crap. Doing too much is not sharing.

Sharing the work will also be difficult if you are the lazy type who naps when the big project is due. For improv, be lazier. An improvisor's work is pleasure and it takes effort to resist pleasure. It takes less effort to share in the labor than to do nothing.

Share Yourself

To share yourself means to reveal something to another. The thing you share is personal; it makes you perceptible as an individual.

Back in our sentence exercise, you shared your mind's inner workings both by the words you chose and the quality of the lines you used to connect them. How your hand recited our sentence also offered a glimpse into you. But you have plenty more to offer, such as how you think and feel, what you know, and even your physical movement.

You will be comfortable sharing yourself in some ways—those are your strengths. You will be uncomfortable sharing yourself in other ways—those are your strengths you have yet to discover. Hidden strengths? Yes, please.

If sharing yourself with a bunch of strangers makes you giddy, you're set. I look forward to your one-person show and its sequels.

If sharing yourself sounds icky, I have good news: we don't have to hear your traumas and darkness; that's your cat's job. But we desperately want you to mine your life and incorporate snippets of it into the work. It proves to other humans that you are human, and that kind of sharing makes friends.

If sharing still makes you feel icky, it may be because you can't imagine you have interesting life experiences. I have more good news: being uninteresting is plenty. Our experiences are rarely profound, occasionally story worthy, and usually trivial. If profound was common in your life, it would be trivial. Bam! Smoke that in your logic pipe.

If you still feel icky, you may have shingles.

You never know what experiences from your life will resonate with others. I vividly recall the pink plastic retainer case adorned with a My Little Pony sticker mentioned by a scene partner years ago. I never had a case like that, and, for the record, I definitely was not into My Little Pony. But her words conjured in me an image that was nearly palpable, and it still takes up room in my brain. Perhaps it jangled the "unfriendly childhood medical device" memories in me. But if it works, it works. We will examine more about sharing yourself in a later chapter.

Wrap It Up

A wind, a sail, and a boat are required for sailing, but they are not sailing. The sail manifests the power of the wind. For improv, the sail is your ability to share.

You must share the focus by taking turns, share the work by participating jointly, and share yourself by revealing bits of you.

3

The Boat: Commit

In sailing, a boat converts the power of the wind and sail into motion. In improv, commitment converts the power of shared fun into motion. Commitment is not improvising, but it is required to improvise.

The best way to understand commitment is with this simple exercise.

Step 1. Get pen and paper. You may be tempted to do this on a computer, but don't. It's important to write this out by hand.

Step 2. Write the details of your most recent memory. You may be tempted to describe a big event that happened today, but don't. It's important to use your most recent memory, most likely from when you started to read this chapter.

Step 3. Repeat this process, going back one minute at a time until you describe every memory that you have. You may be tempted to stop when you run out of conscious memories, but don't. It's important you go back to your birth, or preferably, before.

Step 4. Get highlighters and highlight every verb in yellow, every noun in orange, and every adjective in blue. You may be tempted to highlight other parts of speech in green, but don't. It's important the process doesn't take too long.

Step 5. Get scissors and cut out each of the highlighted words. You may be tempted to use scissors that were purchased at a store, but don't. It's important you discover iron ore in your neighborhood and smelt it so you can blacksmith your own scissors.

Step 6. Count how frequently you used each unique word while you sort them into piles. You may be tempted to use the restroom, but don't. It's important to do all these steps in one sitting.

Step 7. Research the meanings of the words that are most important to you, based on their frequency. You may be tempted to use a dictionary, but don't. It's important you visit each word's country of origin and learn the ancient form of its source language while absorbing the context of the parent culture which, of course, you must adjust for historic developments.

Step 8. If at this point if you don't grasp commitment, go back to step 1.

Phew, that was a lot! I hope before you smelted iron you said, "Screw this." But if you completed all these steps, I would like to say congratulations. Also, I am so, so, so sorry.

This was an exercise in commitment, or hopefully, in not committing. Whether you completed the tasks or not, we have something to examine. Somewhere from step 1 to step 8 you had to decide if you trusted if all that effort was a good use of your resources. That illuminates a pithy definition of what it means to commit, which is so important it deserves its own line:

> Committing is deciding to invest your resources into something based on trust.

Let's look at each of those parts of committing, one of the three necessary conditions of improv.

Decide

Commitment cannot happen on its own. It is something you must decide. Committing is your conscious choice to think and behave in a particular way. Or if you prefer, not to think and behave in many other ways. This is what the proto-Romanians of the seventh century preferred when they invented the word, evidenced by the root Latin term *dēcīdere,* which means "to cut off." They knew that to choose one path requires that we sever others. This is difficult for humans to do.

The English acknowledged this difficulty when, several centuries later, they invented a helpful device that evolved into what we now call the guillotine. The English discovered that people, even surly executioners, found it difficult to commit to the needed task. A half-hearted executioner produced work that was protracted, painful, and messy. No one liked it. A half-hearted improvisor gets the same results.

The brilliance of the guillotine is that once set in motion, once a single decision is made to yank a cord, it unflinchingly executes its job. The commitment is made. We may not like its role, but we can admire its decisiveness. When you vacillate in improv, recall the comforting image of the guillotine.

Trust

The decision to invest resources in something is based on trust. But trust what?

When you chose to ignore my instructions at the beginning of this chapter, you trusted something. Wisely, it was not me. You trusted you. You cannot trust anyone or anything until you first trust your own decision to trust. That is a clumsy sentence but offers impeccable reasoning.

Trust, in this sense, is the belief that something will act in your best interest. The principle thing that should act in your best interest is you. However, you may be leery of that person for good reason.

If anyone is intimate with every one of your screwups in vivid detail, it is you. You also may be graced with friends or family who enjoy reminiscing about your foibles. You and your tribe, regardless of intent, may have quietly eroded trust in yourself.

And even if you drip with confidence from your life's achievements, hopefully you discovered that trusting yourself in one arena does not justify trust in another. You may have confidence to raise a child, but not to broil salmon. No matter how crowded your trophy shelf, you can feel a novel lack of confidence in improv. That's okay, maybe even prudent.

Thus improvisors earn their own trust, just as a stranger would. Through experience we see how we make decisions, improve them, stand on them, and survive them. Occasionally this will produce an exquisitely unpleasant moment. Expect this badge of honor—it is a necessary experience. Even if it feels like you lost, you won.

Only after you trust your decisions and ability to handle their results can you commit. Magically, as you build trust in yourself, it will be easier to rely on other improvisors and the process of improv.

On the path of developing trust, you may be visited by doubt, often accompanied by its good pals, excitement and nervousness. They can appear on any journey into the unknown, such as every time you improvise. Be careful not to misinterpret them.

Doubt and pals cannot predict your future. They are not telling you the unknown contains something unmanageable. For all we know, the unknown holds an endless supply of freshly baked brownies.

Doubt and pals are encouraging you to marshal your resources, to prepare yourself. They sense the unknown and are fortifying you; they are not questioning your abilities or the trust you have placed in yourself.

For perspective, remember that in the world of human improv all challenges are human sized and have human solutions. And fortunately, you are human. You lucky dog.

Resources

"Commitment demands your resources!" That sounds like what you would hear while being fitted for a robe in a cult. It is. But improv is a benign cult. Benign cults are cool. Controlling cults are lame. That's what my cult tells me to say.

There are three resources you invest: time, energy, and money.

TIME

You must invest time into improv. There are no shortcuts. This applies to both mind-time and body-time because mind and body do not always travel together.

When your body goes through a doorway, your mind usually lags. It is wrapping up other business, like remembering your parking spot or wondering if your breath smells like coffee. To get your mind anywhere on time, your body must get there early.

To keep your mind present until the end, don't prepare to leave until after the event is over. Jangling keys, closing a backpack, or checking to see if Destiny left you a voice message are signs your mind has already departed.

Give yourself the best opportunity, no matter what the event—a class, a show, or a kiss. Arrive early, stay present until the end, and leave only after it's over.

ENERGY

When investing energy, I don't mean energy in the woo-woo new agey way. I mean it in a woo-woo science way. It's burning your blood glucose and glycogen stores to create energy at a rate above your baseline metabolic rate. It's no different than going to the gym, and you know how easy that is.

That energy is spent on thought, emotion, and physical movement. It may be quiet, such as paying attention, or it can be big like jumping up and down. How it manifests may differ from moment to moment, but you invest energy continuously.

MONEY

Improv needs people and a venue, both of which can require money. Whether it seems like a little or a lot is relative to your situation. If it's any solace, when parting with your dollars, know that only a few coaches, instructors, and performers live in a diamond mansion built on a mountain of improv cash.

Having someone more experienced, like an instructor, assist you in your improv journey is highly recommended. I can't say it is impossible to learn improv alone, but it seems impossible. Nor can you learn it exclusively from an earth-shattering book, like the one you are reading. Improv requires interaction with others. We'll talk more about schools in part six.

The Thing

To commit is to decide to invest resources into something based on trust. For improv that thing is actually several things, each serving as a foundation for the next (like a multilayered cake). Fail to commit to one, the others will topple.

WHAT YOU ARE

The base layer of what you commit to is what you think you are, which also defines what you are not. This is often reflected in labels. We might walk through the door as a serious patent lawyer, reliable soccer dad, or misunderstood stand-up.

These labels cause unnecessary problems when they clash with a skill you need as an improvisor. This appears as the thought "Oh, I can't do that, that's not me." Sadly, a label can smother your budding skills or, tragically, blind you from recognizing when you are quite good at them.

We give labels power because they help run our everyday lives. They are part of a bigger system. I'm not suggesting you abandon your label to find the real you. The current you is delightful. But set your label aside for the time you focus on improv. I promise it will be waiting for you when you're done.

Instead, commit that at a chosen time and environment you have no label.

Wait, "no label" is a label. Dammit, this is hard. Try this instead . . .

Commit that at a chosen time and environment you are an improvisor. Even if it is your first day and you don't know where the bathroom is, accept this vague label. If that label makes you feel like a fake, if you have never acted in your life, if you think everyone else in the room has done impressive things at impressive places and has impressive talent, if you have never taken a chance—keep all that to yourself.

Never speak of it. Never whisper it. Not even to your cat.

None of that matters. A pedigree is the past. What matters is what you do in each moment. Do what you can with what you have.

This kind of commitment was embodied by a woman I'll call Sharon. Sharon had to miss the next workshop in our series of twelve but would return after that. Her reason? Brain surgery. She had cancer. I suggested she drop class and come back when things were better. But Sharon would have nothing of that. "I've taken this class twice before, and this thing stopped me both times. I won't let it win." Sharon can't remember the day she returned, but I do—if I hadn't known her situation, I'd say "That lady is D-R-U-N-K." But she recovered, passed class, and beat cancer. If she can set aside her everyday affairs and commit to being an improvisor for a few hours, we all can.

THE EVENT

The next layer of our commitment cake is to invest in the event. When you show up to a workshop, or class, or show, or conversation—commit to being there for the duration. Bring all your energy from beginning to end. Even the boring parts.

I admit there are boring parts, especially in class. For one improvisor, it may be boring when he is not the center of attention. For others, it may be boring when that guy is the center of attention.

Even when you are not doing, commit to watching. Committed watching is a secret path of learning.

THE PIECE

Commitment to the piece is the next layer on our commitment cake. When you execute the piece, even if it is a simple exercise in class, it is vital to invest in those minutes.

A lapse in commitment during the piece affects all the participants—you, those improvising with you, and those watching you. Everyone has committed to these minutes with their time and energy and money. Don't let everybody down! If nothing else, commitment is attractive—you never know who is watching.

THE MOMENT

At the tippy top of our commitment cake, is investment in the moment. Within a piece there are many moments; each one requiring your commitment from beginning to end. You must focus all your intellectual power, all your emotional resources, all your physical abilities into the reality of the moment at hand. It is here where your energy is most concentrated. If it smells like Styrofoam is burning, then you are in the zone. It's that intense.

It Ain't Easy

If your commitment softens you may get a note from an instructor, director, or coach that you are "bailing" or "checking out" or "giving up." You might get poked with the corrective command "commit!"

Committing requires a lot, whether you've got a lot or not. We arrive wherever we are with a frayed history that includes concerns and hassles with traffic, and bills, and health, and career, and relationships, and tiredness. It's hard to shake all that off.... But you must.

It's hard to arrive early, show up on time, and keep your mind in the room until the end.... But you must.

It's hard to invest mental, emotional, and physical energy.... But you must.

It's hard to trust yourself and others.... But you must.

It's hard to motivate to chat with people after.... But you should. You really should.

Wrap It Up

You need a wind, a sail, and a boat to go sailing, but they alone are not sailing. The boat harnesses the power of the wind, manifested in the sail, and converts it into motion. For improv, commitment is our boat.

To commit, you must trust yourself and decide to invest energy, time, and money into what you are (an improvisor), the event, the piece, and the moment.

PART TWO

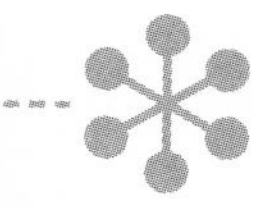

What It Means to Improvise

4

There Is Only One Thing You Make

Our definition of improvise is "to make something from whatever is available," which raises the question: What is the thing I make when I improvise?

The answer to that question will change your life. But only if you want it to. If you don't want to change your life, skip this chapter and make some brownies, but don't continue reading. Now, take a moment to ponder, do you want to change your life?

I'll wait. . . .

You're still reading! I bet you're in a hurry. Well luckily for you the answer is simple. Because there is only one thing that you can make when you improvise. One thing that's mind-blowing. Take a moment to think of the most mind-blowing thing imaginable. Now think of two of them, and that still isn't as mind-blowing as what's coming. Oh boy, we are almost ready! But you know what?

I bet you already know the answer.

WHAT?! *That sounds impossible!* But take a moment to consider that you forgot the . . . okay, okay, I see you're ready! It's time to find out the one thing you make when you improvise. Now let's launch your new life by taking a few moments for a countdown.

Ten.
Nine.
Eight.
Seven.
Six.
Five.
Four.
Three!

Two!!
One!!!
There.
That was it!
The answer.

Let's see how that went. During that world-class hype, did you follow my suggestions to take a moment to ponder and imagine and consider? Did you savor that countdown like a real countdown?

If you did, excellent! At the final moment of the countdown, when you arrived at the "answer," did you feel ripped off or confused? It really doesn't matter. I just wanted you to have a distinct moment. Because that moment is the answer to the question: What is the one thing I make when I improvise?

A moment.

If you blew by all those moments in your rush to find the life-changing answer, you may feel like a failure. You are. Congratulations! That failure made you wildly successful in a different way. You identified a most important trap, one that constantly threatens to ensnare every improvisor: missing a moment because you were rushing to find it in the future.

What Is a Moment

A moment is a short time span that contains content and meaning. A moment is the building block of your life's experience, and improv is just another experience. Thus, a moment is the only thing you can improvise.

You might say "Whoa, I've seen people improvise a scene or song, but never a moment." You're kind of right and very wrong. What you have seen are moments arranged into structures. We'll touch on structures briefly at the end of this chapter and in detail in later chapters.

Moments are the building blocks of everything improvised. You gain power and avoid pain by understanding them. We'll examine moments in everyday life and then see how an improvisor is a specialist at making them.

Your life is packed with moments, like the moment you realized you were hopelessly lost, first saw that impossibly cute barista, or realized your cat is abusive. All moments are not so momentous. There are zillions of less flashy ones, like—oh hey—here's a new paragraph.

A moment is short, measured more handily in seconds instead of minutes. It may feel longer or shorter than its actual duration.

In a moment you experience content. Think of content as "stuff that happens." You can experience external content generated by others (e.g., "I just heard a gruff voice yelling 'watch out below!'") and by the environment (e.g., "It sure is dark in the shadow of this falling piano"), as well as internal content ("My gut feels like something exciting is about to happen!").

You create meaning from that content. In life, your brain is careful to make sure that meaning aligns with your beliefs about the world. That meaning-making process is automatic and efficient, first created and then fed by your experiences or those described by a trusted authority (i.e., a scientist, the news, or your friend's older sister). Is it perfect? No. But it's the process that has sustained our species for a quarter million years. If you have a better idea, start beta testing.

Moments break our uninterrupted experience into discrete units of meaning. They tame the infinite variability of the universe into bite-sized bits. Breaking up a continuous phenomenon is a common tactic. We use it every day:

- ❊ Our thoughts do not exist in tidy sentences, but tidy sentences help express thoughts.
- ❊ A curve is unbroken, but we divide it into discrete rectangles to help calculate its area.
- ❊ Time is continuous, but we break it into seconds so commercials can be less than a minute.

Moments are natural to humans. A child intuitively understands the language of moments in a comic strip. The comic's creators contemplated what were the best "chunks of content" to convey the desired experience. That content appears as words and images framed in discrete panels, each typically representing a length of time. You extract meaning from each, and if the moments were constructed well, you chuckle.

Other disciplines have similar concepts: a photo, a shot, a stanza, a phrase, a sample. All represent a brief but meaningful portion of something larger. Instead of the word "moment" we could just as easily call it a byte, a packet, or a chunk ("I'll never forget the chunk I fell in love with your mother."). Yeah, let's stick with "moment."

The Current Moment

What comes after a moment? Another moment. And then another. And another.

Moments are contiguous and endless like an infinite tray of freshly baked brownies that have been sliced into squares: the end of one brownie is the beginning of another. Or if you are a pessimist: the beginning of one is the end of another. Either way, you cannot see beyond the forever nature of brownies—I mean moments.

Now imagine that you are standing in the middle of that giant tray of brownies, which are moments. You take a step—but instead of walking forward to experience a new moment, the tray moves beneath you, like a treadmill. You huff and puff away as moments speed underfoot, but you never move from where you are. No matter how fast it seems like you are moving, each footfall is the current footfall, and that footfall always lands in the current brownie square—I mean moment.

You are always smack dab in the middle of the current moment. We get lots and lots and lots of current moments. If you mess one up, relax, here comes another.

You can't escape the current moment. Get in a time machine and try. You'll find that no matter where you go on the timeline, each moment will be the current moment to you. If your time machine is in the shop, try the poor man's substitute: memories and fantasy.

But as real as memory and fantasy may feel, you are never really in the past or in the future. You are in the current moment doing some mental activity. Sometimes it feels so real we have physical reactions. That's because it *is* real, a real mental activity in the current moment.

You cannot hammer tomorrow's nail. You cannot bake yesterday's brownie. But you can contemplate them in the current moment.

New Moments

Within a moment, content is consistent and supports a singular meaning. A change in either heralds a new moment. For example, many people try to make sense I once fought a man in Reno just to watch him cry. That last sentence is flawed, but hopefully its flaw let you experience an abrupt change in meaning that marked a new moment. In that example, twenty words are jammed into one sentence, the first eight form a singular meaning, as do the last twelve, but together the twenty do not form a singular meaning. It is a passable example of a sentence that contains two moments and a textbook example of a terrible sentence.

When it feels like there is a new moment, there is. Moments are subjective. They are not always so simple or clear-cut as our twenty-word sentence. Here's an example.

Imagine savoring a delicious brownie. As the chocolatey goodness floods your mouth, endorphins pulse through your body, delivering pleasure at the molecular level. You chew, not out of necessity, but because it is ecstasy. You go blind because your brain's resources are overwhelmed by the unearthly luxury of this brownie. It is one great brownie bite moment. Then your teeth hit a nut. Here are two possible outcomes.

A) If you are a reasonable human, a new moment is created. The original perfect brownie moment is destroyed because some dolt put a nut where both science and religion agree nuts do not belong. The most recent experience, the disturbing discovery of a nut, is different than the previous homogeneous moment of bliss. It is a new moment, one of suffering.

B) If you are an uneducated simpleton, the original moment of bliss continues uninterrupted. Because of reckless parenting or tragic character flaw, you believe the vile fallacy that a nut belongs in a brownie. To you, the discovery of a nut is an unremarkable change in content and is in complete accord with the heretofore sublime brownie moment. The nut would not give rise to a new moment for you. And so your bliss continues, though your soul is forever damned.

All Moments Count

We think some moments are more important than others. We even label them "big moments." "Big" implies spectacular content such as ticker-tape parades, earthquakes, and dinosaur brawls. But "big" also refers to meaningful moments that occur without fanfare. Moments like, "Hey, I'm pregnant, pass the salt please." Do not confuse big-as-in-spectacle with big-as-in-meaningful.

In our everyday lives, we focus on big moments. They are isolated and highlighted in our minds and media. For an improvisor, this is a high crime.

Your moment is influenced by the moments that came before. The moment you discover an oasis is affected by all your prior moments of desert wandering. A note in a song is affected by all the notes that came before. The final number in a countdown has meaning because of the previous numbers. If you skip them, you're just shouting the number one.

Every moment is indispensable. Each forms the whole. An improvisor attends to every moment, big and small.

Make Moments Purposefully

When we recall a moment from our life, its creation seems effortless. It doesn't feel like we did anything to make it. It seems reasonable to say we "have" moments instead of we "make" moments. But let's be unreasonable.

Our "effortless having" is the culmination of brutal work. This work starts as a newborn baby and continues even after that baby grows gray and moves into a retirement condo. Your brain does this work in response to an unforgiving environment that mostly plots to kill you. Consuming content and deriving meaning is a survival skill. Your moment-making ability has been hammered and honed without your consent over your entire life. The result?

You are a moment-making machine.

And that is the dirty improv secret: you already have the basics to do this stuff. Or the dirtier secret: the basics already have you. You've just forgotten that you are doing it . . . and how you are doing it.

What separates improvising from other moment-making in our lives is that improvisors:

- ❋ Respect the inescapable current moment.
- ❋ Generate almost all content filling that moment.
- ❋ Are more purposeful about attending to that content.
- ❋ Are more purposeful about creating meaning from that content.
- ❋ Can change a reality to fit that meaning (instead of the other way around).
- ❋ Are less beholden to the moment-making habits of everyday life.

That last point is key. An improvisor hacks their own sacred meaning-making system. In a fictional staged reality, they free themself from their brain's automatic processes, their own beliefs. They can generate any valid meaning from the content of the improvised piece. They consciously choose a meaning from many possible meanings.

Thus, you don't abandon your moment-making machine as much as you adjust its settings. Open it up and see what that moment-making machine can do. *Vrooom! Vrooom!*

Meanings may differ from what we would conclude in everyday life, but they have a logic and integrity within the staged reality. They can even change that reality. More on that later.

This focus on making moments is not just useful for improv. A man we'll call Al cornered me after a workshop. I had been sharp with Al that night. I was frustrated with his work. Whatever insight he earned was lost by the next workshop, if not the next bathroom break.

"I want to show you something," he said. He grabbed my hand and jammed it into his hair, guiding my fingers to the back of his head until they found a depression that felt like . . . well . . . a hole. He had been in a coma after a car accident, and to relieve the swelling in his brain the doctors removed some of his skull. That saved his life, but forever changed his thinking. He lost his job, his wife, and his old life. "I know I'll never be great at this," he said. "But it's like medicine. When I do it, people say I'm different. I listen. I can track. I can have a conversation. It makes me a better person." He understood the work more than I did, because he was aware that he was fixing the hole in his head. It was humbling. It was also awkward having my hand in his hair.

Moments Make Structures

All this talk of making moments seems far from what we think improvisors make, such as a story. The two are closer than they appear. For now remember moments combine to form different types of structures, like a song or a scene or a story. The difference between forming them lies in the nitty-gritty of how an improvisor makes each moment (something we will explore a little later).

Wrap It Up

When we improvise, we purposefully make the current moment (the discrete building block of our continuous experience) by tinkering with the existing moment-making machine inside us.

Playing with how we create moments exposes the terrain of our minds and our society. It turns out, both are amusing.

5

There Is Only One Thing You Make It From

Our definition for improvising is "to make something from whatever is available." That definition raises a critical question: What is the "whatever is available?"

I found the answer while driving cross country, on a long, empty stretch of Interstate 94. As dusk fell I came upon a historic marker, one of those roadside installations that tell about people and events that made America. Usually I speed by such things, but this marker looked especially lonely, so I pulled off to visit with it for a while. Here is the story it told.

Deep in the forested plains of North Dakota, there lived a tribe of aboriginal lumberjacks. Their lives were spent scratching out an existence in the forest, requiring extreme lumberjack skills. So advanced was their craft that even an average lumberjack could fell a 100-foot pine with a whisper, have it collapse into two-by-fours with a joke, and grow a new tree overnight with just a seed, a pint of sarsaparilla, and three lumberjack tears.

For one week each fall the lumberjacks celebrated the Lumberjack Olympiad. However, more than the competitions themselves, it was the debate that followed they anticipated most of all. For in addition to brawn, the lumberjacks had a robust discourse over their central problem: their village had no women. And as their village was the only village in the entire forest, the absence of women presented a most intractable problem.

When the competitions ended, the tribe gathered in the village center to share bark stew and acorn pudding and debate. Each lumberjack was allowed to speak for however long he could remain balanced atop a twig selected by the previous speaker. After weeks of oration and countless twigs, the lumberjacks made a formal proclamation.

"As we lumberjacks have no recollection, foul or sweet, of womenfolk visiting our humble village, and having taken austere stock of our lumberjack ways, we conclude that to engage said womenfolk we must rebuild our village and ourselves, rebuild with the most exotic material imaginable. We hereby certify, ratify, and petrify to embark on a new future, a future built on hope, a future made of brick."

The lumberjacks knew that brick was their key to happiness. Unfortunately, that was all they knew. No lumberjack had ever touched the mystical material, much less knew how to make it.

Their first awareness and total understanding of brick came from page 97 of a September issue of *Architectural Digest* magazine, found lining an eagle's nest in a tree that was felled during the Olympiad. The torn picture showed a slender brunette woman relaxing in an Eames chair, complete with ottoman. Her hair, cut in a smart bob, hid most of her face yet revealed a coy smile. In the background was a fire in a fireplace. The fireplace was made of brick.

For the lumberjacks, that was enough.

Around that crumpled magazine they constructed the Principle Aboriginal Lumberjack Center for Applied and Theoretical Brick Research, or PAL-CFAATBR for short. The structure was expanded vertically, laterally, and diagonally until the need was so great that they built a second research facility across town, followed by a third, and then a fourth.

Walkways were built to connect facilities that gave rise to an unforeseen scourge: massive foot-traffic jams. In response, high-density tree housing and mass-transit ladders and slides were constructed. The village grew bigger and busier than ever, yet as months wore on all worried, they were no closer to making a brick.

One spring day the village's bustle was interrupted by an unprecedented sight: a flying lumberjack. Launched by the freshly built "news catapult," the diminutive lumberjack soared across the village shouting the latest discovery: bricks had something to do with fire.

The village erupted at the news. Reenergized, the lumberjacks plunged ahead to construct a massive furnace built entirely of wood. This facility came to be known as "That Place That Burned Down Last Night." Repairs were constant.

The village's ceaseless construction demanded a ceaseless supply of wood. The lumberjacks had to improve their already legendary skills and learn the forest as never before. Whatever quality was needed in their wood, they knew exactly where and how to fell it.

Regrowing so many trees demanded more lumberjack tears, giving rise to the art of Extremely Melancholy Lumberjack Storytelling, practiced each evening by lantern light. Not a village to wallow in sadness, the tribe would end each evening with a riotous recounting of the days' various puns, insults, and euphemisms that used the word "wood." No one ever tired of these bits.

As the next Olympiad approached, the lumberjacks grew despondent. In their pursuit of brick, they had crafted an elaborate city of wood complete with trams and byways, laboratories and observatories, lecture halls and particle accelerators, theatres and stadiums. Yet they had not made a single brick.

To salvage their mood, the village declared the day before the Olympiad to be a day of rest, the first in a year. On this day, the lumberjacks again took to the woods to fell trees, but this time—just to relax.

As they came upon a grove on the edge of the forest, the ground shook and the air filled with sickening sound. The lumberjacks became concerned. Each lumberjack paused behind a tree for safety ("Paused behind a tree for safety" is the closest a lumberjack ever gets to hiding). The clatter and shaking grew until the lumberjacks could hardly stand or hear each other yell euphemisms that used the word "wood."

From around the bend the tumult became clear: a team of twelve horses snorted and brayed as their hooves hammered the ground to pull the massive weight of a triple-decker coach made entirely of brick. The carriage teetered and lurched and thumped as the team strained to roll the square brick wheels. Holding the reins was a woman. Her hair blazing red and her skin flawlessly smooth, except where flesh rubbed against her garments which were made of a fine brick weave.

She pulled the reins. The carriage stopped. The lumberjacks leaned from behind their trees. A helicopter made of brick circled above.

The shutters covering the carriage's windows opened. On all three tiers, women peered out. Each gave a slow wave.

The lumberjacks gave slow waves back.

One lumberjack ventured onto the road. He doffed his cap, cleared his throat, and swallowed.

The woman took a breath. Her cheeks glistened. Her hands trembled. Pollen floated in the still air amongst the trees. In a wavering voice she announced, "We have come to see a most impossible city, a most unimaginable city, a city where everything is made from the most extraordinary material, a material called wood."

Whatever Is Available

I don't know when or where you will improvise—we're practically strangers. But I am confident that wherever you go, one thing will always be available. And that one thing is you. You are the only thing that is always available to you.

This may sound like a motivational quote on a refrigerator magnet, but it is a mistake for an improvisor to accept it superficially. It is common to experience your experience as common, and that thought can hide in the dark alleys of you mind, behind the brightest facade of confidence. It will sabotage you. Let's shed some light on it.

You Are Wood

Just like in the story of the lumberjacks (which should probably win several Pulitzer Prizes, if not all of them), we discount the raw material of our lives. The lumberjacks' lives were filled with wood. To them wood was their everyday. Perhaps it was even boring. But to outsiders, it was an extraordinary material that formed extraordinary structures when used with skill.

Your life has supplied your raw material. That material makes your work specific to you. You are an original without even trying.

Your materials are complete and ready right now to improvise. You don't need to read classic literature, or bone up on pop culture, or research geopolitics (unless that's what you're in to). Your mind is bursting with junk, time to use it. Broad categories of that junk look like this:

- **Memories.** Both big and small from home, work, play, and the boring stuff in between.
- **Beliefs.** Facts, opinions, and values, whether original or adopted, "right" or "wrong."
- **Intellectual abilities.** How you process data, drawing connections and conclusions.
- **Emotional abilities.** Discriminating your emotions and those of others.
- **Physical abilities.** How your body knows to move or not move.

Improvisors develop skills to use their material effectively, often entertainingly. Just as the lumberjacks worked tirelessly to improve their craftsmanship and knowledge of wood, so an improvisor works. This is what separates the levels of artistry, not the material.

Your material, used with skill, is enough to build a world from the slightest suggestion, such as a page torn from *Architectural Digest*.

You Are Lacking

The lumberjacks started their journey believing they lacked a special material. But by the end, they found they still lacked a special material. They were horribly deficient. And so are you.

The good news is it doesn't matter. Everyone is deficient.

Who knows if the lumberjacks ever figured out how to make a single brick? They took action with what they had and produced extraordinary results. The lumberjacks had never considered that the world wants to see lumberjacks use lumberjack skills and lumberjack material to create in ways only lumberjacks can.

What makes you *you* is not only what you know, but the gaps in what you know. There are no fact checkers in improv. There are no trophies for talent. The world wants to see you build with what you have and around what you lack. Savor your shortcomings, they are defining quirks. That's not opinion; it's historic fact.

The Roman Republic turned Empire ended over a thousand years ago, and we still admire them for being the smarty-boots of their times with fancy roads, beautiful aqueducts, and classy vomitoriums. They constructed all that without having a unit of time called a minute, a telephone, or a single Ford F-150 pickup truck. Their achievements are a marvel, made even greater because of what they lacked.

Whether you work at being super knowledgeable and talented or, like most of us, are happy being categorically unknowledgeable and marginally talented, you are in great shape. If you have trouble grasping concepts, making connections, or paying attention, let's be frank—you will have challenges. But who doesn't have a big bag of challenges in their closet? It may mean you need to improve some skills, and improv may help. You can find similar minds with which to play and have a grand time. I'd never say, "Don't bother." Please, bother!

I worked one on one with a guy pursuing comedy who we'll call Luke. Luke had cerebral palsy. He used a motorized wheelchair, had limited use of his hands, and had some speech difficulties. We did a drill in which you rattle off the first five things you think of in an assigned category. Under the pressure of time, interesting stuff comes out the more you rattle. I assigned "stores you wish existed" and his third response was a showstopper. With awe at his own idea he said, "A store where they let people in wheelchairs just stop and rest." To which he followed with both optimism and a sense of being over it, "I get tired." We both laughed. Luke expressed his life, his frustrations, and his optimism in that business idea—a store that sold nothing, but existed solely to let him hang out.

You Are Bottomless

You may worry that your material is finite, especially the "good stuff." What happens when you run out?

You can't. Lumberjacks grew trees overnight with sarsaparilla and tears. You can too. You generate raw material every day, including "the good stuff." Pay attention to the details of your life. Pablo Picasso agreed when he said, "Painting is just another way of keeping a diary." So concise, that Pablo. He should have been a writer.

If you haven't been paying attention to the details of your life, relax. You can start right now.

Beyond that, nothing in this chapter advises against actively stuffing more junk into your brain. There is no end to learning (which is another fine magnet for your refrigerator door).

Wrap It Up

To improvise means "to make something from whatever is available." The "whatever is available" is you.

You make from what you are and are not, and that is plenty.

6

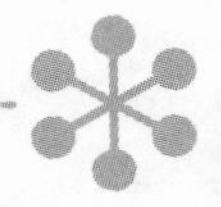

There Is Only One Way You Make It

Our definition of "improvise" is "to make something from whatever is available." The thing that is made is always the same—a moment—and it is always made from you. But how is a moment made? Some say that is a matter of opinion, but art has no room for opinion. Art only has room for science. So let us return to the day when science revealed how we make a moment.

The girl yelled at me in French. I looked up and we locked eyes. She was bathed in the glow of the control panel. I couldn't tell if she was afraid or excited, but the fog inside of her face shield told me she was sweating. She wore a yellow radiation suit with a patch that said "Claudia Odette." Her finger was trembling above a red flashing button. The red was a warning. It's dangerous to tinker with the fabric of reality in a particle collider.

The Large Hadron Collider is the world's most powerful particle collider. It took thirty years to construct a seventeen-mile underground tunnel along the border of France and Switzerland, and costs $1 billion a year to keep it running. For that money, physicists get to smash particles together at 99.9999991 percent the speed of light. Other than the pure fun of smashing things, physicists record what flies off those collisions. By studying how things deconstruct, scientists discover the particles and forces that make up everything, everywhere. Pretty cool if you have that type of money.

The European research organization that has that type of money is known by its snappy acronym CERN. I bought a raffle ticket at their annual $1 billion fundraising potluck. I felt I had to, I forgot to bring a dessert. Those tickets were not cheap. First prize was a weekend of personal use of the Large Hadron Collider. I won that, plus a T-shirt that said, "Physicists Do It with Force."

That's where I was with Claudia, underground in the Large Hadron Collider, seconds before our experiment. Yellow warning lights were spinning. A European-sounding siren was blaring, which was hard to take seriously. But it was serious. In front of us lay a steel pipe that disappeared into miles of dark tunnel, Claudia was about to release a proton down that pipe where it would accelerate to 99.9999991 percent the speed of light and then collide with an idea.

No one had ever smashed a proton into an idea. CERN's scientists had protested—"C'est impossible!" But I won the raffle. It was my weekend in the collider. I had to try.

The idea we were deconstructing was the "make" from our definition "to make something from whatever is available." We were going to smash it and, for the first time since God put the universe into motion, reveal its inner workings.

The Euro-sirens were wailing. Claudia stared, waiting for me to respond. Plumes of steam poured into the tunnel. Whatever she had yelled at me was lost in the noisy tunnel, but it didn't matter—I never understood French. I closed my eyes, forced a grin, and gave two thumbs up.

Then Claudia pushed the flashing red button.

When I opened my eyes, all I saw was ceiling. I was lying on the floor. My head was throbbing with pain. There were no sirens. No spinning lights. No steam. The tunnel was a silent shambles of twisted pipe and torn cables. Our experiment had destroyed the Large Hadron Collider.

I heard crying. Across the tunnel was Claudia, kneeling and hunched over. She held a flashlight, looking at the rubble beneath her. She turned to me. Through her shattered face shield, I thought I saw a smile. She raised a torn sheet of paper, the last output from the collider, showing the deconstruction of *make*. She was shedding tears of joy.

Deconstructing a Moment into Its Six Components

The diagram Claudia held up is a model that serves both the novice improv student and the veteran. Let's go down the layers of the diagram to deconstruct what it means to make a moment, recognizing that the details of the lower layers deepen our understanding of the upper.

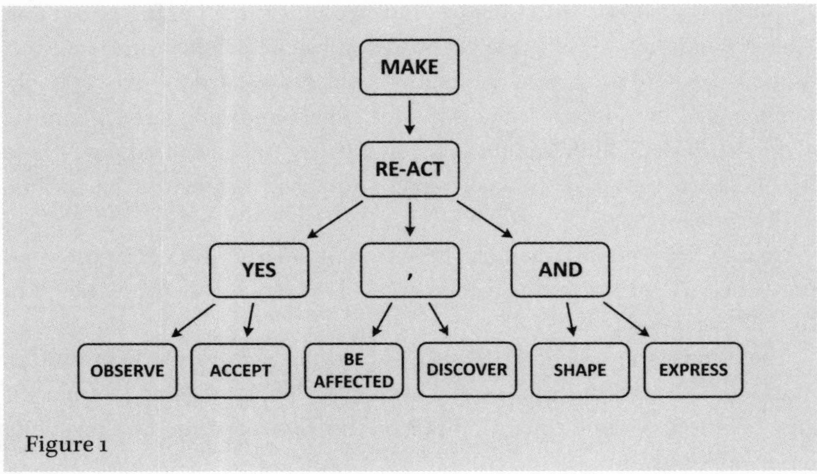

Figure 1

Starting at the top, the core of "make" is to re-act, which means "an action in response to a previous action." Our spelling accentuates the prefix "re," which means to refer, complete, or intensify that which came before. Thus to make a moment in improv you simply react to the previous moment by leveraging it somehow. This understanding is enough for many people to lead happy lives of improvising.

But for those who want more insight, we can deconstruct re-act to discover its components: Yes, And. This is a legendary phrase in improv. But as famous as it is, most are shocked to realize "Yes, And" is not made of two elements, but three. The comma is essential.

Traditional interpretations of Yes, And hold that one must simply agree with what has come before and add to it. This level of understanding is also enough for many to lead happy lives of improvising.

But for those who want to know what it truly means to Yes, And, to understand the inner workings of improv, we must go deeper. We find that each component of Yes, And can be deconstructed to reveal the six fundamental components that make a moment:

- ❋ Observe
- ❋ Accept
- ❋ Be affected
- ❋ Discover

- Shape
- Express

We will take a closer look at Yes, And in the next chapter and then examine the six fundamental components individually, not only because they are that vital but because they are that elusive. Their labels are deceptively simple. We need time to understand them and the traps that make them tricky.

Before forging ahead, we should recognize that although the six components must be presented in a sequence, your experience of them may not feel sequential. Just as subatomic particles can exist at the same time, the components of a moment can happen simultaneously.

Also note, we can refer to a component of a moment as a verb or as a noun. For instance, the component "observe" (a verb) could be also referred to as an "observation" (a noun). However, try to remember our six components as actions—what you do to make a moment.

Sensing the Invisible

A human cannot see subatomic particles, they are super tiny. Physicists developed exotic equipment to detect them and gave that equipment exotic names such as Compact Muon Solenoid or Geiger-Müller Tube.

Similarly, the components of a moment are invisible, except for the sixth component ("express"), which can be seen. Thus, you must develop exotic equipment to detect the invisible and give that equipment the exotic name "your gut." A moment that feels right to your gut means all the components are present. A moment that feels off means one or more are missing.

You can't rely on another person to tell you what went awry in your moments. Even a seasoned improv instructor with a sensitive gut can only take an educated guess. Part of learning is to calibrate your gut by listening to what someone else's gut has to say. Ultimately, it is your job to diagnose what is wonky.

A Framework for Understanding

You will receive lots of notes in improv, which can cause confusion. Concepts and terms in improv are not standardized as they are in physics, cricket, or woodworking. To tame that thicket of ideas, you can relate each note you hear to a bigger concept, integrating it into a whole. At this point, you have a basic framework to organize what you will hear.

Some notes pertain to the necessary conditions we learned from Ernie while on the lake. To sail it is necessary to have a wind, a sail, and a boat, and similarly for improv it is necessary to indulge, share, and commit. If any of those necessary conditions are absent in improv, it is difficult to make complete moments.

Other notes relate to making moments and may be given at the general level (re-act or Yes, And) or at the level of the six fundamental components (observe, accept, be affected, discover, shape, express), which we will explore in the next chapters.

And there are still other notes on structures, character, stagecraft, and so on. These are important but less central. We will visit some of these concepts later.

Wrap It Up

There are six fundamental components that make a moment, but only one (express) can be observed by others.

7

Yes, And

"Yes, And" is an iconic phrase in improv, it elaborates on what it means to re-act, describing how to make a moment. It is typically explained as "agreeing with what has come before and adding to it," which is concise, but misleading. The words are simple, but a simplistic understanding will cause you a lot of unnecessary struggle.

We have to look closer at the "Yes," the comma, and the "And" to start seeing important nuances that will become clearer when we look at the six fundamental components of a moment in the chapters that follow.

Yes

Everybody loves "yes." Books are written on the power of "yes." Seminars are devoted to getting to "yes." Admiration for "yes" peaks in the world of improv, where it receives rapturous love. Is any of this worship earned? And in bitter contrast, why no such love for the rugged and maligned "no"?

It may seem that Yes's status comes from its association with getting what you want:

- Will you marry me? YES!
- Did your ship come in? YES!
- Is school canceled today? YES!

But an honest accounting shows that "yes" is the culprit in plenty of unwanted events.

- Are we lost at sea? YES!
- Are you a werewolf? YES!
- Is that income taxable? YES!

The real reason "yes" gets more greetings cards than "no" at both Christmas and Chanukah is based on function.

- ❊ YES is efficient at the business of what exists.
- ❊ NO is efficient at the business of what does not exist.

"Yes" wields the power of existence by design: "yes" is from the Old English *gēse*, a combination of *gēa sī*, which means "so be it." At least that's what the dictionary told me. Or what I understood of that part of the dictionary. But it fits.

If you're in a bar watching a hockey game and the hometown team scores a pivotal goal, you will hear a chorus of "Yes!" and its kin: "Yea" and "Yeah." Why yell "Yes!"? Who asked a question? These exclamations are spontaneous cries of "So be it!" It exists. What we saw, happened. We are validating a reality.

And we will see that validating a reality is verrrrrry important for improv. The two components of "yes" are:

- ❊ **Observe.** Sense what is.
- ❊ **Accept.** Believe it to be part of reality.

We will examine these two concepts in more detail in the following chapters.

Comma

The unassuming comma was invented somewhere in the thirteenth century and has served writers dutifully ever since. Unfortunately the comma is often neglected when spoken. Such a slight may be tolerable for other phrases, but for Yes, And it is devastating. When hearing "Yes, And" an improvisor must remember the comma exists. It is a meaningful symbol just like the word "yes" and the word "and." It symbolizes a pause.

In that pause we do work. The work is silent. It takes digging. It is an adventure.

That silent, digging adventure is a search for gold. When gold prospecting you have two activities: find where the gold is using your instincts and smarts, then unearth the gold with your tools.

The good news is that, as an improvisor, no matter where you look and no matter which tool you use, you can always find gold! The bad news is that this is a metaphor. There is no actual gold.

We prospect for meaning instead of gold in the silence of the comma. The comma involves two components, which we will look at more deeply a few chapters from now:

- ❊ **Be affected.** Sense where meaning lies.
- ❊ **Discover.** Uncover the meaning.

And

The common explanation for the meaning of "and" in "Yes, And" is "to add to what has come before." This belittles the full abilities of And. And is a master craftsman, who wields hammer and fire just as deftly as calipers and file. We need the artisanal skills of And not to slap things together crudely, but to combine things seamlessly.

We often ask And to add similar items in an almost mathematical way, like 1 inch + 1 inch = 2 inches. This bores And. It is too easy.

A challenge that makes And grin is when we want to combine dissimilar elements. This is when And stokes the fire, sharpens a pencil, and rolls up its sleeves. It's time to show off. And lives to figure out how dissimilar things can go together and to marry them. And wants us to marvel at its entertaining unions of disparate elements—whether an inch and a meter, a flamethrower and a wedding, or toast and vengeance.

And presents us perfectly mated unions by relying on its two components:

- ❊ **Shape.** Make information compatible.
- ❊ **Express.** Assert that information into reality.

Wrap It Up

"Yes, And" elaborates on what it means to re-act, and both describe how to make a moment. Deconstructing each part of Yes, And reveals the six fundamental components of a moment, the only thing we can make when we improvise. We will look at each component over the next six chapters.

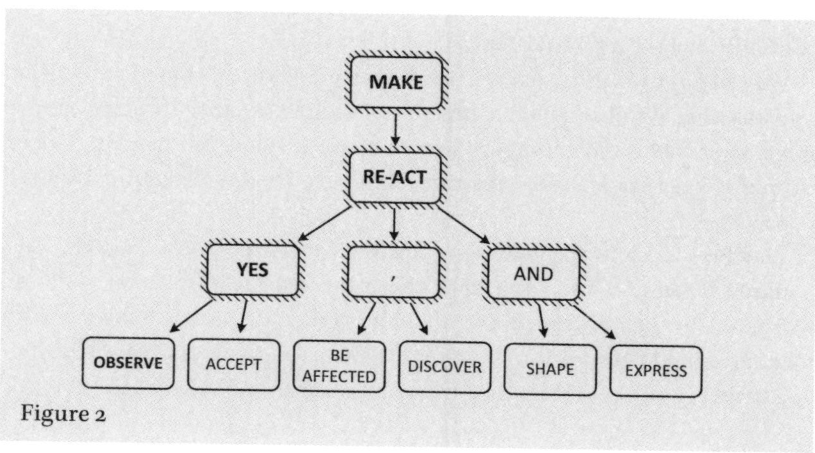

Figure 2

8

Observe

Observing is directing your senses to gather information.

Observing Is Sensational

Our senses gather information about the environment and ourselves. They provide the raw material from which we form moments. An improvisor relies on all their senses . . . the more, the merrier.

Exactly how many senses you have is controversial. Traditionally, lab-coat-wearing people agree that humans have at least five: vision, hearing, taste, touch, and smell. Many other senses have been proposed, but defining our "sixth sense"—a term reserved for any super-cool power like predicting a closer parking spot—is hotly debated. Regardless of how many senses science may decide we have, improvisors observe with them all, both external and internal.

Your externally directed senses gather information about your surroundings. Your internally directed senses gather information about you—what is going on emotionally, intellectually, and physically. All our senses are critical. Sadly, not all get our attention.

We often miss our full experience because we are infatuated with vision and hearing. We obsess about this power couple because they are easy to relate over: light and sound are external stimuli that can be experienced by many observers at the same time. They are ideal for creating a shared experience.

This bias leads to the common improv buzzwords: "look," "watch," "eye contact," "listen." When you hear those buzzwords, remember they are shortcuts for the more accurate, albeit less graceful, phrase "Observe with all your sensory resources." If you are short a few senses, work with what you have. If you have extra, then by all means use your echolocation.

Observing Takes Special Effort

You don't need special observational skills to improvise. You recruit those skills that you use in life. That's the good news. The bad news is you are careless with those skills. We need to observe with more effort than in our everyday lives.

This effort is not about furrowing your brow and grunting, "I A-M C-O-M-M-I-T-T-I-N-G M-Y S-E-N-S-O-R-Y R-E-S-O-U-R-C-E-S!" That kind of muscular tension makes it more difficult to observe. Those muscles are trying to help you, but they aren't equipped for the job. Let 'em relax. Our effort is about directing attention.

Observing is like using a flashlight, where quick, relaxed, and fluid movements are most productive. The following guidelines apply to both flashlights and your attention. None require you to furrow your brow.

- **Turn it on.** Your attention is either on or off. Always check the switch before venturing forth.
- **Be aware of where you direct it.** The power of your attention is the same regardless of where you point it, whether at the carpet, an embarrassing date you once had, or the meaning of life.
- **Alternate between a narrow and broad focus as necessary.** The power of your attention is limited and can be either concentrated on a specific detail or broadened across a large area. Both cannot be done at the same time.

What You Observe

There are just three things you can observe. That's all—three!

1. **You.** Observe what you do, which includes how you do it. Strive to observe yourself as the world does, because what you intend to do is not always what you do. That's why they invented the word "oops." Observe your internal world. It will be forever unknown if you don't pay attention to it. No one can do this for you.
2. **Your partners.** Observe what your partners do, which includes how they do it. That is all you can access of them.
3. **The environment.** Observe the environment, which is anything and everything that is not you or your partners. This includes the

audience, the lighting, a noisy pipe, the vibrations from a truck passing outside. Anything that intrudes upon the shared space is a legitimate target. Anything.

Level of Detail

You probably have a name, a nose, a hobby, and some anecdotes. Those details define you to most of the world. Don't feel bad. Almost everyone and everything can be viewed as a collection of details.

What we call something is often based on the level of detail we are observing. For instance, the punctuation mark ";" is one semicolon, or two periods—one of which has long hair. Any detail is a target for further observation, which will reveal more details.

When observing your partner, there are countless details to which you might attend: their feet, or hands, or eyes, or the color of their eyes, or the distance between their eyes, or how often they blink their eyes, and so on. Once you recognize the overwhelming details that make up the world, where do you place your attention?

The answer: don't worry about it. Your lumpy friend the brain is going to automatically tell you where to point your flashlight and when to focus its power, you just need to listen to it.

The seven billionth "office cubicle" scene ever improvised provides a simple example of observation. The scene started as nearly all cubicle scenes do: two characters typing away, but when my scene partner passed behind me to go to a filing cabinet, I felt him graze my shoulder with his hand. It was purely an accident, but we both noticed it. We made eye contact and realized that shoulder touch was going to matter. It's not a dramatic example, but that is the point—observations don't have to be profound.

Intimate Curiosity

The word "observe" sounds clinical, which is only partially true. An improvisor is like a scientist, but instead of a scientist studying a boring rotavirus, imagine a scientist studying a sexy rotavirus. Or a sexy norovirus. Or whatever virus turns you on. The point is you are engaged. Observation sounds clinical but it's an intimate curiosity.

Wrap It Up

We observe by directing our senses toward details of ourselves, others, and the environment to provide the raw material of our reality.

Observation is one of the six fundamental components of a moment, the only thing we can make when we improvise.

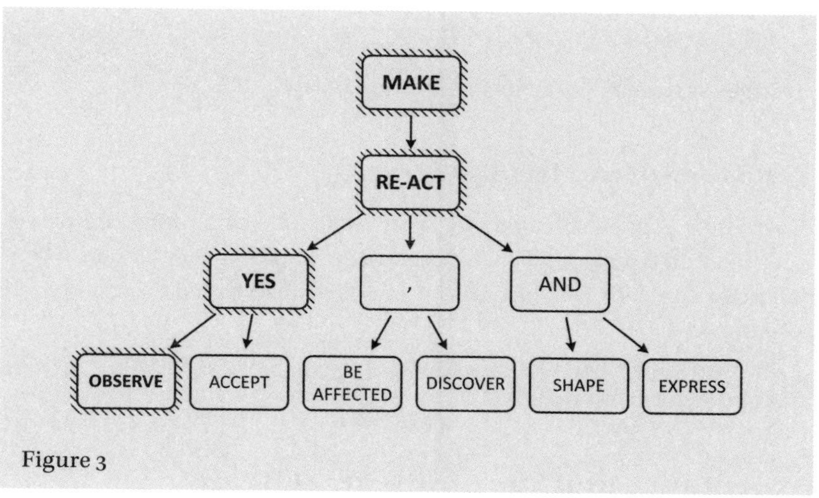

Figure 3

9

Accept

To accept is to believe that an observation is valid.

You Don't Have to Like It

Acceptance is about recognizing what exists. It has nothing to do with what you would prefer or allow as a character, improvisor, or human. If your preferences get involved here, they taint your observations. For now, only accept.

The observations we accept form our reality, or, more accurately for the improvisor, form our realities.

Acceptance and Your Individual Reality

From the observations you accept, you create your individual reality: what you think the universe is and how it works. Through interacting with your environment, you keenly conclude things such as rocks are hard, water is wet, and the sun is bright. Making your own reality is impressive, but don't get cocky—your work is shoddy.

Your individual reality is based on your limited and imperfect observations of a sliver of the universe over a tiny span of time, cosmologically speaking. That rickety approach is good enough because it turns out you don't need a perfect model of the universe to survive. In the school of "getting by" you must only avoid an F.

A good-enough model is how we interact with any complex system. Even with the crude understanding of right pedal go, left pedal stop, turn wheel to where I want to go, we can be ignorant of the achievements in science, commerce, and government that make automobile travel possible, yet still drive a car successfully across the continent—or at least until it runs out of fuel.

So, if you ever say someone is driving like an idiot, they are—and so are you. We are all idiots when it comes to interacting with our complex universe.

Acceptance and Our Shared Reality

When our imperfect individual realities interact, headaches abound. Ancient philosophers honored this when exchanging the morning greeting, "Who gives a shit about your reality?"

To avoid headaches, we try to agree on our observations about the universe. We compare individual realities and refine them. If all goes well, our realities become more accurate, useful, and less headachy.

Where our individual realities overlap, we form a shared reality. A shared reality rests on a set of observations that are accepted by all participants. If you and I both accept that rocks are hard, water is wet, and the sun is bright—odds are we share the same reality.

A shared reality is essential to improv. When we share a reality with others, everyone can comprehend what is going on and feel safe. Remember, safety is required to indulge fun. And it is not fun to be outside of a shared reality.

We might call someone outside of our shared reality "the crazy dude yelling at invisible people," while he calls us "the blind morons." More commonly, you may have had the *Am I crazy?* feeling a few (thousand) times while in an intimate relationship. That outsider feeling happens when participants do not accept each other's observations as valid. Avoid this in improv. And in relationships.

You leave the shared reality when either you accept what others cannot or you cannot accept what others do. Leaving the shared reality can lead to becoming that crazy dude, a magnate, or the Buddha. Life can be a crapshoot.

The observations you accept of your internal world, although private, can be part of the shared reality. If you are a human, odds are that what is happening inside you is happening inside other humans participating in the same event. Accepting your internal world connects you to the experience of others.

Acceptance and Our Staged Reality

Humans form shared realities because we experience common features in the natural world (i.e., rocks are hard, water is wet, the sun is bright), but we also go to tremendous lengths to create shared experiences. One could argue that news, science, and entertainment exist in part so millions can share a reality. I hate to admit it, but humanity needs boy bands.

Improv is an explicit, concentrated effort in building a shared reality. We carve out this shared reality from our everyday shared reality by a boundary, often a stage. We will call this shared reality the "staged reality." Other disciplines mark a shared reality with their own boundaries, like a picture frame, movie screen, or newspaper.

Our staged reality begins with almost nothing defined. It usually doesn't have the abundant natural features of reality to help us have common observations, like rocks, waters, or suns. It usually doesn't even have props, costumes, or set pieces to help. It sounds like a terrible idea.

And it would be a terrible idea were it not for the one magical thing we are left to observe in our staged reality: what people do. What people do is the most powerful creative force in our staged reality—but only if every "what we do" is accepted as valid.

Making Acceptance Easy

Accepting is easy if we recognize that an observation is always from an individual's imperfect reality. A character's observation is valid, but we may discover it is not complete or accurate in the shared reality. This liberates us to accept observations that appear to be in conflict.

For instance, you may hold up your hand to display an imaginary coin and declare that it is engraved with an image of George Washington's head. We accept that observation from your point of view. When I look at that same imagined coin, I say it is engraved with an image of a bald eagle. We accept that observation from my point of view. Both are accepted as valid, although they appear to disagree.

For this discussion on acceptance, we could stop at that—robotic, mindless, automatic acceptance of the participants' observations. But if we were to continue, we may discover these two observations mean we are looking at different sides of one quarter, that George Washington bears a striking resemblance to a bald eagle, that the coin was minted to commemorate your bald eagle named George Washington . . . or . . . well, you get it.

The conflict in our coin example was reconciled relatively easily, but do not fear observations that appear irreconcilable, such as: it is night and day, I am dead and alive, his name is Gary and Garry. It is the improvisor's job to discover the reality that allows such seemingly conflicting observations to coexist.

Point of view is a concept grander than just spatial relationships, such as our coin example. Point of view is the imperfect but functional model we use to navigate life. We will explore it later in part five on character.

Acceptance becomes simpler if you remember we are not beholden to real-world facts from our everyday reality. If we shackle ourselves to real-world facts, we can't explore any other world. Our coin example would be two people referring to a point in space where no coin exists. That does not sound like fun.

Our closest equivalent to fact is any assertion about the staged reality that does not deny the possibility of what has already been asserted. For instance, in the staged reality let's say you admire the sun setting in the east. If the sun hasn't previously been established as setting in the west (or any other direction), your eastern-setting sun becomes a "fact" of the staged reality (although it is not a fact in our everyday reality). We may eventually discover why our staged reality differs from everyday reality, or it simply may be "how it is."

Clearly, ideas like truth and fact are elusive when interpreting through a character's point of view in a fictional staged reality that is being created spontaneously. That's why concepts like "valid" and "observation" are more fitting.

Acceptance becomes easier when we know that whatever the observation, we get to choose what it means and what action it inspires. We cover how that works later, when we examine other components of a moment, but knowing it now helps with our immediate task: simple, uncomplicated acceptance.

Making Acceptance Difficult

Our minds meddle with acceptance. A point of view helps navigate the world, but it also likes to filter observations to meet its desires. This is such a pervasive topic that it gets its own chapters where we will closely examine the treacherous behaviors that sabotage our moments. But for now, here are some tactics your brain uses to swap what is with what it wants. The following manifest in many ways. When you bump into them—and you will bump into them—just give a polite nod and keep your hand on your wallet.

- ❋ **Deny.** That did not happen.
- ❋ **Distort.** That happened differently.
- ❋ **Discount.** That doesn't matter.

Denial, distortion, and discounting sneak in wherever they can. In one show, we were part of an oyster business, and we were shucking and eating oysters in multiple scenes while dealing with various stuff. It wasn't until well into the show that my scene partner was the first to fully accept that yes, we run an oyster farm and yes, all we do is eat oysters. Once accepted, the issue became clear, "We need to talk about our business model." The audience responded. As improvisors we had observed everything but had discounted our oyster eating. But the audience knew the eating mattered.

Oops

No matter how diligent, an improvisor will fail to accept some elements of the staged reality. But when they miss a lot by getting stuck in their individual reality and losing touch with the staged reality, you may hear confessions like: "I was writing," "I was in my head," "I checked out," or "I went somewhere." We all take a trip to that somewhere eventually. It's okay. Just don't lose your return ticket.

Wrap It Up

We accept an observation of both the external and internal as valid even if it appears to conflict with other observations. Acceptance is one of the six fundamental components of a moment, the only thing we can make when we improvise.

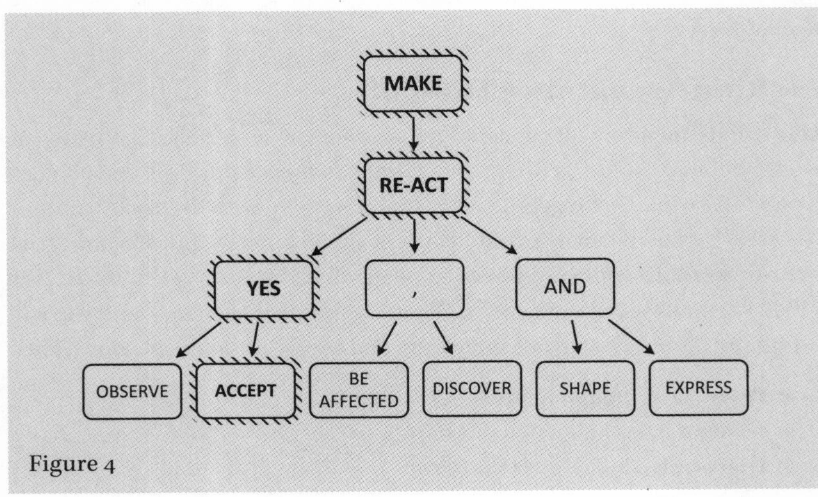

Figure 4

10

Be Affected

To "be affected" is to recognize when an observation stirs you intellectually, emotionally, or physically. It signals what has meaning.

Pointing to the Meaningful

Of all the things that enter our perception, we isolate a limited number that matter. Why we notice one thing from the ocean of other things may be a mystery, but it is a mystery an improvisor learns to trust. We don't have to know what the thing is, or what it means, or where it leads; we just need to recognize we are affected by something and allow it to move us.

Different Flavors

We can be affected in three basic flavors: emotionally, intellectually, and physically. Each is a type of feeling, which is a broad term for an emergent bodily experience.

EMOTIONAL FEELINGS

These get so much attention that we often use "feelings" and "emotions" interchangeably. But emotions are just one type of feeling. An emotion is a short-lived spontaneous physiologic and mental state. That is a dispassionate definition for a passionate phenomenon, but it will have to do. There is no agreed upon definition of emotion, nor is there consensus on how many emotions we have or if there are "core" emotions. Nevertheless everyone is happy to agree that emotions exist.

INTELLECTUAL FEELINGS

These are rarely discussed, which may leave you quertorqued. Hopefully you don't know the meaning of "quertorque," partly because this example relies on your ignorance and partly because I invented the word. Before you considered burning precious calories to research its definition, an intellectual feeling made you take notice. Such a feeling is on display when a dog perks up his ears and tilts his head when you make an odd noise. The dog is stirred intellectually. It's fun to see, but kind of irritating to them. Fortunately dogs are super cool. By the way, when a dog tilts his head in that fashion, he is quertorqued.

PHYSICAL FEELINGS

If you have ever been at a traffic light, drumming away on the steering wheel as you rock out to your sweet summer music mix, only to be interrupted by the honking of drivers informing you the light has changed, then you have been affected physically.

You will be more attuned to one type of feeling: emotional, intellectual, or physical. This bias comes from both biology and environment. Your environment may have encouraged or discouraged certain feelings, which is a rough ride since no one controls when feelings occur. For instance, if an environment discourages an emotion—let's say anger—we may cope by denying the existence of anger in ourselves or others. We become conditioned to ignore that emotion, maybe even all emotions. To compensate we might develop superhuman sensitivity to physical or intellectual feelings.

Your biases influence how you improvise. And just as you are biased, so is a school, instructor, or classmate. If your biases differ from others, working together will be either a raw chafe or a growth opportunity. It depends on everybody's mood that day.

You Choose Your Threshold

We can observe a feeling, but that feeling must reach a certain intensity before it affects us. That threshold may be big (like a lightning bolt from the gods) or small (like "Hmmm, I came up the stairs for a reason but can't remember why.").

Our thresholds in everyday life are high, especially for common transactions. Feelings go unaddressed throughout our day so the world can turn, and we can get home to unload the dishwasher. Normally only a powerful feeling can exceed our threshold and interrupt a routine.

In improv, we consciously choose to lower our thresholds. We choose to be more sensitive. Normally, if I hold a door open for you it is a courtesy that elicits a "thank you" in response, but with a lower threshold it becomes an act of loving self-sacrifice that demands a clutching embrace.

An improvisor is sensitive, but the character may not be. An improvisor's low threshold will fuel a character who is a histrionic train wreck as equally as one that is a stoic lump.

Thresholds change and become selective during a piece, such as a scene. In the beginning our thresholds are low and we are affected by any slight event. As the piece takes shape, we can raise our thresholds but remain sensitive around certain dynamics.

A threshold set too high means nothings affects you, so nothing matters. You may hear the corrective note "be vulnerable," which does not mean sob more, it means lower your threshold. Even a slab of granite is eventually affected by its surroundings. You can be better than a slab of granite, I know you can.

In one scene we visited the grave of Wolfgang Amadeus Mozart. We read from the engraved stone that Mozart died in 1791, at the age of thirty-five. One of the improvisors let that sad fact hit him, he began to weep, then wail, then throw himself on the marble slab, lamenting that Mozart not only died too young but cursed God that Mozart died at all, he was too much a genius to be taken, ever. That is an improvisor who knows how to be affected. The emotion revealed what mattered.

What Affects You

There is no rule for what can or can't affect you. It may be dramatic or trivial, beautiful or grotesque, rational or random.

Being affected is preverbal: words, meaning, and actions come microseconds after the feeling. But if we *had* to put words to your internal monologue, it might say:

- Oh my, that's fun.
- Oh my, that's confusing.
- Oh my, that's bold.
- Oh my, that's unusual.
- Oh my, that's sweet.
- Oh my, that got everyone's attention.

The "oh my" happens inside an improvisor and represents interest, not judgment. Even if something could "ruin everything," the improvisor views it as yet another "oh my." (The character, however, may view it quite differently.)

Context changes what affects you. A steaming mound of horse manure on the floor may not affect you in the context of a barn. That same mound may affect you in the context of an operating room. Unless it is in a hospital run by horses.

If many things affect you at the same time, increase your sensitivity to find what stands out, even if just by a little ("That tall tenor is the most off key."), or recognize that you are affected by the aggregate ("This chorus is horrible.").

An improvisor can choose to be affected by what affects others. You might find a newborn baby boring since he has nothing interesting to say, but the group you are in gets excited around him. To build a shared reality with that group, you can choose to be affected by that baby, "Oh my, he drools so effortlessly!" In a performance, an improvisor can choose to be affected by what affects the audience.

What affects you may be unique to you; no one has your brain or life. But despite each person's uniqueness, we share a lot: we are all human personalities with human bodies living in the same era, traveling the same roads in the same weather to be in the same room at the same time to share the same staged reality right up to the current moment. It's a wonder we're not best friends.

Therein lies some magic: by attending to what affects you, you discover what affects others. Staying grounded in your experience builds a bridge to strangers because we come from a different but similar place. This is how the work of an improvisor can be personal yet resonate with others. Without this magic, there is no improv.

This magic does not insure you from an exquisitely awkward moment when no one gets you. If it helps, I relate.

Wrap It Up

To be affected is when a feeling (emotional, physical, or intellectual) rises above a threshold, identifying what has meaning. You don't need to know where the feeling leads, it simply stirs.

To be affected is one of the six fundamental components of a moment, the only thing we can make when we improvise.

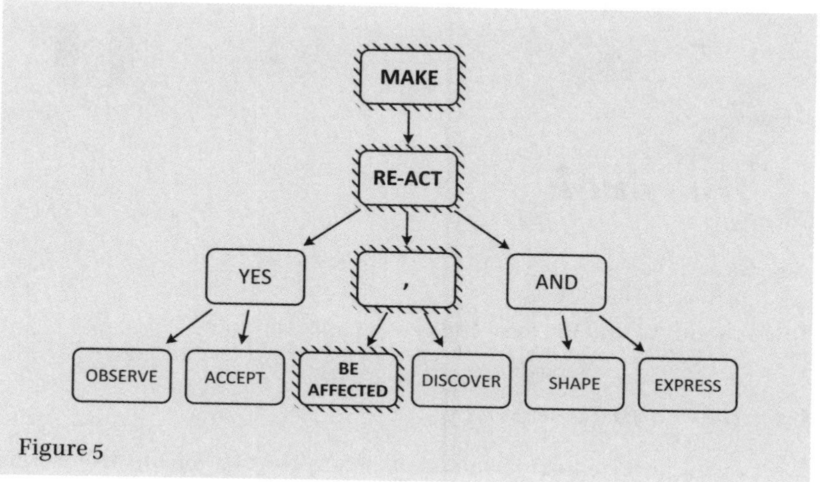
MAKE
RE-ACT
YES
,
AND
OBSERVE
ACCEPT
BE AFFECTED
DISCOVER
SHAPE
EXPRESS

Figure 5

11

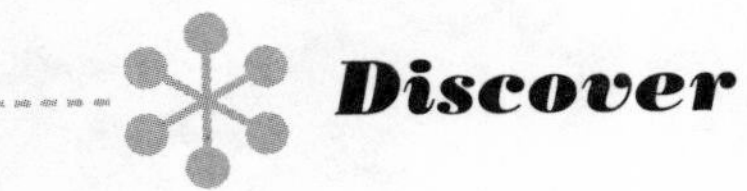

Discover

To discover is to find the meaning of what affects you.

Earmarks of Discovery

Discovery is an adventure in your skull. It may feel like you are discovering things "out there" in the staged reality (it's okay to think of it that way if you prefer), but what is "out there" is only accessible if it's inside you. Every discovery you make comes from what is in your mind.

A discovery occurs silently, just like observing, accepting, and being affected. For example, let's say you observe your right hand, and the position of your fingers reminds you of holding a hammer. Your observation leads to the discovery that you hold a hammer in the staged reality. Your discovery becomes part of the shared reality when you express it. You may say "I am holding a hammer," or swing your arm as if you are hammering, or comment on the quality of your hammering. You can manifest a single discovery many ways.

Until you express your discovery, it is only a potential—hold it lightly. The staged reality may evolve to render your discovery impossible or irrelevant before you can express it. If that happens, cuddle your potential—then snap its neck. It is not for this reality.

For example, before you say, "I have a hammer," someone else says "You are holding a bottle of champagne!" This is a different but valid discovery based on your hand position. That which is first expressed, exists: you hold champagne. You must abandon your hammer idea, or you could discover how it fits with the new information—perhaps you use the bottle as a hammer, the bottle is in the shape of a hammer, or the bottle is labeled "Hammered Champagne."

This mental agility lets you act even when your discovery is fuzzy. Let's say you have no idea what you hold but swinging your arm seems fitting. So you swing away, not sure if you have a hammer, a flyfishing pole, or a bull-whip. You can act on the fuzziness of swinging a "thing." You will discover the specifics of that thing eventually.

A discovery should, in general, feel like it comes from—or fits with—the existing staged reality. It should connect to what comes before. If it doesn't, you may get the note "you're inventing," or the more flowery note, "now you're just making shit up." Each is a reminder to discover from what has come before. Do not fabricate haphazardly. A popular analogy is to "Drive forward by looking in the rearview mirror."

This does not preclude randomness and non sequiturs, which improv adores. But those are spices rather than main ingredients. More on that when we examine your big discovery skills later in this chapter.

Improv lacks standard terminology. Some terms in this chapter are common and others are my approach. Terms are necessary, but they don't help when improvising in the moment. Rely on your training and experience. If things go sideways, follow your gut. It's a street fight.

What You Discover

Our everyday reality is made of countless things. We can ignore most of them until they affect us because each asserts its own existence (or nonexistence). Your car makes its presence known every morning by sitting in the driveway. Its lack of fuel or charge demands your attention. A jelly stain on your seat perpetually reminds you toast is a dangerous car snack.

In contrast, our staged reality starts as a blank slate; nothing asserts its own existence. Improvisors are responsible for each element. We discover everything including the trivial, because the trivial can change an entire world in improv.

Everyday reality in the world is stuffed with countless things, but God took seven days to create it—and who has that kind of time? Instead, like an artist drawing a sketch, we discover a limited number of elements to portray a larger world. Some are crisply drawn; others are left vague.

The zillions of things we could discover fall into a scandalously small number of categories. The following are elements that make a reality: objects, characters, relationships, locations, movements, emotions and ideas, structures.

An **object** is an entity, usually having a physical presence, that lacks the ability to think, feel, and express—a coffee cup, an electron, the Eiffel Tower, an orb of energy. In improv we may not have the actual physical object, but we treat an imagined object as if it has a physical presence.

A **character** is an entity, usually having a physical presence, that has the ability to think, feel, and express. This includes not only people but also anything we endow with those abilities: a coffee cup, an electron, the Eiffel Tower, an orb of energy.

A **relationship** is a connection that carries expectations about the behaviors, feelings, and knowledge between the related. The most common relationships are between characters, such as parent-child, enemies, or best friends. But other relationships exist, such as between a character and object or location, which we call ownership.

A **location** is a defined space: an apartment kitchen, the interior of your stomach, a lunar landing pad. A location carries with it expectation about the objects, characters, and movement that occur within that space.

A **movement** is any act of doing by a character, object, or location. It sounds odd to say objects and locations can "do," but they can: an acorn can fall and the Earth can quake. Character movement is covered more in chapter 13 on expression. Movements relate to each other in a hierarchy:

- **An action** is a short, limited movement: a human cracking an egg, a robot raising its appendage, a gust of wind.
- **An activity** is a combination of related actions: a human making brownies, a robot killing its master, a storm of nature.
- **An event** is a collection of movements, objects, characters, and locations that are related: the County Fair Brownie Competition, the robot uprising, the Earth's revenge.

Emotions and ideas typically belong to a character but can exist independent of characters. An idea or emotion can have broad influence beyond just a character. This is covered more in part three on structures and part five on character.

A **structure** is a sequence of moments that relate. When we say we are improvising "a scene," it is more complete to say we are improvising "moments that relate to form a recognizable structure we call a scene." We could improvise other structures such as a song, a poem, a show, or a conversation. The power of structures is examined in more detail in part three.

The Specific to General Spectrum

Elements of everyday reality exist in full detail, whether we notice the innumerable details or not. But an improvisor can't fuss with so many details in the staged reality, so we must rely on both the specific and the vague. We need a mix.

Specifics affect us. Few people have a strong response to the generic word "food," but salivary glands rouse at "a warm chocolate brownie with slightly crisp edges." Specifics are evocative: they pull focus, simulate reality, stir feelings, suggest meaning, and help connect our various mental items (memories, facts, expectations, and so on).

Generalities have their uses too. For instance, "The two made love like wild animals" paints a different picture than the more specific "The two made love like hippos." Generalities do a great job of conveying ideas, backgrounding the less important, avoiding conflict with other information, and engaging people to furnish their own often familiar specifics.

Each element discovered in the staged reality falls on a spectrum of specific to general. At one end of the spectrum is "He sauteed diced shallots in salted butter on a 320-degree Fahrenheit cast iron skillet, which had an engraving on the handle that read 'Happy belated 18th birthday, Frederick, from your loving, younger, half-sister, Adelheid,'" and at the other end is "A thing did stuff to things." We can go too far in either direction. (There will be times when going too far is fun . . . you'll know it when it happens.)

New improvisors, in general, avoid getting specific—evidenced by their use of nonspecific words such as "this," "that," "these," "those," and "things" but never defining what those words refer to. It's natural to stay general in situations that are unclear but, ironically, clarity comes through specifics. Generalities also mean different things to different people, so to build a shared reality we must use some specifics.

A good habit for an improvisor is to sprinkle specifics liberally. Like scattering seeds, some may lie dormant while others take root and grow. You can't predict which will thrive, so don't bother. Scatter away.

When hearing the note "get specific!" an improvisor will often go into a mania, tacking on endless details. This result is often tedious. When indulging fun you may need to pursue a more precise type of specific. That is, you need to get "speunausible."

The word speunausible (spew-NAWZ-uh-bull) does not exist outside this book. It means specific, unique, and plausible: specific in that the instance is clear and distinct from others, unique in that it is uncommon, and plausible in that it could exist in its given reality. This is fertile ground for improvisors.

For example, in our everyday reality, "a sandwich" is plausible but not specific or unique. A "turkey sandwich on rye with mustard, pickle, and cheddar" is specific and plausible, but not unique. An "angel-wing sandwich, hold the mayo" is specific and unique, but not plausible (in a given reality). A "ham and Swiss on graham crackers" is specific, unique, and plausible . . . and ill-advised.

Specificity may not come out in one plop; it often can take several moments. For instance, from a glance you may discover that your character is attracted to the person next to you, then discover you two are engaged, then discover you are getting remarried after just divorcing each other. That specific relationship takes time to uncover.

We get specific by discovering attributes that discriminate one thing from another (i.e., aggressive, crinkly, 250 pounds). Without attributes, our staged reality only contains generic blobs of existence. You will hear words like "label," "quality," "trait," and "characteristic," which all mean the same thing.

Not all attributes, however, function the same. Let's examine how different attributes create specificity.

- An **objective attribute** describes with minimal interpretation: green, sixteen kilograms, man, biological mother, silent, wooden. There is little confusion about their meaning, making them perfect to create a shared reality.
- A **subjective attribute** describes relative to the values of an individual: fat, smart, bad, rude, generous. Each person interprets these words differently. Most people like a nice dinner date, but your values determine whether that involves a flight to Paris or a drive-through liquor store.
- A **type attribute** identifies a set of generally agreed upon features that describe a thing's nature: lamp, ocean, minivan, submarine. A type attribute seems just like a noun—but thinking of it as an attribute is useful for improv. We often can't birth our creation in one push. Discovering the existence of a thing can be separate from discovering what it is. We open a present to discover an

object but have no idea what it is. We may carry it around, wave it about, toss it . . . but only after we label it with a type do we know it is a softball, an ostrich egg, or a grenade.

A well-chosen type is economic, cutting a precise image with few words. If you doubt that, ask a nocturnal predatory feathered flying animal; or a nocturnal predatory bird; or an owl.

- ✻ A **style** is a set of attributes that describe a thing's form, but not its function or nature. A Shakespearian style would recruit the attributes we associate with a play written by William Shakespeare—including the words, diction, and clothing. We can apply that style to a newscast, dinner, or trench warfare. Each would retain its nature as a newscast, dinner, or trench warfare but have Shakespearian qualities. A style can refer to an artist, genre, culture, or any group of things. For instance, ballroom dancing in the style of a brick would recruit the attributes you associate with bricks.
- ✻ A **sensory attribute** refers to the sound and feel of a word, independent of the word's meaning. "Fussy" and "persnickety" feel and sound different when spoken. The names Dick Gurtz and Porsche Ellingham can inform us about the qualities of those characters. Sensory attributes are always available. You don't need the definition of a word to extract meaning from it.
- ✻ A **handle** is the phrase we use to point to a thing: John Doe, Serial Number 0538-MG7550-2831, the Black Plague, 50 Albemarle Street. A handle is how we linguistically grab something, but it can also communicate other attributes such as with the name Blackbeard the Pirate.

Your Big Discovery Skills

You have three big, all-purpose skills you use to discover elements and their attributes. For this discussion we treat these skills as separate, but in practice their boundaries blur.

- ✻ Associate
- ✻ Infer
- ✻ Intuit

ASSOCIATE

To associate is to follow a perceived connection from one thing to another. Association may be the mother of all discovery skills because it is reliable, quick, and comprehensive. Everything in your head is associated to some other thing in your head. If an item in your head has no associations, good luck remembering it.

No matter how we categorize our mental items (memories, facts, fiction, images, procedures, grudges, and so on), they all mingle in the same pool when associating. A character in a movie can remind you of your coworker's mustache, which reminds you of an elevator inspection certificate, which reminds you that in the United States, grounded electrical wires are color coded green, which reminds you of the panic you felt in a urine-splashed stairwell of a deserted parking garage. You forged each association at some point, and they are, de facto, valid. Use them. It's as if you've been preparing for improv your whole life.

Leading statements that can spur your association engine:

- ✻ "That reminds me of . . ."
- ✻ "This feels like . . ."
- ✻ "What I know about that is . . ."
- ✻ "Those are related by . . ."

INFER

To infer is to reason a conclusion that is suggested by the evidence, although it may not be proven by evidence. For instance, if you see two people talking on a park bench you could conclude they are either friends chatting with each other or strangers talking to themselves. Both conclusions are possible, but neither is for sure.

Inference is concerned with a clear reasoning, not a conclusion that is "right" or even probable. It's about making a sense that can be followed, not a sense that others might agree with. In our everyday reality "right" is determined by comparing your conclusion to what exists, but in improv what you conclude usually defines what exists. Infer boldly.

If "inferring" scares you, try its complement "implying." Shift perspectives from "What do I infer?" to "What does it imply?" Putting the focus outside of oneself can relieve the stress of making bold assumptions. It is mental trickery because the work is the same, but if it helps you then trick, trick, trick, away.

Leading statements that can jump-start your inference engine:

- ❊ "And what that means is . . ."
- ❊ "If that is true, then . . ."
- ❊ "What you are really trying to say is . . ."

INTUIT

To intuit is to make a conclusion by nonrational means. Intuition's lack of logic does not mean it lacks sophisticated processing; it just means we aren't privy to that processing. Be careful, intuition's inscrutable nature makes it susceptible to the biases of your brain and your brain's evil desire to control outcomes.

Intuition carries risk because to share a reality we need a minimum of logic. Usually we make sense of an intuited discovery or we enjoy the sprinkling of arbitrariness. But when intuition is overused, we fall behind justifying each discovery—too much information doesn't fit the staged reality. This is called crazy-town, crazy-train, or just plain bat-shit crazy. It can be fun, it's just crazy.

The brain frequently unleashes this beast if association and inference come up empty. Some different flavors of intuition include:

- ❊ **Gut feel.** Sometimes something deep inside you rumbles and vomits a discovery. It seems dangerous to ignore that kind of mojo. Obey.
- ❊ **Muscle memory.** Your body make choices on its own by how it moves, forms words, or simulates interacting with objects. Let it do its work. Then figure out what it means.
- ❊ **Reflex.** Your fastest emotional, intellectual, or physical response is often better than anything deliberated.
- ❊ **Random-ish-ness.** Generating truly random information may be impossible since the brain has its own patterns, but the attempt is productive.

Tactics and Terms

Improvisors use big discovery skills for specific effects, and these tactics are often perceived as special skills with special names. No matter how many of these you hear about, or how they are taught, they are just specific uses of your big three skills. Let's look at some tactics and terms you may run into. The following is not complete, not exhaustive, and not shabby.

Improvisors make discoveries that fulfill what has been set up explicitly or implicitly. You might hear this as "Pay it off!" If your character is labeled a hot head, you can get upset at a common inconvenience. If labeled sophisticated, pour a snifter of cognac. If someone says it's cold, *manifest* that by putting on a jacket.

This includes fulfilling a *pattern* or *rule.* A rule that "you must sit when another person speaks" helps discover what to do. This includes what some call fulfilling the "game of the scene," a pattern with rules that drives discovery. Fulfilling an *analogy,* or *mapping,* also aids discovery: when looking for who ate the last brownie, your knowledge of a police procedural is there to help.

We will cover structures later in the book, but progressing through a structure, such as a scene, song, or poem, also helps discover what is next, and is a kind of pattern fulfillment.

The note "justify," means to make sense of what seems to conflict within the staged reality or with everyday reality. If you were named Chris in a scene but someone just called you Pat, a justification could be that Pat is the name of your twin. If you chew glass without flinching, a justification could be your dental braces are so painful you didn't notice.

A technique to justify when you have no idea how to make sense of something is to build rungs of a *ladder* with simple, reasonable statements until you reach a connection to the principal issue. For instance, to explain to your boss why sleeping on the job is good: sleep requires quiet; if I sleep, everyone is quietly working at their desks; my sleep measures the workgroup's productivity; I am your most valuable employee; I'll take that raise now.

Improvisors often *isolate* an element to explore its meaning. You may simply *call out* what affects you: "Okay, we blew the world up and now we're in Central Park talking about it." You can *confess* your character's internal state with an "I feel . . ." or "I prefer . . ." or "I think . . ." statement, which is a classic tactic when things get wacky. You can also isolate on one part of a whole by *deconstructing.* The line "I fed the cat this morning," could be *parsed* to focus on who took action (I), the act (feeding), what was fed (the cat), or the time of day (morning). You can also isolate with emotion, "WE ARE BAKING BROWNIES!!"

Repetition is another way to isolate an element and increase its meaning. Improvisors can *mirror* each other's attitude, posture, and voice to foreground character. And you can surprise everyone with a *call-back,* by repeating an element that has slipped from everyone's immediate memory. But if you wait too long people may not remember what you are calling back—at least that's what Ernie says.

Heightening is to make something more extreme. If Claire finds a penny on her way to work, we heighten by discovering how her day goes from good, to great, to ecstatic. We could juxtapose her with Gary, who lost a penny and sees his day spiral into catastrophe. Repetition can also heighten.

When you *sharpen,* you continue getting more specific. Look at this candlestick holder . . . there is price on it . . . for $99 . . . with a red tag discount to $60 . . . and hand marked down to $10 . . . it's labeled "imperfect." You can sharpen any element: locations, objects, relationship, actions, and so on.

You may hear the general advice "advance and explore," which sounds amazing but is slippery to define. It refers to alternating between expanding the staged reality with discoveries and then discovering how that new information relates. For instance, once you advance a scene by discovering you are half-sisters neurotically baking apple strudel in the kitchen of the local Eagles club, you then explore the details and dynamic of that situation. A similar piece of advice is "create and reuse."

Most of the staged reality is revealed through what a *character* says and does, which is driven by the character's point of view. A point of view is like a diesel-powered industrial strength discovery machine. We'll go into character more in later chapters.

Tricky Discovery

A murder mystery in improv is notoriously tricky. Creating any kind of whodunit with no plan is nerve-wracking and high risk. Everyone's internal writer desperately wants to decide on an answer and drop a trail of breadcrumbs throughout the piece, leaving little room for true discovery.

In one performance we were about to reveal the murderer, who stood in a closet. Our mystery had been no Agatha Christie, but it was pretty good, a rare achievement for the genre. When we opened the closet door, however, our suspected murderer was a contorted mess on the floor, herself murdered.

The audience loved her bold choice, but my stomach dropped—we had to run back into the fire we had almost escaped. And then I received a lesson. Robbed of an easier solution we continued to play and, due to some astute minds, organically discovered the true murderer—the facts made perfect sense. It was a real, legitimate, mystery—solved. By being denied good we found great, but only because we kept discovering.

Chaining Discoveries

You can chain together potentials (unexpressed discoveries) to arrive at an unexpected discovery far from the observation. For instance: you make observation A, which spurs discovery B, but instead of expressing B you use it to spur discovery C, which you express. You make a chain: A→[B]→C. Others sense the implied existence of B, and it becomes a part of the staged reality. (Notice that "B" is placed in square brackets to indicate that it is not expressed. We'll use that convention in the next few paragraphs.)

You can chain more than two discoveries. For example, someone hands you an imaginary document→[it must be an exam paper]→[you are a stern professor of macroeconomics]→[the student has failed]→[the student will not survive academia]→[you have a parting gift]→you present an object and disdainfully say, "Here's a plunger, good luck as a plumber."

Such a long chain built in the solitude of your mind has risks. The longer the chain, the less likely others will divine the intermediate discoveries. Others might make sense of what you express—but it may not be your sense. In this example they might see a dystopian future where, after being presented with paperwork from the Ministry of Nepotism, a bitter bureaucrat grants the coveted tool needed to become a plumber.

Short chains are less risky. Think A→[B]→C.

Exploiting Implicits

An improvisor can recognize and use an implicit discovery to influence future discoveries: it becomes a powerful, invisible organizing force. A typical use is to infer a general attribute from an observation and use that generalization to fuel more discoveries. The general attribute could describe a character, a scene, a show . . . anything.

- **Character.** You interrupt someone before they finish speaking. We'll call that observation "A." From that you discover your character is rude, which is discovery B. You could say "I am a rude person," making that discovery explicit, A→B. Instead, you keep silent on that and discover how to be rude while advancing the scene A→[B]→C (e.g., perhaps you relieve your bladder on the breakroom floor while you make coffee).

✻ **Scene.** Your partner looks away when they talk to you. That is observation A. You discover the scene feels like a soap opera. That is discovery B. You could say "This feels like a soap opera," but you don't. You let the soap operaness inform how you conduct the rest of the scene (a bunch of Cs) with melodrama and scandalous revelations. The other improvisor recognizes your implied discovery and plays along.

✻ **Show.** You notice the audience laughs during a scene. That is observation A. You discover the underlying premise that provoked laughter (discovery B) but keep silent on it. You then start subsequent scenes (a bunch of Cs) with different characters at different locations, with each a more extreme situation of the same premise.

Taking the Third

Some improvisors follow the philosophy "Don't take the first thing that comes to mind, take the third." Using our previous notation, this looks like A→[B1], [B2], B3, where observation A leads to three discoveries, unrelated and of different nature, of which only the third is expressed. (Instead of three you could take two, or twenty—whatever you fancy.)

For example, when you observe the position of your fingers you silently discover *I'm holding a hammer* [B1], *I'm wrangling a snake* [B2], only to express your final discovery B3, "I'm strangling a teddy bear."

This approach isn't searching for the "best" discovery. It is exploring your brain and running with what you find. This burns off initial discoveries that tend to be predictable, maybe even cliché.

This silent process is sometimes exposed. During an improvised scene, an instructor or director might interrupt an improvisor with the command "new choice," and the improvisor must express an alternate to what they last said or did. The command is repeated until arriving at a particularly difficult or surprising choice, and the improvisors must deal with that discovery in the staged reality. If you can't find fun, this is one cure.

Wrap It Up

To discover is to infer, associate, or intuit what exists, on a spectrum of specific to generic, from what has come before. Discovery is one of the six fundamental components of a moment, the only thing we can make when we improvise.

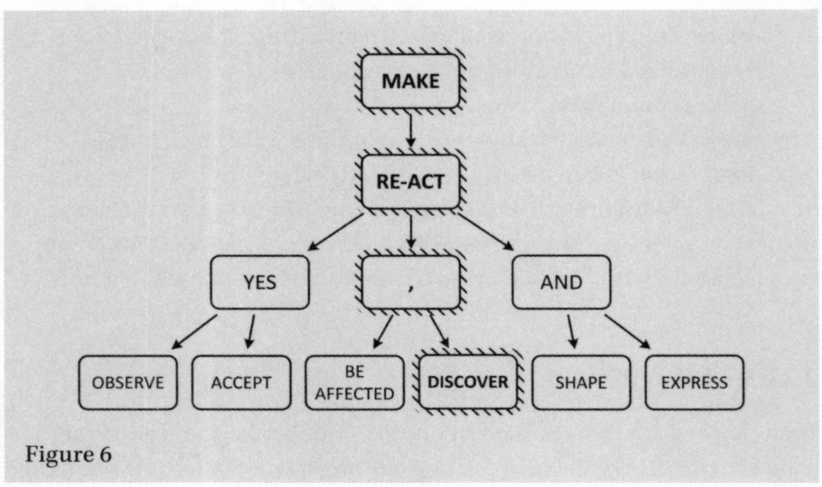

Figure 6

12

Shape

We shape the expression of a discovery to support both the integrity of the staged reality and our creative needs.

Many Shapes to Express One Discovery

There are various ways to express a single discovery. That's right. Correct. Amen. Affirmative. Uh-huh. Bingo!

For example, a waiter approaches your table and says, "I hope you're enjoying the soup," and you feel you are not enjoying it. For now, we don't care how you discovered that feeling, we'll assume it was sound. There are many ways to shape the expression of your displeasure. Here are a handful:

- Confide to the waiter "I prefer less cumin."
- Inch the imaginary bowl off the table.
- Burst into song about disappointing soup.
- Take out a sheet of imaginary stationary, write a letter, mail it, time dash to a week later, open a newspaper, and publicly read your scathing review of the soup.

Discovery and shaping have similarities, but they are different. Discovery is like having an idea, whereas shaping is like finding the words to write that idea in a sentence. Discoveries originate inside us and bubble up until they are expressed into the staged reality. As they are bubbling between discovery and expression, they are shaped by two forces: the integrity of the staged reality and our creative needs.

Integrity of the Staged Reality

The integrity of the staged reality is the feeling that the staged reality is whole and consistent: all its elements make sense within it. Without integrity, our staged reality fractures into disjointed fragments or, worse, a mess of nonsense. Humans are constantly uncovering vast deposits of nonsense; we needn't make more. We give the staged reality integrity by respecting what already exists and creating new elements that can coexist with that.

What already exists includes hard features that pass from our everyday reality into the staged reality such as walls, railings, and time constraints. We must respect these features; they are unforgiving. Let's say in the staged reality you are walking in a wheat field, but while doing so you step off the edge of the stage. That edge is inconsistent with a wheat field; it destroys the staged reality's integrity. However you might justify your fall by discovering a silver mine in that field, restoring integrity to the staged reality—although not to your ankle.

In addition to hard features, what already exists includes everything previously expressed by improvisors. What an improvisor expresses does not enforce itself like hard features. It is up to us to honor them. If careless, you can destroy the integrity of the staged reality without noticing. Nothing prevents your bad Australian accent from morphing into a bad Japanese accent except your vigilance.

Your Creative Needs

You have a duty to support your creative needs, which includes indulging what you think is fun and avoiding what ruffles your moral feathers. No one knows what will unfold in improv, and you may face two possible conflicts: 1.) the staged reality wants you to do something you don't prefer; or 2.) you want to do something the staged reality doesn't prefer.

For the first conflict, it feels like you are skating the edge of your moral code or into unsafe territory. It is more than just the reluctance of leaving your comfort zone. You are responsible for your actions: if you decide something is out of bounds for you, it is. However, you must still find a way to support the staged reality or at least do it no harm. Shaping solves this conundrum.

For example, let's assume you feel strongly about not cursing. One day you find yourself in a staged reality that was built with textbook-perfect improv, impeccable in every way, to create a reality in which everyone swears like angry sailors.

You could shed your moral code for a few minutes and shape your discoveries to be expressed via the filthiest language you can imagine. When the piece is over, you can pat yourself on the back for supporting the staged reality, take a soapy shower, and return to your respectably articulate life.

But what if you really, really, really don't want to swear? That's okay. You can shape your discoveries so that everyone wins: perhaps you curse with gusto but with words you invent; or substitute a beep for every curse; or use language at the edge of your personal limits, thereby defining your character's "bad" language; or write your curses on an imaginary sign and display it for others to say. Shaping discoveries allows you to keep your personal code but also support the staged reality.

Shaping also remedies the second type of conflict, when your creative voice wants something that doesn't seem to fit the staged reality. We must remember that we often don't see the logic of our urges until after they are expressed. Shaping helps these situations.

Let's say you find yourself in a staged reality in which you are enjoying a perfectly romantic picnic, on a perfectly romantic hilltop, with a perfectly romantic partner. And through textbook-perfect improv, impeccable in every way, you look in the picnic basket to discover an object. It's undeniable to you. Your mind sees it—a flamethrower.

You could drop your discovery, sensing it would break the integrity of the romantic reality, and look around the picnic basket to discover, beneath that flamethrower, a perfectly romantic poem to read. When the piece is over, you can pat yourself on the back for supporting the staged reality, take a bubble bath, and go light a dumpster on fire.

But what if you really, really, really want to use a flamethrower? That's okay. You can shape that discovery so that everyone wins. Perhaps the flamethrower is a romantic gift of self-defense complete with ribbon on top, or it's a tool to build a romantic fire, or it's a weapon to incinerate approaching unromantic zombies. These, and much better options, allow you to support the staged reality and accommodate your personal flamethrower needs.

The Clash

Balancing creative needs with the needs of the staged reality is a constraint, but an essential one that propels specific, personal, and interesting work. Constraints enable creativity.

A vast majority of the time, all the needs can be satisfied. Happiness abounds. But when your discovery cannot fit, your creative need must be the one that is sacrificed—never the staged reality. The integrity of the staged reality must be the dominant goal, for two simple reasons:

- ❊ The staged reality is the vehicle through which your creative needs get fulfilled; if it gets sacrificed, your fun ends.
- ❊ The staged reality is the shared product of our collaborative effort; if it gets sacrificed, the collaboration ends.

You Always Shape

There is at least a small amount of shaping that occurs with every discovery. You are like a mason building a stone wall—even if you find a rock with the ideal form you will have to chip it slightly to mate with the stones you have previously set.

Each expression from a character needs shaping because what people do and how they do it has its own integrity. Can you imagine how anger would be expressed differently by a squirrel, a supercomputer, or the Sun?

Sometimes you must fully shape your discovery prior to its expression. For example, if the staged reality is created for a young audience and your contempt for another character is reflected by naming him "J. J. the Asshole," that name is difficult to integrate into the squeaky-clean staged reality once it is expressed. It must be fully shaped before expressing, perhaps yielding a more appropriate "J. J. the Jerk."

Other situations are more forgiving, and your discovery can be roughly shaped. You know your expression doesn't perfectly fit the staged reality, but it's the best you could do in the moment. Then you and others get busy discovering how it fits. In our romantic flamethrower scenario if you couldn't figure out how the flamethrower supported the staged reality, you could roughly shape it and then you and your partner could discover how it fits over the next several moments.

- ❊ You remove the flamethrower from the basket and feeling its heft say, "I brought you a flamethrower." ("I brought you" roughly shapes it to be relevant to the relationship and event.)
- ❊ Your partner strokes the flamethrower, "A candy apple red paint job, mmmm . . . sexy."
- ❊ "I borrowed it from my dad," you say as you gaze into your partner's eyes. "I told him I wanted this to be a special evening."
- ❊ Your partner grasps the handle, "Oh Gary, I've never lit a forest on fire before."
- ❊ You touch your partner's cheek, "Claire, I swore I never would . . .

until I met the right person." Then you and your partner proceed to torch the surrounding hillside.

In addition to this rough shaping, remember that components of a moment can happen at once. Shaping a discovery can occur while it is being expressed. The act of doing affects the doing while you are doing. Knowing these are valid approaches will hopefully liberate you from feeling you must have "everything figured out" before taking action.

Keep in mind shaping occurs not just to words, but with your movements. In one scene my character was disgusted by the actions of another and was compelled to spit on him. The idea was brilliant. Its execution was not. I didn't fully shape my spitting action to be a "stage spit." To my horror, and my scene partner's displeasure, I realized mid-action that actual spit came out. How much doesn't matter; any spit is too much spit. If you are lucky, you'll play with people whom you have built up a lot of goodwill with, and who will take anything you give them to fuel their work—even spit. That day, I was very lucky.

Wrap It Up

You shape the expression of a discovery to support both the integrity of the staged reality and your creative needs. These two factors help make our work personal, unique, and interesting. Shaping is one of the six fundamental components of a moment, the only thing we can make when we improvise.

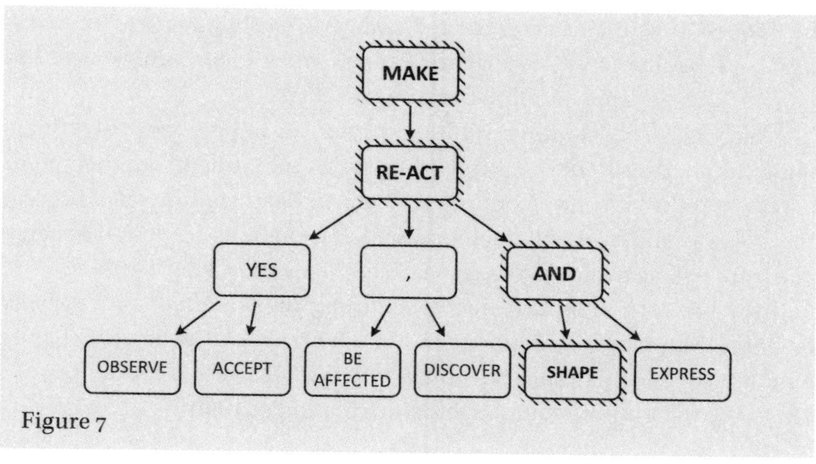

Figure 7

13

Express

Your expression is a discovery born into reality; it is the only way to affect others. To express is to share information by doing something in the staged reality.

The Point of No Return

You express a discovery that has been shaped. Recall that until a discovery is expressed, it is only a potential in your mind. It can be made impossible or irrelevant at any time by the unfolding staged reality until the moment you express it. Stay alert!

You express by doing. What you do must be observed by others. Obvious? Obviously. But noteworthy since expression is the only one of the six components of a moment that is visible to others. In a staged reality, if something is not observed, it does not exist.

When we express in the shared reality, we pass a point of no return. Whatever you express, whether it was what you intended or not, cannot be undone. If your character is tired and says "Gosh, I am tire," then it is highly probable you are now a tire. An improvisor incorporates what has happened, as it happened, into the staged reality.

Avoid expressing the inner workings of you, the improvisor. It's common for an improvisor to have a surge of emotions that differ from their character's, whether it be joy, confusion, or panic. Keep your internal process tucked away and let the character present. It is the secret of your butcher: if you want people to enjoy the sausage, don't show them how it's made.

If you break the staged reality by exposing your internal state (usually laughter), you may hear the warning "don't break" or the corrective note "commit!" When this happens, think *So this is what it feels like to have a good time,* then incorporate your laughter into the staged reality.

You Are Always Expressing

You're always doing something, even when "doing nothing." What we often call doing nothing is resting, or standing, or staring, or thinking . . . something like that. It refers to having little physical movement for prolonged periods or when movement is expected. There is never a moment you do nothing—your boss may disagree, but an improvisor understands.

> Claire: My house was on fire, and you did nothing!?
> Gary: No, I watched it burn.
> Claire: Oh, right. Sorry.

Since we are always doing, we are always expressing. Whether the doing is big like dashing across a room or small like raising an eyebrow.

We label what we do with simple words, but what we do is rarely simple. It takes years of struggle to master what we casually call "tying your shoes." The concept is simple but the execution difficult, one reason why childhood is a campaign of frustration. Our doings are almost always complex and compound, made of many what-you-do's.

There is always specificity in those complex and compound doings. Gary can stroll, saunter, sulk, sneak, or storm into the room. The difference between those actions lies in the nuances of how Gary does the complex and compound act we could simply refer to as walking.

What You Do

In the staged reality you can do anything we do in everyday reality, such as stuffing a pillow or vacuuming a pool. You can also do things we can't do in everyday reality, such as cutting a hole in time or rummaging through someone's memory.

You may have no actual knowledge about the activity or event in which you are engaged, but that must not stop you from taking action. In any moment your doing is always a simple action. No matter how fantastical or complex the situation, you can only do a simple action. Then do another, then another, and so on.

Let's take a closer look at some common things we do: interacting with objects, vocalizing, and bodily motion.

Interacting with Objects

A lot of life is spent fiddling with objects, but improv is usually performed without props or costumes or set pieces. That means we must make what we need in the fastest and laziest way possible. The fast and lazy way to make objects is called “spacework” or “object work.” I will use the term “spacework” since it sounds more mysterious.

Spacework is the realistic interaction with objects in space that do not exist. Think of it as the practice of using imaginary things. Spacework allows the improvisor to create any object they need, for any setting, at any time, for zero dollars. That’s a good value.

Spacework is not indicating an object. Indication, in this sense, is a visual symbol that points to the existence of a thing. If you pretend to rob your friend at gunpoint you will probably point your index finger to indicate the barrel, extend your thumb up in the air to indicate the hammer on the revolver, and fold your remaining three fingers as if making a fist to indicate the grip. That’s a well-indicated gun. But your fingers are not a gun. They are your fingers, shaped into a symbol of a gun. That is indication.

For our purposes, simulation is more useful than indication. A simulation tries to replicate an everyday reality as closely as possible. A simulation of holding a gun would have your index finger extended yet curved to be on a trigger, your thumb is wrapped around the back of the grip, and your remaining three fingers are wrapped but not closed, so they leave enough room to account for the volume of the grip. It’s not perfect, but it gets us closer to simulating an actual object in your hand. Your fingers get to remain your fingers, which makes them happy.

Indication is less useful for improv because it requires us to ignore the details of what we observe. When indicating, our body stops representing itself and starts representing an idea.

Simulation is more useful because we can accept what we observe exactly as we observe it. For instance, if we simulate lifting a beachball-sized boulder without muscular effort, we can discover any of the following: we are incredibly strong, the boulder has low density, or gravity is weak. But if we work in the less precise world of indication, we may never notice how easily we moved the boulder because, after all, it’s just the idea of lifting a boulder. We would look past what we actually observe in favor of the indicated meaning.

In practice, any spacework falls somewhere on the spectrum between sloppy indication and perfect simulation. Strive toward perfect simulation. Despite your efforts, your simulations will rarely be perfect and involve some degree of "yeah, yeah, yeah, we get it." Minimize those "yeah, yeah, yeahs."

SPACEWORK TIPS

For your spacework to be a mindbogglingly realistic simulation you can spend a lifetime studying kinesiology or you can follow a few simple rules. These are "rules of existence" that objects enforce in everyday reality, but which improvisors must enforce on their behalf in the staged reality—or notice when we violate them. If you follow these rules people will ask, "Wow, did you spend a lifetime studying kinesiology?" Respond coldly, "It is the only way."

✻ **Volume.** An object has dimensions in space and occupies volume. For most rigid and semi-rigid objects, dimensions are constant regardless how they are translated or rotated. Notice if your objects grow or shrink magically, especially work surfaces such as tables or countertops.

✻ **Mass.** An object has mass, and when gravity acts on mass we call it weight. Weight is typically constant for a location. Notice if your object lacks or has variable weight. Express muscular effort in proportion to an object's weight when interacting with it.

✻ **Permanence.** An object has permanence, which means it doesn't pop in and out of existence on its own. If you need an object, you must get it from somewhere, and when you are done with it you must put it somewhere. Where you left it is where it will be unless something acts upon it. Attend to where things come from and go to. Pro tip: objects typically don't float in the air.

✻ **Structure.** An object has a structure that dictates how it responds to forces and how we interact with it. Structure accounts for the materials and construction that give an object form and paths of motion: drawers slide straight out, a door handle swings in an arc of constant radius, a pillowcase collapses, your hand enters the top of a cookie jar and exits by the same path (i.e., not through the side of the jar).

Two additional tidbits make your spacework clearer to observers. The first is to over-articulate when you grab and release an object. When you over-articulate your speech you focus on pro-noun-sing ehv-ree sih-lah-bull, by slightly exaggerating mouth movements. Similarly you slightly exaggerate grabbing and letting go of objects. This might violate perfect simulation, but it helps.

The second tidbit is to always give thin objects some volume, even if it seems silly, such as for a piece of paper. That small space allows an object to exist. It is the difference between "pinching a piece of paper" and "pinching your fingers together." Similarly, if you scrub the floor with an imaginary towel, your hand should not touch the actual floor. Leave space to accommodate the imagined object and avoid causing sound (hand rubbing against ground), which would conflict with the sound we expect from the imagined objects (wet towel on floor).

You don't have to know the object you are working with to interact with it. Take a specific movement, such as grasping and turning an unknown object, and see what you discover: you could be tuning a ham radio, removing a uranium rod, or gently twisting a stake into a vampire. It can be any of those things because the spacework you express is just that—spacework. Until the object or action is asserted, they are potentials.

WORKING WITH OBJECTS THAT STRADDLE REALITIES

Most people perform improv wearing clothes. It can be confusing how to navigate between your real clothes and your imagined clothes in the staged reality.

In general, it is preferable to use spacework for all wardrobe concerns. If you take off your pants, take off spacework pants. That goes double for someone else's pants. If you reach in a pocket, use a spacework pocket. If you need a wallet, spacework a wallet. This keeps the staged reality and our everyday reality separate both for clarity and flexibility. If you interact with your physical wardrobe too much it becomes confusing as to what we should accept or ignore from everyday reality (e.g., are your mismatched socks part of the staged reality or not).

If a physical object is used in the staged reality, then that is where it lives. Thus, if you accidentally or purposefully use a piece of wardrobe, like a hat, then that hat is part of the staged reality for its duration. Our minds can magically keep track of which items are in the staged reality and which aren't, but be consistent and judicious.

Physical objects straddle realities and can have attributes in each. If you use a rickety black chair, we can add to or reinterpret its features in the staged reality to become a golden commode, a dirty throne, or a deep-sea diver's helmet.

Your body is also a physical object that straddles realities and can have attributes in each: the fat can become thin and the thin become fat. You can even lose your humanity; you can be an object. Is a coffee table needed? Be the table. An atom? Why not. A robot? Slam dunk. As an object you may or may not be a character (an entity that possesses thought, emotion, and the ability to express), but objects can perform actions that affect the staged reality. Clocks tick. Doors open. Meteors crash. Even mountains can move if you discover they do.

When you portray an object, your body is condemned to be less a simulation and more an indication. Against those impossible odds you should still strive to simulate as best you can. Fight the good fight.

I learned the "spacework your clothes" lesson the hard way. In one of the first classes I took, I had to read an imaginary correspondence that explained why my letter to the editor would not be published. The objective was to get emotional over something minor. As I read that imaginary letter, I got angrier and angrier. Unsure of how to heighten my anger further, it seemed like a good idea to rip off my shirt. So I did. I finished my tirade as a bare-chested maniac. I sat down and put my shirt on. As I watched others do their work, I noticed they kept their clothes on the whole time and it dawned on me—I have poor judgment. A week later the instructor told everyone to "keep your real clothes on." He was speaking to me, but he was kind enough to pretend everyone needed that message.

Vocalize

Vocalizing includes any sound that emanates from your pie hole, whether it be singing, sound effects, humming, grunting, or gibberish. If you noticed, I omitted speaking.

You don't need to be reminded of speech. It is everybody's favorite form of vocalization. Our love blinds us from seeing that talk is cheap, lazy, and complacent. You deserve more. There are expressive options that don't use words and they are dying for your attention.

Bodily Movement

Moving your body from one place to another expresses information about the character and space. If you are on the west side of a space and then you move to the east side, the path you take expresses information about the staged reality. Perhaps you avoid a specific area that we later discover is a tar pit, a freshly shampooed rug, or where you once saw a ghost.

You can move on stage and off, amongst the audience, lobby, and even the parking lot. It's all fair game, so long as it supports the shared reality and remains fun.

The quality of our movement also expresses. A walk, hop, hobble, skip, or roll all say different things. Similarly, we can trudge through muck, brace against the wind, glide through air, or feel through fog.

The absence of motion is also expressive. It is common for improvisors to get stuck standing in one spot. Usually that provokes the note "move!" But recognize that stuckness, if accepted, can also be viewed as an important expression. Stillness can say plenty about the space, character, or situation. You can exist in a closet, have your feet nailed to the floor, or be a statue.

Bring Your Best Acting

Simulation is preferable to indication for all doings in the staged reality, especially our emotions. We have depended on reading the emotional states of others since birth and we are sensitive to nuance. If an emotion doesn't feel authentic enough it becomes an indication, it is a symbol. A common note for this is that you are "playing at." A less tender note is "bad acting."

The message: be a good actor. The good news is that "good" is relative. What constitutes good acting is different from place to place, decade to decade, medium to medium, fashion to fashion.

Improv typically has wide latitude for what constitutes acceptable acting because we are not specializing in acting, we are specializing in improvising, of which acting is a single skill (an improvisor is also writer, director, choreographer, stuntman, and so on). Improv is also spontaneous; it does not allow the same preparation as other actorly endeavors.

Regardless of those factors, you still must act to the height of your abilities. The more refined your skill set, the more engaging the experience will be for both the audience and you. Fortunately, wherever your acting skills are now is exactly the spot from which you should start.

If you are a trained actor, you are a specialist with superpowers. These superpowers will serve you well. To challenge you, improv is going to remove some of the tools you rely on for your craft. This may be uncomfortable but is necessary for you to develop new superpowers. You will not be allowed to prepare as you may have been trained as an actor. You will be stripped of prior knowledge of character, plot, arc, dialogue, circumstance, objective, and relationships. You must still forge ahead when nothing is defined. This often requires emotional choices that have opaque motivations. If all that sounds tawdry, try to find the fun in tawdry.

If you have no acting training, do not worry. Your job is to pretend like you do. Acting requires a range of skills that you can hone for years. The following is your four-paragraph crash course, which is probably four paragraphs more than you need to begin improvising.

"Acting is behaving truthfully under imaginary circumstances." Those words were spoken by a guy named Sanford Meisner. He gave a reasonable definition for the acting you need in improv. It jettisons the baggage we may have around what it means to act. Do what makes sense if the situation in the staged reality were true.

Untrained actors often find it challenging to express emotions in public, especially for an imagined situation. Perhaps this is because in everyday reality we mute emotions to grease social interactions. But in the staged reality, that hides what is happening. You must let it shine.

Whatever your comfort with emotion, keep in mind there are two ways to work. If you commit to an imaginary situation well enough, you often connect to an authentic emotion. When that happens, your job is to let it freely come through your body and voice so it can be seen and heard. Other times we might not feel an emotion that fits the staged reality. When that happens, your job is to simulate emotion with your voice and body the best you can, even if you don't feel it. Surprisingly, sometimes this makes you feel it.

Here are three emotional tips to help the untrained actor in improv:

1. Get comfortable living an emotion without knowing its cause or purpose. The meaning of the emotion will be discovered, but it often takes time.
2. Stay open to emotional nuance and shifts; don't cling to a state.
3. Action reveals emotion. You can chop parsley while saying you feel fragile, but the world wants to see you chopping parsley the most fragile way possible.

The trained and untrained actor share a common goal—to live naturally on stage without concern if anyone is observing. A guy named Konstantin Stanislavski captured this idea with the phrase "public solitude." It is to act as freely in public as if one were in private.

Improv is a path to public solitude. The problems and tasks that need to be addressed while improvising consume vast amounts of brainpower. There is little capacity to be concerned with an observer's judgment, or our own. Improvising is the antidote for self-consciousness.

Whether trained in acting or not, all eventually find this truth: our best acting leads to our best improv, and our best improv leads to our best acting.

Wrap It Up

Expression is a discovery born into the staged reality through what you do, and do not do, with your voice and body. Simulation is more useful than indication. Be your best actor. Expressing is one of the six fundamental components of a moment, the only thing we can make when we improvise.

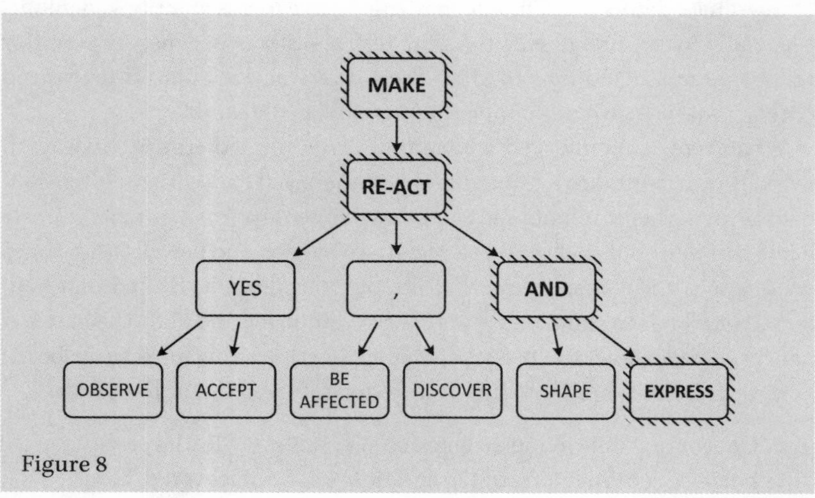

Figure 8

14

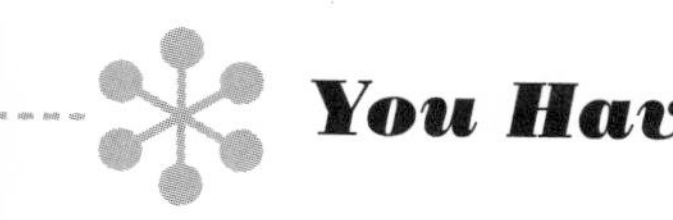

You Have Arrived

Congratulations! You have covered the basics of improv. I hope you feel a sense of achievement—because it is an achievement. You climbed this peak and deserve to relax on the summit: make a mimosa, microwave some popcorn, and plant a flag that says, "I Made a Molehill Out of This Mountain!"

Look at this view, you can see everything we just navigated. That was some tough country.

We started our journey in a lake, where Ernie showed us the necessary conditions to sail, which were really the necessary conditions to improvise. You need all those conditions met before you dare embark.

- You need the wind—the power behind all movement. The wind is your ability to indulge your fun, another's fun, and the audience's fun.
- You need a sail to manifest the power of the wind. The sail is your ability to share the focus by taking turns, to share the work by participating jointly, and to share you by revealing bits of yourself.
- You need a boat—it harnesses the power of the wind, via the sail, and converts it into motion. The boat is your ability to commit, which is to trust yourself enough to invest energy, time, and money into what you are, the event, the piece, and the moment.

With those three conditions we can improvise. But what does that mean?

Our simple definition for improvising was "to make something from whatever is available." But that definition prompted three crucial questions: What is the something that we make? What is the whatever we make it from? How do we make it?

It turns out that the only thing you can make, the only thing anyone can make, is a brownie . . . I mean a moment. A moment is a discrete building block of your continuous life experience, and improv is just another experience. Moments in improv, however, are made more purposefully than those in your everyday life; you tinker with the moment-making machine already inside you.

To understand the "whatever" from which we make moments, we traveled deep into the forest to visit a tribe of aboriginal lumberjacks. They developed skills working with their raw materials to build a world that astonished others. We found that the raw materials from our lives, no matter how common they seem, are enough to improvise. You make from what you are and are not, and that is plenty.

Then we went underground with some pliable French scientists and destroyed one of the world's most powerful particle accelerators to glimpse how to make a moment. We deconstructed the word "make" to reveal the components of a moment, diagrammed as follows.

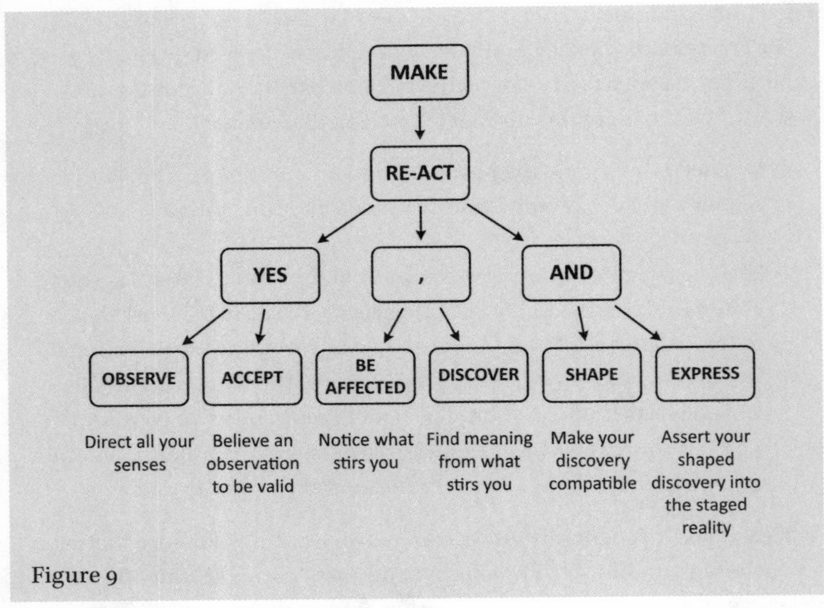

Figure 9

Well, now we're on the peak. I can't see anything else to climb, I guess this is it. So, let's savor these minutes before we pack up and say our goodbyes. Take a deep breath of that crisp air. It's been quite a journey. Watch those clouds wander by. I'm kind of sad; I had a great time. Close your eyes and soak in the sun as it breaks through. Yeah. That feels good. What a beautiful . . . oh . . . shit.

Wait. Keep your eyes closed!

Shit, shit, shit!

Okay. Deep breath. You will find out sooner or later so . . . open your eyes and turn around.

Look up. Keep looking up. Up. Up. Up. . . .

That is where we are headed. That is the true summit. I thought we were on *the* peak, but we are just on *a* peak. Now that the clouds have cleared, we can see the whole mountain.

Can you imagine the view from up there?

I could say I'm sorry, but I'm not. Not at all. I'm antsy to pack up and get moving. The weather is good, the company is swell, and our adventure continues. That's pretty damn good in my book.

PART THREE

Structures

You can have rock-solid skills in making a moment, but struggle mightily to improvise a story, scene, or song. The frustration makes you want to scream, especially when other improvisors make it look easy.

You are not alone. This struggle is ancient. Therefore we will look to two ancient screams that can help our improv.

She threw her hard hat on the ground in front of the granite card table she had just flipped over, unbuttoned her safety vest, and inhaled.

This was supposed to go smoother: ancient space aliens teaching ancient Egyptians how to build a pyramid in time for Egypt's first Pyramid Day. "Easy peasy," both sides had said. But they had not made it through a single construction meeting in the past decade.

The construction trailer was filled with aliens and Egyptians sitting in folding chairs, watching her melt down. She squatted slowly, fists clenched, eyes tightly closed, and began to scream—a scream that sounded like she was shitting lava.

She was frustrated. Pyramids were a national obsession. Every Egyptian was confident of what made a pyramid: sides that were triangular, a point that was pointy, and a doorbell that was inviting. But when they tried to build one, no matter how many sides or points or doorbells they cobbled together, all they ever made was a rocky mess. They were desperate. When the aliens landed in Egypt on their spring break, the Egyptians saw it as salvation.

Her scream rattled the windows of the trailer. Kilometers away, jackals lounging in the desert dunes pricked up their ears.

The aliens were a difficult lot—they were impossibly precise. Every meeting they would theatrically choke on their doughnuts when an Egyptian referred to "the pyramid" and "the pyramid parking lot" as separate things. To the aliens, space was one contiguous system of blocks, with each block having its own quality and relationship to other blocks; no block or group was considered separate. The aliens had to trace the galaxy's entire system of connected blocks until they arrived at the blocks of interest, blocks the Egyptians simply called "the pyramid." The aliens viewed time similarly, recounting their civilization's entire history before arriving at the time of interest, what Egyptians simply called "Tuesday."

The Egyptians would listen to these recitations until they snapped. Every meeting ended prematurely with the same tantrum: a scream like someone was shitting lava, a pot of coffee smashed against a wall, and a whine of "we just want to build a pyramid," as the final Egyptian stormed out of the trailer.

Her scream ended. She stomped to the coffee maker and stared at the device. Everyone in the room gasped. There was no coffee. She had smashed Egypt's last coffee pot a day earlier. In the distance, a dinosaur crowed.

With no coffee pot to smash, it was clear that this was not their usual meeting. She remained standing. No one stormed out. The alien foreman cleared his throat and continued recounting the interconnected blocks of the galaxy.

He droned on through day and night.

On the third day, she collapsed on the floor, broken. She then whispered words no Egyptian had ever uttered, "Please, I just want to place blocks sequentially that have pyramid relations with each other, with an intent they eventually give a satisfying feeling of pyramid." Her eyes opened.

That was the moment the Egyptians understood a crucial lesson: they could not build a pyramid with just the features they found most memorable. Every structure required the meticulous laying of blocks. Egyptians soon mastered making a block, then mating a block to the previous block with the proper relation, and then laying consecutive blocks that collectively gave a feeling of "pyramid." Ten years later, the Egyptians put the pointy top on their first complete pyramid, just in time for Pyramid Day. It was a day of national pride.

The aliens had an equally valuable epiphany heralded by a remarkable scream of their own. The aliens and Egyptians were completing a ropes course in a grove of redwood trees high in the Nile Mountains as part of a team-building retreat. As the final alien navigated the swaying rope bridge, urged on by cheering teammates, he slipped, lost his grip, and fell. All gasped as he plummeted toward the rocks below.

Throughout the forest and mountains his scream echoed, "I have lost my footing on the ropes serving as conveyance between our final waypoints and am being pulled by gravity at a speed dangerous to my survival of impact and wish for assistance in arresting my descent in an effort to spare my life." Although the trees were extraordinarily tall, they were not tall enough to afford the alien time to complete his plea before smashing onto the rocks below. Most of his words were delivered after impact.

Looking down from the treetops at the fallen alien's shattered body, both Egyptians and aliens cried, hugged, and applauded. The gravely injured alien laughed between coughs of blood and summoned a thumbs up. All were celebrating. The alien had uttered the most succinct cry for help in the history of their species. It did not involve a recounting of history or a tracing of the galactic interconnectedness of blocks. A lesson had been learned. The fallen alien was airlifted to a local hospital and recovered fully. Helmets save lives.

This lesson allowed the aliens to finally fulfill their spring break. Instead of killing the mood by tracing the galaxy's connected system of blocks, an alien could now simply say, "Wanna make out by that keg?" It was a day of intergalactic celebration.

Pyramids and Improvising

The Egyptians used blocks of stone to build structures in the physical world. They placed blocks, one at a time, each with its own quality, in relation to other blocks, that together gave a feeling of pyramid. Those same skills could make different patterns that felt like temple, fortress, or sphinx.

Our blocks are moments, and we build structures in the mind. We do this by making moments, one at a time, in relation to other moments, that together give a feeling of a structure, like a scene or a song.

When watching skilled improvisors we forget they are making moments. We get enamored with the feeling of the structure. If you try to make that structure directly, especially the cool parts, you will forget to work moment by moment.

Recognize two different skills: making a moment and making moments to form a structure. Just as Egyptians had to master making blocks and mating them with relations that gave a feeling of pyramid, so must you.

If you confuse the skills, you will erroneously conclude "I'm no good at improv," when you invariably make a rocky mess. You might even scream as if you are shitting lava. However, like the Egyptians, when you recognize structures then your work will become a wonder.

What Is a Structure?

The aliens learned that although they understood the limitless and interconnected blocks of space and time, it was just as valuable to recognize and label groups of blocks that had similar qualities and familiar relations, to name a structure. It could be "a pyramid" or "a cry for help."

A structure is a group of moments that cohere. Their content and meaning differ enough to justify separate moments, but they retain enough commonality to bond. There is continuity of characteristics.

For instance, we might experience moments with someone that cohere into a structure we call "a greeting," followed by moments that cohere into what we call "small talk," followed by moments that cohere into "a goodbye." If the moments across all those structure share characteristics, such as the same people, setting, and subject, they form a larger structure we call "a pleasant conversation."

Life is filled with structures, official and unofficial, many of which we name. Some names are formal (baptism, inauguration, arraignment) while others are natural (getting ready for bed). Sometimes they are generic (piece, work, job), while other times they are jargon (notes, bars, measures; lines, stanzas, quatrains; scenes, acts, plays).

How Structures Help

Structures help us lead our everyday lives and we leverage them in a staged reality. Just as we are more aware of making moments when improvising, so too are we more aware of structures. Structures can help in the following ways.

- **Interpret what is occurring.** Each moment we experience is new, but we usually interpret them as part of a structure that is familiar. Our expectations around a structure influence how we make moments. A clown at your front door is fun in the structure of trick-or-treating, it is not fun in . . . well . . . any other structure.

- ✻ **Discover what occurs next.** We have expectations about what is typical and atypical within a structure. When getting ready for bed one frequently sets an alarm clock, but rarely opens a can of varnish. Similarly, we have associations for what comes after a structure feels complete.
- ✻ **Consolidate our experience.** Instead of tracking every pesky moment of our lives, we account for many moments via a structure. We assign general attributes to a structure that are distilled from, and then applied to, all its moments ("I remember that wedding, what a miserable time!").
- ✻ **Mark progress and closure.** With structures we can tell someone "I've gotten ready for bed," exchange high fives, feel satisfied, and sleep soundly knowing we are masters of our world. Without structures we would experience a sense of accomplishment only on our deathbed ("Soooo, this is what it's like to finish something.").
- ✻ **Increase productivity.** By agreeing on structures, people communicate more concisely and become more efficient and effective. It allows us to work in groups and build things like pyramids and shared realities.

For our work, structures help in three broad areas. Examples in this chapter mainly illustrate the first two, and subsequent chapters examine the third.

1. We structure our everyday lives. It's natural.
2. The media we consume uses structures. Movies, podcasting, radio, publishing, theatre, and so on have crafted their own structures that exploit our natural structuring abilities.
3. Improv has its own structures, designed to entertain, that borrow from both our everyday lives and the media.

What Structure Am I In?

In any moment we need to know the structure in which we are participating to get their benefits. This can be a nuanced affair. A single moment can cue us to expect a certain structure ("Ah, a business card, this must be a business dinner.") or we might choose the structure we desire ("Ah, a business card, a formal start to a romantic date!"). We then continuously check our structure against our moments.

Moments influence our structure, and a structure influences our moments. In this dance, moments always retain their wild nature. Nothing must unfold as expected.

When our moments don't fit the structure we thought we were in ("Wow, this HR manager just fired me.") we can respond a few ways: we make the meaning of our moments fit the structure ("That is a fun way to flirt!"); we revise our expectations of the structure to make our moments fit ("I guess love is complicated."); or we identify a more fitting structure ("Okay, maybe this was a business dinner.").

There are times we experience a feeling of no structure—when there are no structural expectations to influence us. It shows up on vacation: wandering streets eating frozen custard, petting stray dogs, and buying a hat you will never wear. An unexpected delay can grant it, like being stranded at an airport with nothing to do and nowhere to be. And it is a hallmark of childhood, where walking home is a parade of distractions.

But no structure can be uncomfortable, especially under stress; we are robbed of the guidance structures provide. An improvisor develops comfort with no structure, it exists at the beginning of most pieces, at a minimum.

Switching Structures

Within your life you are constantly switching between structures. Where one structure ends and another begins may be clear, such as the final buzzer at a sporting event. But that boundary is often nuanced, such as where the plains turn into mountains. You are the judge of when you switch structures. Here are some signs.

- **Discontinuity.** We switch structures when we feel a discontinuity in content and meaning. If in the midst of getting ready for bed you discover a spider in your sheets, you may switch to the new structure "burning the bed."
- **Closure.** We do stuff associated with a structure until we feel a sense of closure, even if we can't articulate why. It may not be the same stuff, in the same order, in the same way. Some nights you

do not floss but you do take a bubble bath, but neither change the structure of "getting ready for bed."

- ✻ **Declaration.** We switch structures when we say so. One moment two people are "hanging out," the next moment they're dating—simply because someone states it. The universe has not changed, but the declaration of a new structure changes our subsequent moments, influencing how they are made and what they mean.
- ✻ **Recasting.** When we recast, our previous moments are reinterpreted in the current moment because we have identified a different, more accurate structure than what we originally thought. We may believe we are "carpooling" and during that drive, or years later, realize "Oh, that was falling in love." It is a quirky kind of switching.

When we switch from a structure before it feels closed, it becomes fragmented. The fragment may be continued if a later moment shares enough content and meaning with it. It is similar to returning to school after fall break or picking up an argument after using the bathroom. Unclosed structures stack in our mind in a pile labeled "to be continued." If that causes you stress, I'm afraid you are doomed to finish every book you start—even the stinkers.

EXAMPLE 1

To illustrate switching structures, we return to ancient Egypt, where, in addition to pyramids, aliens and Egyptians pioneered talk radio with the popular show *Blockheads,* a cutting examination of the issues of the day by a leftist Egyptian and a right-wing alien. All pyramid work stopped when it aired, as everyone ate lunch and tuned in.

Radio stations, struggling to survive, aired commercials that fragmented a show into segments. To avoid confusing the audience, station managers introduced and concluded each commercial with sixty seconds of tone while announcing "you will now hear a commercial," and "you just heard a commercial."

Advertisers balked at paying for two minutes of announcements for a thirty-second commercial. Station managers experimented and found, shockingly, the audience understood when a commercial started and ended even if the tones were so short they couldn't be heard.

Listeners understood structures had switched because the content and meaning were discontinuous. The commercials had different voices, sounds, and topics. Station managers admired their own cleverness.

Advertisers scorned the new format. The recently eliminated tones were when the audience ate alien potato chips, which were wildly popular and notoriously crunchy. Without the tones, all one could hear throughout Egypt during a commercial break was the deafening sound of potato chip crunching. No one heard the advertisements.

Station managers retaliated: they made the commercials sound like the show so no one would suspect a change in structure. The hosts would debate pyramid politics one second and effortlessly slip into pitching dubious products to relieve back pain the next. The unsuspecting audience never discerned the switch from show to commercial. Potato chips remained bagged and silent.

However, a few astute listeners did recognize the change in structure and recast those previous moments as what they really were—advertisements. They felt tricked and soothed their hurt feelings with slow potato chip crunching.

Station managers, drunk on success, dared one final scheme. They created a show for each host, one called *Blocks Good!* and another *Blocks Bad!*. With no opposing viewpoint to explore, station managers booked twice as many commercials, both overt and clandestine. They christened this new structure "hard-hitting news," and introduced each show with a dramatic theme song. This cued expectations to interpret what followed as fact, when in truth the show was an advertisement for itself, the station, the host, and a specific point of view.

Most listeners understood the game but tuned in anyway. It was a diversion from the hard work of constructing pyramids. And even though Egypt was divided into fans of *Blocks Good!* and *Blocks Bad!*, everyone benefited from a shared reality in which all agreed that blocks exist.

EXAMPLE 2

Our structure-making ability is hard at work even when the content we observe is nuanced.

If we watch an ancient video of an alien and Egyptian talking in a café, those moments stick together as a structure we call "a shot." If that is followed by a close-up of the same alien talking about the same topic in the same café, we perceive that we have switched structures to a new shot. But since much of the content is like the previous, the shots cohere into a structure we call "a scene." Next we see the same Egyptian and alien holding torches inside a pyramid tunnel. This content differs enough from the café that we perceive not only switching to a new shot but also switching to a new scene. The tunnel scene still shares some content with the café scene and coheres into a larger structure called "an episode." Shots form scenes, scenes form episodes, and episodes form seasons—in this example, of the ancient hit sitcom *Who's the Block?*

We can tell the difference between this sitcom and other sitcoms because each has its own characters, settings, topics, and relationships. We differentiate a sitcom from a drama from a sporting event because of an even greater difference in content, yet they retain enough similarity to stick together as "premium entertainment," or something like that.

YOU ARE ASTONISHING

Although it feels effortless, your mind's ability to structure a continuous torrent of content is miraculous. You are exposed to nonstop images and sounds through an expanding world of devices, which adds to the relentless sensory experience of your everyday world where rocks are hard, water is wet, and the sun is bright. In that bedlam, your mind grinds the avalanche of stimuli into countless moments and structures and realities well enough to survive, entertain yourself, remember your dog's name, and know that when you look at a device called a mirror what you see is yourself. If you don't think that is astonishing, you are wrong.

What Is Improv: The Mode of Production

How we improvise a structure depends on our mode of production. A mode of production is the tools and people involved with a structure. The more people involved, the more challenging it is to share expectations and a reality amongst everyone. This challenge can be overcome by introducing tools such as rules, schedules, computers, cameras, and lights. Each addition represents a greater investment of resources and introduces constraints.

The more complex our mode of production becomes, the more our moment-to-moment choices are limited by both practicality and the weight of meeting expectations. A complex mode of production offers benefits, but is paid for in freedom. The simpler a mode of production, the greater our liberties.

For instance, a backyard football game has a simple mode of production. We can adjust the number of people, the shape of the field, the rules . . . we don't even need a ball—anything we can throw or kick will do. And all participants can be satisfied with this football game structure.

A professional football game has a complex mode of production. It involves many tools and people, including a big stadium, ticketing systems, broadcasting equipment, and at least one official football. With all these tools and people, each person gives up some freedom to meet everyone's expectations of this game. Making spontaneous changes to it is effectively impossible.

EVERYONE IMPROVISES, BUT ALL IS NOT "IMPROV"

We still improvise in a complex mode of production. We make moments from whatever is available, but our ability to observe, accept, be affected, discover, shape, and express is limited and our "whatever is available" often includes inflexible tools.

In such environments, we can feel like cogs in a machine with little choice and it becomes possible, even practical, to operate on "automatic." If that happens, we risk making the moments of our lives with less purpose. We dull or forget our abilities. Possibilities narrow. Outlooks harden. These are the complex environments in which we spend much of our daily life. Very little feels as lively as "improvising."

Which is why in our context the words "improv" and "improvise" refer to a specific environment and purpose; improv can be more than just a shortened version of improvise.

Improv refers to a simple mode of production in which we improvise: modest venues, small groups, live performances, low costs. It maximizes freedom, requiring us to be more purposeful. We create moments more purposefully, structures more purposefully, meaning more purposefully, and a shared reality more purposefully. And through that purposefulness, we see how we construct reality.

In this stripped-down environment we isolate a fundamental life skill, maybe *the* fundamental life skill—our ability to make something from whatever is available. In improv we sharpen the tools dulled in our everyday lives.

Perhaps more than any other time in history, technology and culture intertwine to produce a complicated world vying for influence in our minds and lives. It may be no coincidence that improv has gained in popularity as our environment has gained in daunting complexity. Improv is an antidote.

THE MODE OF PRODUCTION IS THE ATTRACTION

When someone says, "Let's go see improv," their words do not identify the structure that will unfold. "Improv" is quirky in that its primary association is not a structure. Compare that to when someone says, "Let's go see a movie . . ." or ". . . a court case," or ". . . a duel," they are primarily referring to a structure.

The simple mode of production and purpose is what is attractive in improv. People are interested in participating in the process, not the polish of the product. It cannot meet the expectations of complex modes of production, so don't try.

The ability to improvise wildly different structures leads to wildly different conceptions of "improv." Thus, it is incorrect to consider any one structure as *the* structure of improv. It is true that some structures seem attached to improv such as theatre games, a Harold, or a montage (explained in later chapters), but those are structures, not improv itself.

Respect for improv's natural habitat is critical when porting it to mediums with more complex modes of production, such as video. We risk cueing expectations of that medium (editing, sound, pacing, scripting) that won't be satisfied. Even if we record a performance with a single camera from a fixed point, as if you were in the audience, we will satisfy neither the expectations of a live performance or of a recorded program. If we capture it with several cameras and edit them together to achieve some expectations of video, it counters the expectations of improv as a simple, continuous, spontaneous event. It's a tough nut; crack it wisely if you must.

Examining Improv Structures

The following categories of structures are typical to what is commonly called improv, which skews toward entertainment and performance. If performance is not your thing, that's great. Improvising is a life skill; if you have a life, you can use the skill.

- ✻ An **exercise** is a structure that is designed to isolate and develop specific skills. Usually exercises are done in a workshop setting, although many have entertainment value.
- ✻ A **spot scene** is a structure with entertainment value that lasts a few minutes or less, contains characters interacting in continuous time in a single setting, and, aside from limited information to initiate the scene, all information necessary to understand it is discovered within the scene.
- ✻ **Short form** includes structures with entertainment value that last a few minutes or less, in which rules of the structure are established before it starts. The rules heavily influence the structure and are designed for entertainment value. Often, short form is a spot scene with rules imposed upon it.
- ✻ **Long form** includes structures with entertainment value that last more than several minutes. Aside from limited information to initiate, each long form is self-contained. A long form structure can be composed of many other structures, usually scenes. The scenes share bits of content and meaning so the structure coheres.

In the following chapters we will look more closely at two of the most essential structures: spot scenes and long form. We will also briefly touch on short form.

The structures you focus on will change over time, so keep an eye out. The first character-focused class I took had a final exercise to show whether we grasped the material enough to pass. I did not do well. I was told to repeat, and my instructor added, “Yeah, I don’t think you understood the exercise.” And I didn’t. I didn’t understand most of class. It was different than all my previous classes that focused on spot scenes, which I was marginally competent at and in my mind defined “improv.” Now I felt incompetent again. It was like bringing scuba gear to a yoga retreat. It took me a while to recognize we were doing something different.

Wrap It Up

We can only improvise moments, one at a time, in relation to other moments that together can give a feeling of a familiar structure (like a scene or a song) in our minds. We recognize, rely on, and are entertained by structures in our lives.

We perceive our world continuously with information streaming through our senses. We break those continuous streams into moments, packets of content and meaning. When moments share characteristics, they cohere to form structures. Structures can be familiar, have names, and cue expectations. Structures influence how we make moments. We constantly check the structure we think we are in against our moments, which always retain their wildness.

A structure involves people and tools, which is its mode of production. As the number of people and tools increase, the mode of production becomes more complex, and we have less freedom if everyone's expectations are to be met.

What people commonly call "improv" refers to improvising in a simple mode of production where we are more purposeful with moments, structures, meaning, and shared realities—but does not refer to the structure that will be made. This environment allows us to isolate a life skill, perhaps *the* life skill: our ability to make something from whatever is available.

15

Spot Scenes

You can build many structures in improv. One structure that is important to feel at home at is a scene. But strict rules on how to build a scene, or any structure, have oppressive consequences—as the ancient Egyptians found.

Ancient Egypt had a construction boom and every family soon lived in their own pyramid home. This blessing, however, was a curse. For an Egyptian would stumble home after an exhausting day at work, crawl into bed, kiss an eager spouse, and realize upon spooning the body in bed that this was not the correct home, not the correct bed, and not the correct spouse.

Pyramid homes were so standardized, they were indiscernible. Children bounced from incorrect pyramid to incorrect pyramid for weeks, months, and years. Adults never knew if it was their own child staring at them from across the dinner table, as all youth sported the same bowl haircut and Egypt Unified School District uniform. Each morning, bags labeled "child lunch" were handed to all present, a kiss on the forehead was dutifully provided, and after passing through the picket gate a child would turn and shrug a goodbye to the stranger before trudging off to school through blowing sands.

When asked "How's the family?" the standard reply became "A handful," which meant "a handful of sand," which meant "unremarkable and indistinguishable." Everything was a blur when living in identical structures.

To save family life, builders began tweaking relationships between blocks to make structures that were still recognizable as pyramids but gave different living experiences. Soon one could open the real estate section of either major paper, the *Egypt Times* or the *Times of Egypt,* to find variety: "split-level pyramid, perfect for entertaining," "3 br Spanish Revival pyramid, landscaped sand," "Cozy Victorian pyramid with noon view of Ra!"

The variety in pyramids allowed each to be distinguished from another, families were reunited, and life in Egypt achieved new levels of happiness.

Pyramids and Scenes

The Egyptians found they needed variety; that building structures per some prescriptive formula only creates the unmemorable and indistinguishable. Similarly, with a prescriptive formula for how to build a scene, we only produce monotony. Thus we have no formula.

We do have the tactic of the Egyptian builders, introducing variety that appeals to the inhabitants while maintaining the basic features of our structure, a scene. This leads to the tragically overlooked question: What do we mean by "scene?"

Your favorite movies, shows, and plays are filled with scenes. Some are riveting while others are a chance to void your bladder. All those scenes floating in our heads confuse us about what, exactly, is to be created when we say a "scene." We have different ideas about what is being built, which explains why certain people can evaluate an improvised scene as "good" while others consider that same scene "not good."

To minimize our confusion, we will examine an essential type of scene: spot scenes, alternatively called open scenes.

Our Definition

The qualifier "spot" carries several helpful meanings: something of interest ("This nightclub is a hot spot!"), a situation ("We are in a tight spot!"), and a mark with clear boundaries ("There's a spot of ink on my linen!"). Such meanings help inform the definition we will use for spot scene: characters going through minutes that matter to them.

If we unpack that short definition, we find some notable qualities of our spot scene.

- ✻ **Efficient.** The scene lasts in the order of minutes, typically two to three. This requires improvisors to be efficient; everything must have relevance to the staged reality.
- ✻ **Contained.** We will never see these characters in this situation again. We must contain the scene to the here and now by keeping the characters, actions, and emotions in the time and space on stage.
- ✻ **Complete.** Characters must "go through" these minutes regardless of whether they like or dislike their experience, or if they succeed

or fail. Going through something, positive or negative, is how character is revealed and allows a sense of completion.

- ✻ **Character focused.** Characters are the main attraction, not plot or story, which are unhelpful in a short, unplanned piece. Character drives what is done and how it is done.
- ✻ **Affective.** The minutes matter to characters based on their points of view, and is shown by emotion, whether happiness, sadness, anger, and so forth. Spot scenes must find emotional intensity.

A spot scene is a complete piece that occurs in a short time with few improvisors. Its exacting nature quickly exposes how well we make moments and a structure. The ability to repeatedly build a successful spot scene requires rock-solid skills that prove invaluable in short and long form.

We could also call our spot scene a "day when" scene because it is the day when something meaningful occurs from the character's points of view.

Structure of a Spot Scene

The structure of a pyramid home could be viewed as a group of substructures such as foundation, chimney, and pointy top. Each has a feel and function.

Similarly, our spot scene has substructures with a unique feel and function. Recognizing these structures prevents us from making moments higgledy-piggledy. Instead, we can get a sense of what substructure we are in, which influences each moment until we feel "Ah, that part feels complete—next!" Let's examine the following substructures of a spot scene.

- ✻ Suggestion
- ✻ (Preparation)
- ✻ (Transition)
- ✻ Start
- ✻ Context
- ✻ Dynamic
- ✻ Progression
- ✻ End

Although these substructures are presented in a chronological order, the bits of each may not occur packed together. They can be interrupted and resumed. For example, the contextual information about a scene may not come out all at once; some bits may be delayed. It's like placing blocks of a pyramid, there is an optimal sequence but also flexibility. We might even forget a block here or there, but when we place enough with the right relationships we achieve the feeling of a pyramid.

These eight substructures are necessary to form a spot scene, although the audience may not be privy to them all. The "preparation" and "transition" substructures can be private to the improvisors. Like a foundation of a home they are necessary but out of sight, sometimes occurring when the stage is dark prior to the start. To reflect their potential to be private, our list sets them in parentheses.

A warning before we begin. Most media we consume compresses time for dramatic effect. This conditioning causes stress when, in a spot scene, an improvisor is forced to live every moment in real time—there is no escape. This causes us to rush, racing to the "good parts." Lower the stress: remember that while most media cuts to the meaningful moments, an improvisor can make each moment meaningful.

Each substructure description that follows will have a section labeled "Help!" that gives simple advice to the performer regarding that substructure. With everything that can be floating in your head, it helps to dramatically simplify your thoughts on stage.

SUGGESTION

A spot scene originates before an improvisor speaks a word, before they move a muscle, before they think a thought. A spot scene originates when an improvisor listens to a suggestion, also called a prompt.

The suggestion is the first sharing that occurs and is often the audience's only opportunity to provide content. The suggestion is our key to the new world and ensures that what is about to occur cannot be planned. Honor the suggestion.

One suggestion for a scene is sufficient, but more can be solicited. The more suggestions, the more constraints. At some point the entertainment value becomes paying off multiple suggestions, which leans toward short form improv.

A suggestion often relates to the context of a scene, such as an activity, location, or relationship, but could just as easily be an object, a lyric, or a gesture. Almost anything can be a suggestion because almost anything can be an inspiration for the scene.

In fact, instead of an audience suggestion we could use tea leaves, a page from *Architectural Digest*, or an entry from your cat's diary. "Suggestion" is the common term, but it points to a broader idea. It is any inspiration that acts as the origin of the shared reality of which the improvisors have no prior knowledge.

Our Spot Scene Preferences

For our spot scene, we prefer a single suggestion that avoids a premise, plot, or story.

HELP!

It is embarrassingly easy to screw up the suggestion: you forget it, miss it while wondering how your hair looks, or fixate on a different suggestion that was offered. Thus it's useful to repeat the suggestion to yourself or out loud.

(PREPARATION)

We enter the preparation immediately after the suggestion is accepted. We use the suggestion to prime ourselves about possible elements of the scene (objects, characters, relationships, emotions, actions, ideas, location, and any attributes). All are potentials; none are part of the staged reality yet. The preparation is usually brief, perhaps a second or two.

The preparation is typically private, occurring silently inside the improvisor. It can be a dreamy cascade of images, feelings, and ideas or a more intentional hopscotch through your mind. How you operate your brain is your business.

But the preparation could be public, where improvisors vocalize and even physicalize what is happening in their heads, working off each other. It can have its own unique structure, which can be interesting and entertaining. Public preparations take more time and can generate many ideas so are more typical in long form improv. A public preparation in long form is called "an opening."

Our Spot Scene Preferences

For our spot scene, the preparation is private.

HELP!

The preparation can lure you into planning or panicking, especially if you know little about the suggestion. A few reminders:

- ❄ Simplify.
- ❄ Don't think too hard.
- ❄ See what image arises when you hear the suggestion.

(TRANSITION)

The transition is where we shift from everyday reality to the staged reality. We discover the first elements of the scene based on our preparation.

First, pluck one or two elements from your preparation. If you generated more than that, congrats. Choose a couple that strike you and let the others go. They might make a surprise appearance later, but they sit on the bench for now. From those elements your job is to discover an attitude and an action, then commit to both physically.

Let's say the suggestion is "barn" and the image of rough, natural-fiber rope strikes you. You may discover the action of coiling rope, tying a horse to a hitching post, or mending a hole in a fibrous sack. You can adopt an attitude or emotion that is barn-inspired, whatever that means to you—rough, simple, rowdy. Commit immediately to that activity and attitude, even if the stage is dark, and knowing your choices may ultimately be labeled different from what you think they are.

Typically it's useful to avoid vocalizing in the transition, especially dialogue—the staged reality hasn't yet formed and words in the transition are premature in our version of a spot scene.

If your brain gives you nothing from the preparation to work with, don't panic. You have two bulletproof options.

- ❄ **Option 1.** Make a choice—any choice. Pick an attitude and some spacework, whether you know what they are or not. At the minimum, hold an object. You don't need to know what it is—just hold something with specific weight and shape. You will figure it out as the scene advances but at least give yourself something to figure out.
- ❄ **Option 2.** Observe what your scene partner is doing and feeling, and either harmonize or contrast. The simplest form of harmonizing is to copy; it is a time-honored tactic. You don't need to understand anything to execute, just do and be like your partner is doing and being. Or, to contrast, use your partner to discover choices that are markedly different from theirs, even "opposite."

Harmonizing or contrasting with a scene partner are more than just tactics of the desperate. It can be a primary strategy, especially harmonizing. When both improvisors harmonize, their mirroring evolves their attitudes and actions into something neither chose but which both created. This process can be made public for everyone to see, in which case it can be given more time because it is interesting to watch.

If the preparation occurred in darkness so does the transition, which lasts a second or two. The transition can be private, where you make choices that apply to just your character, or it can be public, where you make choices that apply to your character while observing your scene partners, which may influence your choices. Sometimes, when the transition is expected to be in the dark, the lights come up before improvisors have transitioned and the audience gets a peek of them in this gray area, settling into choices. That's okay, it is interesting.

Whether private or public, in light or darkness, one might call this the "pre life," because the scene has not started but living it has.

Style Influences

Schools, theatres, and individuals have preferences that influence your discoveries in the transition. The preferences relate to how the suggestion will be incorporated into the scene and the style of start that will follow the transition.

Some prefer to incorporate the suggestion as soon as possible, liberating the scene to go where it wants. For instance, if the suggestion is "banana" you may prefer to "hit it on the nose" by peeling a banana, or maybe you prefer to be indirect by digging on the beach of a banana republic. Others prefer to delay incorporating the suggestion, allowing the entire scene to transpire before discovering how it ties back to the suggestion.

The transition is also influenced by preferences for the start that will follow. These preferences fall on a spectrum from "neutral" to "loaded" starts. (Note: the dialogue mentioned as follows is not spoken in the transition, only in the start, but it illustrates preferences that can influence your discovery in the transition.)

A neutral start portrays everyday characters in an everyday situation, reflected in unremarkable emotion, spacework, and dialogue. Unremarkable dialogue means the ideas expressed are not extreme or dramatic. A neutral start does not mean the scene will remain neutral, it is simply how it starts.

A loaded start portrays unusual characters and/or a situation, reflected in heightened emotion, spacework, and/or dialogue. Only one of those three must be heightened to load the start. Heightened dialogue means the ideas expressed are more impactful ("The volcano is about to blow!").

When loading the start with emotion, an improvisor often chooses the maximum human intensity, as if emotion only exists as either absent or over the top. Such over-cranking is okay but has risks. It leaves little room to heighten, floods the improvisor emotionally, and strains plausibility before bringing the audience along.

Our Spot Scene Preferences

For our transition, incorporate the suggestion early and directly, give yourself spacework, take an attitude that is at least slightly loaded to prime your character's point of view, and do not worry about dialogue—like, at all.

HELP!

Staring into the void of a blank staged reality can freeze your brain. These tips help the thaw.

- ❄ Simplify.
- ❄ Make a choice.
- ❄ Shamelessly copy your scene partner.

START

The start is when the staged reality begins, and where you establish it. Typically it lasts from a few seconds to maybe fifteen seconds. The start is the beginning of action to the audience, but it is the middle of action for the characters. The start merely marks when the audience becomes privy to the characters' lives that are already in motion.

Where the transition ends and the start begins is debatable, just like the boundary between the plains and the mountains. It may be clearly signaled by a change in stage lights, but even with such external cues, we only truly switch when the content reflects a reality separate from everyday reality.

Improvisors switch by ignoring elements of everyday reality (like the presence of an audience, lights, stage, and their roles as performers) and validate what has emerged from the transition. You do this simply by connecting with your scene partner and maintaining a consistent attitude while performing spacework. No words are necessary.

Before you speak (if you choose to speak), take in the staged reality as it exists. The attitudes and actions carried from the transition combine to create something different from their original conception. We often overlook what is in front of us to hold on to what we thought it was.

In this nascent reality, discover what the relationship, activity, and location feel like. Allow the fog to clear. The discomfort of ambiguity tempts an improvisor to rush or invent. Resist. If you engage in spacework with an attitude and connect with your scene partner then that is plenty in these first seconds. Everyone is figuring things out alongside you.

It helps to remember that those who created the scenes you remember from movies, books, and plays spent time figuring out what to withhold, what to reveal, and how to reveal it to create interest in the audience. In improv, the process does that for us. If you are discovering, so is everyone else—that is interesting.

The scene may start whether you are ready or not. Lights may come up while you are still checking your zipper. Your partner may be at full throttle while you try to remember the suggestion. If you sense the scene has started but you are unprepared, perhaps caught in an awkward position, that awkwardness is now your choice. Whatever you have will work. The scene is now in charge, everything counts.

Abandoning the Start

In the start, a frequent dysfunction is to abandon choices to find something "better." This occurs when you change your character or drop your spacework and never justify the change.

For instance, if at lights-up Gary appears to be mixing ingredients in a bowl and Claire appears to be chopping a tree, Gary may panic if not able to immediately solve how those two implied activities could occur in the same location. To help, he drops the mixing and starts chopping. Both improvisors pretend the mixing didn't exist and carry on with the world's greatest chopping scene. Life rolls on. But at what cost?

There are characters and a world where mixing and chopping are lovely activities that occur in the same space. Is Gary mixing flapjack batter at a campsite? Is Claire violently tenderizing beef for Gary to marinade? Or perhaps they weren't mixing and chopping at all; Claire was waving a flag dramatically and Gary was beating a steel drum. We never discover if we abandon our choices.

Abandonment is a futile attempt to avoid the discomfort of not knowing.

It rewards us by replacing the old unknown with a new unknown—an unprofitable trade. Eventually we must make meaning of what we choose in our limited time, our first choice is as good as any.

In fact, the fun often comes from figuring out how your first choices work. One spot scene started with me lovingly installing carpet and my scene partner lovingly unpacking clothes. Within a few lines we discovered we were a couple on their first vacation who wanted their hotel room to feel just like home. We never would have found those interesting people had either of us abandoned our start.

Confusing Your Starts

Remember, we are dropping into the middle of our characters' lives. An improvisor's brain can get confused and think the start of the scene coincides with the literal start of some activity for their character, complete with an entrance, a pleasant greeting like "Hi, Molly," then looking around empty-handed for what to do and how to get started.

If this is your brain making a conscious choice, that's great. If this is your brain getting confused, that's also great. You still can work with that start, but it's a handicap. Explain to your brain its confusion and that you both deserve more engaging starts.

Our Spot Scene Preferences

Take time to fully connect with yourself, your scene partner, and what you already have created before spewing words. Commit to your attitude and spacework.

HELP!

If the scene starts and you are caught like a deer in headlamps, here are some helpers.

- ❊ Breathe.
- ❊ Connect with your scene partner.
- ❊ Commit to what you have in the first seconds; it's good enough.

CONTEXT

Establishing context is like setting a table so we can enjoy the food that is about to be served. Context establishes the framework of what follows. It cues expectations of structures from our everyday reality, such as "getting ready for bed," to help interpret the staged reality. Improvisors must assert context because there are no set pieces, costumes, or props to express it for us. Context includes:

- ❊ Who the characters are (their names and relationship).
- ❊ What they are doing, including specific actions, which are part of an activity, which is part of an event.
- ❊ Where they are doing it; a location specific enough to infer what objects are within arm's reach.

Discover context from the moments of the start. If we observe two people exchanging amorous looks while licking envelopes, you may feel they are flirty coworkers at the office. For someone else, the old-school nature of licking envelopes may cause them to hastily label it as flirty grandma–grandson at the office. Sure, that's weird. But the mind is grinding a lot of meat to make this sausage. It will work.

"When" the scene takes place could also be part of context. An improvisor can find meaning in anything, so time is useful but has low priority as context—often entirely omitted without issue unless the scene occurs in a far future or past era. Perhaps time has less relevance to our everyday lives and relationships than we think, which carries over to our fictional realities.

"Why" is a tricky word that often gets lumped into context. It includes the practical and personal motivations behind actions. Asserting the why before the characters and context are glimpsed usually requires invention, because we simply haven't discovered enough to put things together. Prematurely tackling the question of "why" results in the dramatic yet arbitrary, "To Win the Contest to Get Stuff and Avoid Trouble with the Boss Who Is also Mom," or some variation. Don't force why; it is best considered in scene dynamics, covered a little later.

Organic

Labeling contextual information can make for awkward dialogue, such as "Chloe, my wife, I am stirring cake batter in this kitchen of our home." In everyday reality we rarely say this unless we are annoyed with someone.

Label context as organically as possible. To help produce more natural speech, try to limit how much you reveal in each moment; express a quality about the activity, location, relationship, or character and relate your information to what was just expressed.

Claire: "This cake batter is thick to mix."
Gary: "I always wanted a wife with toned arms. Now I have one."
Claire: "I'm glad we installed mirrors in the kitchen. Check out my triceps."

Don't wait to label context until you find elegant words. They may never come. We forgive minor clunkiness because context is vital to understanding.

Explicit and Implied

Context can be stated explicitly, such as "This cake batter is thick to mix," which tells us with specificity the action and object of the action. Being explicit isolates information to help discover its meaning and link it to other contextual information such as "I was expecting higher-quality ingredients at the county jail."

You may believe your words are explicit, but often we are blind to their ambiguity. For instance, you might call your scene partner "darling," "honey," or "baby," thinking the relationship is clear, but those labels can be used for a child, an automobile, or a lover.

Context can also be implied. The spacework of stirring a bowl implies the classic combination of cake and kitchen, but we can't be sure until we label it.

Implied context, whether accidental or purposeful, has risks. If too much is implied, the scene becomes softly generic. It is difficult to discover from this blurry world. It is unsatisfying to the audience and most damaging—we jeopardize the shared reality. Where one person is sure you are "mixing cake batter" another is confident you are "cranking a generator."

Contextual ambiguity, however, can be fun if we recognize and play with it. For example, if a couple is having an intimate discussion lying down, we assume a location of privacy such as a bedroom. Later we may defeat that expectation by declaring: "We better wrap it up. The mattress store is closing." We have more to discover about that couple once the context became clear.

Note that there is almost always some degree of ambiguity with words. In our example, Gary doesn't say exactly "You are my wife." With his line "I always wanted a wife with toned arms. Now I have one," he could be bragging to his personal trainer, boss, or daughter. Claire could assert any of those, or many others, and Gary would roll with it.

Context Stew

It is a trap to assume or label the context as what we think it should be rather than what it feels like or what is fun, as if mixing cake batter could only take place in a residential kitchen. This is the Reasonableness Trap, which is explored in more detail in the chapters on character.

With some reflection you'll find most any combination of activity, attitude, location, and relationship is possible. Some combinations are unusual, and in everyday reality you might avoid them—but your characters don't. Contextual elements are like a stew—a lot of odds and ends can go into the pot and consistently make a tasty meal.

Handicaps

Some context handicaps our spot scenes. If our characters are meeting for the first time, have no desire for a relationship, are overly task-focused, or are beholden to their social roles, we have less opportunity for the minutes to matter since those moments are transactional. These transactions often appear as purchasing, negotiating, commanding, or teaching. In those cases, it is useful to pierce the transaction to reveal or establish a personal relationship.

No Context

It is possible to do a scene with no context: no names, no location, no relationship, no objects. The characters can even have no past, no future, and no outside world to refer to. It can be just two people existing in a void with each other and the current moment. The improvisors work solely with their reactions to each other. The clarity and honesty of such scenes is interesting and entertaining; however, they are niche.

Our Spot Scene Preferences

For our spot scenes, we prefer context that is expressed explicitly through characters who have, or quickly develop, a personal relationship.

HELP!

If you are foggy or unsure about what to do, odds are you don't know the context. Remember to:

- Trust that whatever a relationship, location, or action feels like is exactly what it is.
- Everyone else is probably unsure too; be the hero and label.
- Get specific.

DYNAMICS

A dynamic describes how things move, the path of a scene. Without a dynamic, the scene is a hodgepodge of bursts and lulls in haphazard directions—perhaps fun but not a scene by our definition. Similar words for dynamic are the engine, the game, or the deal of the scene.

Discovery techniques are used to find scene dynamics. A simple one is the question "Why are these characters, with this relationship, doing this activity, at this location?" You may prefer the short version: "Why?" We have a few big categories of scenic dynamics.

- **Action.** Actions to achieve a tangible goal; whether unclogging a toilet or disarming a bomb.
- **Relation.** What characters mean to each other and how that meaning changes; this includes status.
- **Character.** The characters' points of view: beliefs, values, wants, and tactics.
- **Law.** How the world works, the rules of both humans and nature.

These dynamics intertwine; we see character expressed and relationships change through actions performed against the backdrop of society and nature. They are interdependent. This allows us to see thousands of scenes with a similar relational dynamic, such as falling in love, without it growing (too) tiresome. Each scene is unique in how its characters advance their specific love through specific activities at a specific location. When these elements are based on a random suggestion, it is hard to re-create the same scene.

One dynamic usually dominates, and that dominance is often what differentiates the scene preferences of improv schools—some prefer character, others relation, and yet others prefer law (akin to "the game of the scene").

Imposing a Dynamic

The natural desire for a dynamic often drives an improvisor to impose one, to "make something happen." Ironically, forcing a dynamic often eclipses the one that already existed. There are a few commonly imposed dynamics to keep an eye on.

A reversal is spuriously flipping a character's feelings or injecting a problem or interpersonal conflict. For instance, if a scene starts with happy bomb makers happily building a bomb, a reversal may appear as spontaneous regret, inexplicable clumsiness, or discontent between bomb builders ("Hey, happy bomb maker, remember when you slept with my girlfriend last year? I've decided to get angry about it now.").

Such a reversal is problematic when it feels invented or premature. Your information feels invented when it does not flow from, or relate to, what has come before. It is premature when it occurs before we understand the characters and situation, so it has no meaning. We undercut what came before to start over.

Another type of reversal is a character admitting their previous words and deeds were fake, although perceived as earnest at the time. It is a capricious change of character.

Conflict between scene partners can be an imposed dynamic without having to reverse anything. We might begin with such conflict because it gives us a false sense of knowing what is going on—we're fighting! We are also primed with the theatric tradition that "there must be conflict," too readily interpreted as conflict between scene partners. We frequently impose this dynamic if we begin with an antagonistic attitude. Anger is a fine emotion to start a scene, but your mind usually assumes your scene partner *must* be the target of your anger simply because they are the only other tangible thing on stage. Conflict between scene partners may arise, but we needn't court it.

Other imposed dynamics are characters that obviously deceive others and interminable subtext, saying one thing but meaning another. Shifty, cunning, indirect characters are fun, as is word play and subtext, but a shared reality in which characters go through minutes that matter require us to eventually deal with truths the world can plainly see.

Our Spot Scene Preferences

Our spot scene focuses on dynamics related to character and relationships and, to a lesser degree, action, all discovered within the scene.

HELP!

When in a pickle and you feel the desire "to make something happen":

- ✻ Be more easily affected; allow something to matter.
- ✻ Observe and ask yourself, "Why?"
- ✻ Magnify what is already there.

PROGRESSION

In the progression we progress through all dynamics, with one taking primacy. We fulfill what we have set in motion. We see ideas manifest, emotions build, and action advance through various points of view until they are exhausted. We will never pass this way again.

Think of the discoveries made in the early part of the scene as promises, and the progression is where we deliver on those promises—then over-deliver. Or, the scene is a laboratory where we set up an experiment at the beginning and let it run rampant in the progression.

To contain the scene and give a chance for completion, avoid tangents or new lines of exploration in the progression.

Withholding: Tension and Release

Energy varies over the progression. Humans like "more, more, more," so energy in a scene often builds to a peak. But it can go the other direction, descending to a nadir. Or it can have changes like a rollercoaster. There is no prescription, but there is a warning: do not withhold.

Withholding energy—that is, refusing to ride the rollercoaster—produces a "flat" scene. It damns us to a world of dialogue. We talk about what to do instead of doing it. Claire can say, "I'm so angry I could burn my house down!" Or she can burn her house down. We talk about personality traits instead of living them. Gary can make stew and claim he is tough, or he can make stew like a tough guy. Rip that beef with your hands, Gary, then hold it above the stove burner as it browns. That's tough.

Withholding also shows up as half measures, resisting the full indulgence of fun. If you are on a spaceship you could endow the ship with gravity, or does a part of you want to simulate zero gravity? You have the power.

It is also common to withhold as we approach what seems like peak energy, because no one knows what comes after. Forge on, past what you feel is your top, to find what is on the other side. Worst case—energy resets only to build again. Thus, scenes may have one single build, or go through rounds of tension and release.

HELP!

When you feel internal resistance, or a scene feels flat:

- ❋ Do it.
- ❋ Pour gas on the fire.
- ❋ More more more! Or less less less!

The End

The end is the last portion of the scene, starting when we feel enough time has elapsed and the exit point is on the horizon. The end, like all structures, influences how moments are made.

A willful brain can get excited and engineer the end it wants, abandoning the fundamentals of improv. Don't do this.

Continue to make moments one at a time. Feeling you are in the end structure will influence your discoveries, making you more sensitive to opportunities to heighten and find completion. In this way you continue to play, knowing the scene will eventually terminate.

However, characters are oblivious to the mortality of the scene in which they live. They existed before and will exist after we are privy to these minutes of their lives. They pursue life ignorant of the finish line that looms. They always have a new high or low, a new task to complete, a new stage in the relationship to plumb. In this way, you play as if the scene goes on forever.

The exit point is where we leave our characters' lives and the staged reality dissolves. The exit point is recognized in retrospect. We play until we realize, "Holy crap, that was it!" Do not predict the exit. As soon as we think "Here it comes; there can't be any more," commitment fades—and everyone is betrayed. Another moment is always, always, always possible.

The exit point is usually crisp and definitive. It may be called a blackout, referring to stage lights going dark, even when there are no stage lights. Endings can also be gentle, where the staged reality drifts away as lights fade to black.

The exit point is called by an individual. Usually, it is someone outside the staged reality such as a director, instructor, or a sound and light technician. Without those helpers, an improvisor may call the exit from within the scene.

The exit point relies on three things: timing, timing, and timing.

- ✻ Timing applies to scene length in absolute time. Usually a scene has a range of expected lengths. When in that range, we are primed for the exit.
- ✻ Timing applies to the quality of the moments relative to the structure. We can sense an exit from a feeling of closure, energy that hits a high or low, or a scene that simply needs to be put out of its misery.
- ✻ Timing is related to the quality of the most recent moment. Sound advice is to exit on an up note such as a laugh, surprise, or big shift.

You have consumed a lifetime of media that has secretly trained you to recognize exit points. Listen to your gut.

HELP!

When you feel the urge to engineer a desired ending:

- ✻ Keep playing!
- ✻ Look back to the beginning of the scene to make connections and find closure.
- ✻ Keep playing!

Side-coaching

While working on spot scenes, you may get "side-coached" by an instructor. These are notes given as you work. Don't break the staged reality when you are side-coached, treat the notes as if they are thoughts from your own brain. The point of side-coaching is to help reveal options and remind you of principles, so that you internalize them.

Not everyone likes side-coaching, especially by an instructor who is heavy-handed with it. I say that as an instructor who has been heavy-handed with it. It wasn't until one student, frustrated with my constant interventions, grabbed his hair with both hands and with knees buckling said, "Get . . . out . . . of my . . . head." Note taken. I now side-coach gingerly.

Beware of Story

A scene may tell a story, but do not try to tell a story with a scene. Live the scene moment to moment—characters going through minutes that matter to them. Visions of story do not help you spontaneously create a scene that is efficient, contained, character-focused, affective, and complete.

Chasing story leads us outside of the moment and into our heads to think about what happened in the past and what should happen in the future, concocting in the mind's solitude *what will be amazingly entertaining with clever twists and novel turns and wild reveals and whoops—I just missed the interesting thing that happened right now.* Focus on the scene. Story will look after itself.

Psychic Weight

There is something magical that happens when an improvisor rises to do a scene. With training and practice, a skilled improvisor can calmly stand on stage in front of a crowd of strangers, reflect on a random suggestion, and from absolutely nothing start a scene where they inexplicably lose their mind.

Chaos ensues: words are vomited, nothing is heard, actions are not seen, insanity is pursued.

It happens to everyone.

There is a psychic weight about doing "a scene" that urges us to abandon all our improvisational skills and grasp for a personal theatric fever dream to ensure THIS IS THE MOST DELIGHTFUL SCENE IN THE HISTORY OF DELIGHTFUL. It usually isn't.

There is no antidote—except to towel off, change undies, and get up again—with less caffeine maybe. And remind yourself, it's just a scene, one of many types of structures, built moment by moment.

Wrap It Up

A scene is one type of structure that can be improvised, and there are different types of scenes. Our spot scene definition is "characters going through minutes that matter to them." This implies that our scenes should be efficient, contained, character-focused, affective, and complete.

A spot scene has the following substructures as experienced by the improvisor. We can produce tremendous variety while still respecting this basic structure:

- **Inspiration.** A suggestion from the audience.
- **(Preparation).** A cascade of potentials.
- **(Transition).** Engaging in an action with an attitude.
- **Start.** Seeing and validating the initial elements of the staged reality.
- **Context.** Discovering the who, what, and where of the scene.
- **Dynamic.** Discovering what propels the scene.
- **Progression.** Pursuing the dynamic and heightening.
- **End.** Closure and exit.

The pursuit of story hinders the creation of our spot scene. The desire to make an amazing scene can cause you to temporarily lose your mind.

16

Scene Physics

Mothers covered their children's eyes. News crews crowded the alley. Protesters shouted to stop the madness. They called it a mistake, an eyesore, an abomination, but the owner of the pyramid called it a back door. Egypt held a congressional hearing on this new technology, and, under oath, the owner testified on the reason for inventing it, "I needed an easier way to get to the backyard."

Egypt was shocked. Pyramid owners hadn't realized how technology could change life in a pyramid. Innovation became the rage, leading to developments like doggy doors, cat exits, heated roofs, and more exotic offerings like afterlife transitioning and central vacuuming.

With so many technologies, homeowners learned to be thoughtful about which was right for their structure.

Playing God

Improvisors can create a staged reality that is radically different from our everyday reality. We can bend space, time, or any other laws of nature. This is great fun.

But with these powers comes responsibility. These powers must be used to serve the structure being made. The structure is king. So just like the Egyptians who considered which features were appropriate for their pyramid home, we will identify choices that help our spot scene. Let's look at how an improvisor can remodel reality.

Time

As measured on the surface of Earth at human scale, time continuously runs forward at a constant pace with no end. It may feel fast or slow, but the ticking clock says it's constant. In a staged reality we can handle time in several ways.

- **Continuity.** We can jump ahead or back in time.
- **Direction.** Time can travel forward or in reverse.
- **Tempo.** We can speed up, slow down, or pause time.
- **Dominion.** We have the ability to step outside of time, to before it begins, after it ends, or into alternative timelines.

Our spot scene is helped by leaving the clock as it is; a single timeline that is savagely inescapable, continuous, forward moving, and running at normal speed.

Space

The space in which you improvise will have its own physical features fixed in our everyday reality. In the staged reality, those features are malleable.

- **Scale.** The playing space can represent any scale—from the expanse of the universe to the interior of a subatomic particle.
- **Continuity.** The stage is naturally continuous, but we can break it into discontinuous space, like a split screen. For instance, one half can be a deck of spaceship, and the other mission control.
- **Stability.** We can change what the stage represents. It can be the kitchen when we exit and the den when we re-enter.
- **Architecture.** We can modify the architecture of the playing area. We can add imagined features like doors, walls, and windows, as well as remove features such as peering through the ceiling to gaze at the stars.
- **Boundary.** There is typically a perceived boundary between audience and improvisors represented by a physical feature such as the edge of a stage. Improvisors can redefine that boundary by venturing into the audience or other areas.

Our spot scenes are facilitated by a space at normal scale that is continuous, stable, and honors the stage boundary. We can manipulate architecture.

By messing with time or space, such as jumping to the future or popping to a new location, we can change content enough that we perceive a new structure, a new scene. This is great for structures that accommodate multiple scenes, but not great for our spot scene. Don't be not great.

Character

You are you. You have one body. Your body can only exist one place at any time. But in a staged reality, these facts are flexible. Here are options on how we can represent characters on stage.

- **Number.** We can have zero or more characters on stage; thousands are not a problem.
- **Presence.** Characters can enter and exit or remain on stage the entire time.
- **Projections.** You can interact with someone that is not embodied by a human such as a conversation with an imagined bartender.
- **Jumps.** One improvisor can be multiple characters, such as exiting the space as one character and entering as another, or by portraying a character by jumping to their last position and assuming their stance.
- **Contemporaries.** Characters typically interact with each other in the same time and space. But characters can also exist in an adjacent plane, where others can't interact with them such as a narrator, a ghost, or a god.

For our spot scene, we limit ourselves to two or three characters. Each improvisor represents a single character, and all characters are contemporaries. It helps if everyone remains on stage, but a brief exit or interacting from off stage does not spell doom. We eliminate, or greatly curtail, character projections. Dammit, sometimes you need an imaginary bartender.

Magic

Magic, by definition, is supernatural. When we veer from our everyday understanding of nature it takes precious time to explore the rules of the magic and its impact on the world, which is difficult to contain in a spot scene. Magic also can overshadow character because, let's face it, magic is cool. Magic includes such things as inscrutably advanced technology, superpowers, and spiritual gifts.

For our spot scenes, avoid magic.

Bridging Realities

We can play with the boundaries between realities. This is most applicable to multiscene long form, but it also pops up in shorter pieces.

- **Bridging.** We build a bridge between realities by taking an element from one reality and incorporating it in another that had seemed separate. For instance, a character reading a book can meet a character from that book. We can also bridge to our everyday reality by playing a well-known character such as a celebrity or politician.
- **Breaking the fourth wall**. Usually, the audience is silent witness to the staged reality, viewing it through an imagined wall. However, we can endow characters with the ability to interact with the audience. This breaks the imagined fourth wall, bridging both our staged and everyday realities.
- **Collapsing.** If we bridge many elements, we make realities collapse into one. If you are in your kitchen microwaving popcorn with Napoleon and are interrupted by your neighbor whining about French grenadiers stealing his Wi-Fi, we have collapsed worlds.

For our definition of a spot scene, we avoid all these tactics. It is preferable to keep the staged reality simple, clear, and independent.

Imposed Rules

We can impose rules on a scene in the name of fun, limiting or compelling what an improvisor says or does. Rules are only limited by the diabolical nature of humans. The weightier the rules, however, the more the entertainment lies in the acrobatics needed to satisfy them. This is the realm of short form.

For our spot scene, we prefer ever-so-light or no rules.

Wrap It Up

An improvisor can define reality however they wish, and other improvisors will support those choices. This godlike power requires guidance, often provided by the rules of instructors and schools. But these guides, if well considered, are reduced: What best supports the structure? What supports the scene?

Our spot scene is best served by resembling our everyday reality.

However, if you are killed and feel your ghost must transport everyone to the end of time to sit and chat with the audience in a hot tub because the scene absolutely, unequivocally, unavoidably demands it . . . then do it. Rules are happy to be bent if it serves the scene.

17

Long Form

"Can you hear me shouting?"

The ancient Egyptian researchers in the room exchanged looks. He was their best shouter. If he couldn't get a response, no one could.

"Can you hear me shouting?"

He was speaking into the newly invented "shouting tube"—a series of short hollow reeds spliced together to form one long hollow reed. The tube ran from the kitchen of this residential pyramid to the rec room of the neighboring one, where a team of their best listeners sat.

"Can you hear me shouting?"

This was their last hope. Egypt needed a way to connect the exploding number of residential pyramids. Without such a link, each family lived in isolation. What was the point of building all those structures if they couldn't connect to something larger?

"I hear you shouting!" a voice responded. "Can you hear me shouting?"

And with those historic words, Egypt changed. Shouting tubes that connected structures became essential. Friends wanted to shout at friends. Businesses wanted to shout at customers. The government wanted to shout at everyone. It didn't matter what they shouted about; it was just fun to shout.

To any falcon soaring high above, the desert below was transformed into artwork: a canvas of sand dotted with structures connected by silvery threads, a map of the relationships that formed the larger structure of Egypt.

Definition

Like the vast deserts of ancient Egypt, long form is the untamed frontier of improv that is the home of limitless structures. Long form includes any piece that sustains itself over the arbitrary mark of six minutes. That definition encompasses a mind-boggling number of possibilities. No single structure represents all long form.

If we let our spot scene run longer—perhaps thirty minutes instead of two minutes—it would magically turn into a long form piece called a monoscene. The monoscene, however, is not our focus.

We will examine multiscene long form, which is eminently malleable and allows us to venture wherever our impulses lead. It is a flexible counterpoint to our exacting spot scenes. Multiscene long form is defined as a sequence of scenes, employing liberal scene physics, based on one suggestion, which sustains itself without break for its duration, typically targeted between ten and sixty minutes.

But even within the category of multiscene long form there are variations. With so many possibilities, our discussion must be general and brief so you have more time to go do.

Just as each pyramid home in Egypt was linked to other pyramid homes with shouting tubes, so our scenes in multiscene long form are linked to each other. Each scene is a structure in a network of structures, connected by information. And like a falcon flying high above Egypt, and peers down on a network of connected pyramids, so too can we visualize our scenes and how they are linked (see figure 10). We'll see more of this type of diagram later in this chapter.

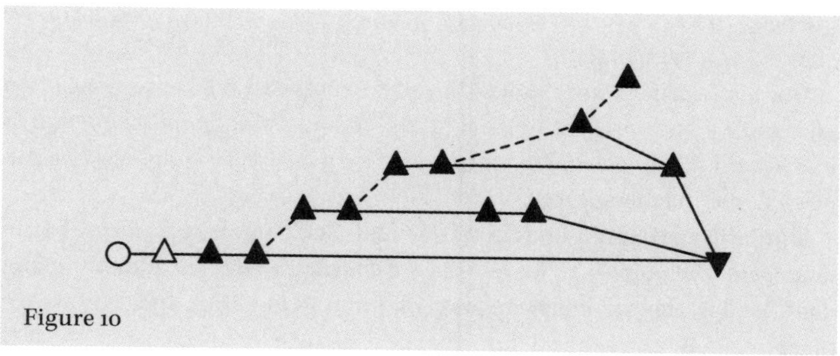

Figure 10

For convenience in this chapter, multiscene long form may be referred to as simply "long form." Don't forget, we are using this imprecise shorthand.

After starting out in improv, I wasn't sure it was for me. It was fun, but I was thinking of moving on to another interest. It wasn't until I saw my first long form show that I pointed and thought *How do I get to do that*? I can only trust my feelings at the time, but that show felt like it was the best ninety minutes of entertainment I had ever experienced. Improv was a nice neighborhood, but long form was the address that caught my eye.

Scenic Differences

Multiscene long form is made by several improvisors who spontaneously create a sequence of scenes that link together to build worlds, follow characters, and explore ideas. Compared to our spot scene, long form has more: more time, more scenes, more improvisors, more characters, more options.

But a spot scene and long form share similar goals: to be efficient, contained, and complete. A spot scene meets those goals in isolation, whereas long form scenes achieve them collectively. Long form has a portfolio of scenes that allow variety within it. It is not a series of spot scenes. Let's look at how long form scenes differ from spot scenes.

Our spot scene originates from a limited shared reality: the suggestion (which, if you remember, is a broad concept that includes any inspiration for a scene). However, in long form most scenes do not come from an audience suggestion—long form scenes propagate themselves. An inspiration for a long form scene is pulled from the pool of previous scenes, which is the ever-expanding shared reality. That allows us to get intimate with the elements of the piece (characters, locations, ideas, and so on) and alleviates the need to label everything, every time, in every scene. In long form, we gain perceptual shortcuts.

Our spot scene stands alone. We must express all relevant information and make sense of it within that scene. If something is unexplored, it is forever unknown. But in long form what we miss in the current scene can be explored in later scenes.

Similarly, we cannot leave the time and place of our spot scene; but in long form, the point is to leave. When a character refers to something not contained in the current scene, we can jump to any time and place to explore it and, if we feel like it, jump back.

For our spot scene we avoid loading the start with a big idea, because the suggestion that inspires it is not a premise—we give the scene latitude to find its own direction. However, the start of a long form scene can be loaded with an idea if everyone experienced the origin of that idea in a previous scene, which allows a scene to be more targeted.

We don't play with scene physics in our spot scenes, preferring to stay close to everyday reality. But in long form, we have no problem bending space and time, bridging realities, endowing objects with life, or exploring the ramifications of magic.

Our spot scene has only a few improvisors who remain on stage for its duration and each improvisor portrays a single human character. But in long form improvisors are free to enter and exit as needed. A scene can have many persons, one person, or no person on stage. It also can have more characters than improvisors, a few can portray an angry (or happy) mob. An improvisor can play multiple characters, both central and peripheral, as well as inanimate objects.

The Back Line

Long form typically has between two and nine improvisors. Improvisors who are not in the current scene stand along the back or to the sides of the stage and are referred to as "the back line" or "the sides." They are not perceived as part of the current scene.

The back line does not lean against the wall. Walls suck energy. Plus, walls get dirty. Plus, wall-leaning lulls you into thinking you are relaxing. You are not.

The back line has a duty to pay attention, support the current scene, and switch scenes. Each improvisor on the back line must be ever prepared to pounce.

The back line supports the current scene by clarifying, advancing, and heightening. They can often see what the scene needs better than those in it. Back line support is not intended to change the nature of the scene, but if it happens organically, that's okey-dokey. The back line can intervene with a side-call or walk-on.

✻ A **side-call** is when an improvisor vocalizes from the back line, they don't even need to move. If a scene takes place in a forest, they could support by hooting like an owl, howling like a wolf, or whooshing like the wind through trees.

- ✻ A **walk-on** is when an improvisor enters the scene to support and then, typically, returns to the back line. For instance, a member of the back line can walk on as a waiter to bring salads to Gary and Claire sitting at a table in a café, offer to grind some pepper, say "Bon appétit," and exit.

Sometimes the character who walks on becomes integral to the scene, either as a recurring or constant presence. Perhaps the waiter is so helpful they go on to assist Gary and Claire in making small talk. In retrospect, we see that walk-on as the entrance of a central character, but at the time of the entrance no one could know that.

In contrast, an improvisor may enter that scene expecting to be central, such as the friend for whom Gary and Claire were waiting, only to discover they aren't. Everyone discovers how the entering person fits in the existing dynamic; perhaps they perform the duty of a waiter while the actual waiter chats. But equally possible, they may enter, see the couple's small-talk needs are taken care of, say "Ah, bon conversation," and exit. Their big entrance turned into a walk-on.

We don't know when an improvisor steps into the scene if they are going to enter and exit quickly or stick around. The only thing a back line improvisor can do is walk on with intent. The scene decides what they become.

In those examples as a hooting owl or waiter, the supporting improvisor is a contemporary character in the scene, but we have greater powers than that.

An improvisor can walk on to point out a detail such as "These characters have chocolate smeared on their faces," or announce from off stage "It begins to rain." In such cases, the improvisor walking on is not acknowledged by the characters in the scene. It's as if they are a ghost, but their assertions are immediately accepted. Thus, the back line can provide music, sound effects, direction, descriptions of objects, internal thoughts . . . whatever supports the cause.

Switching Scenes

Switching from one scene to another requires us to edit the current scene and discover who joins and who initiates the next. Editing, joining, and initiating are essential activities when improvisors self-direct their long form, which is almost always. Let's look at each of these actions.

EDITING

Editing is a signal that we are switching to a different scene. If reckless, you could think of editing like "ending" the current scene, but since we may resume that scene later the word "end" is misleading.

Each improvisor has authority to edit the current scene, whether from the back line or in the scene. If editing from within the scene, an improvisor simply breaks character and then executes an edit technique just as they would if they were outside the scene. We'll look at those techniques shortly.

You edit for several reasons: you have an inspiration for a new scene, the current scene feels complete, the current scene is a train wreck, or time is running out.

Long form has various editing techniques. Some are quick, useful to introduce a scene that is closely related to what just occurred. Others are more elaborate, introducing a scene that is less related to the last, perhaps relating to a scene much earlier or from a different thread.

Some editing techniques fuse the edit with the initiation: the improvisor who edits is expected to initiate. Other techniques decouple those functions, allowing an improvisor to edit at the optimal moment even if they have no desire to initiate, which makes it unclear who will initiate. That's okay.

Shows, and sometimes improv schools, have preferred editing techniques. Here are several examples.

- **Sweep.** An improvisor walks, trots, or runs across the front of a scene to signal an edit and the current scene's improvisors return to the back line. Flourishes to the sweep include vocalizing while crossing, moving expressively, and having more improvisors join the sweep once it starts. The editor signals they will initiate the next scene by immediately taking the stage but may be preempted if someone steps out earlier. The editor can signal they don't want to initiate by returning to the back line—some brave soul will step forward to initiate instead. The sweep may be called a wipe.
- **Fade.** An improvisor enters without acknowledging the current scene and initiates a new scene with spacework and dialogue. Improvisors recognize the discontinuity signals a new scene; those in the current scene drift to the back line while others join the new scene. The new scene and old scenes may coexist briefly. This may also be called a soft edit.

* **Clap in.** An improvisor on the back line claps to signal an edit. At the instant of the clap the current scene ends and its improvisors return to the back line. It's important to end the current scene when the clap occurs. Sneaking in an extra line fouls the crispness of this technique. Whoever clapped is expected to initiate. Any crisp signal could be used in lieu of a clap, but clapping is inexpensive.
* **Side-call.** An improvisor interrupts a scene by announcing a change in time, location, or characters such as "We cut to grandma's house," "Flash forward ten years," or "We see their wedding night." Improvisors enter and exit as they see fit, and any can initiate the scene after the call. The side-call can come from the back line or, despite its name, from anyone in the scene.
* **Tag out.** An improvisor enters a scene and tags a character on the shoulder, signaling them to exit while other characters remain in the scene. The tagging improvisor then initiates. Tags can occur in succession to make a tag run, a series of rapid fire miniscenes. When tagged out, it's important for the previous scene to halt so that the pace and energy of the piece does not drop. For the same reason, tags in a run are best executed with speed.
* **Swinging door.** An improvisor enters behind a character in the current scene, and with one hand pulls the character's shoulder, "swinging" the person to face them and then initiates a new scene. The previous scene may dissolve or be suspended until the character is swung back. A character can swing back and forth through miniscenes. It's important for the previous scene to halt when a swinging door is initiated to maintain the speed and energy of the piece.

INITIATING

After an edit, someone initiates the next scene. This is usually done by taking the stage, although it is possible in long form not only to initiate from the sides but to conduct an entire scene with no one on stage. Who initiates may be clear based on the edit, but it can be a nuanced affair. There may be pregnant moments of eye contact on the back line until one person takes action. That's okay.

An initiation is the first words and actions of a long form scene. The initiation must be inspired by what has been shared in the piece: either the suggestion, the opening, or any scene that has transpired.

A "strong" initiation has intent and is shaped so others can infer what the scene is about and their roles in it. The initiation does not have to be perfect, just good enough so everyone can guess what the angle is. Your fellow improvisors have paid attention; if you point them in the general direction, they will glean your intent and immediately support.

For instance, let's say we have a long form piece that has several scenes about building a pyramid, and the current scene has the entire town waiting in anticipation to see the pointy top of the pyramid put in place. The following are initial lines for the next scene that, when combined with knowledge of previous scenes, convey where the initiator thinks fun lies:

- "Gary! You're in bed. You were supposed to deliver the pointy top this morning."
- "You are the pointiest top I've ever chiseled, but today you must leave the quarry, my child."
- "Sorry to barge in, Mr. Ra, but they're placing that pointy top this morning and everybody kind of expects a booming voice, or sun beam, or other god stuff."

A strong initiation may involve quickly signaling who the initiator wants in or out of the scene with eye contact, pointing, or waving people on or off before words or actions are taken. The initiator may also indicate staging with a quick gesture to chairs or the floor, and may mutter a directorial word such as "car," "bed," or "crowd." Pay attention!

Note that not all initiations must be strong. The improvisor can start with little in mind, using just a minor element from what has come before. The initiator can have no idea what will transpire but is willing to start with almost nothing and discover the rest—much closer to the spirit of a spot scene. We could call this a weak initiation, but we won't—it's a brave way to create long form.

Initiating with strong or little intent are equally valid, but expectations may promote one over the other. Also keep in mind that no matter how brilliant an initiation may be, the initiator must let go of their intent if the scene wants to be something else.

JOINING

When the initiator takes the stage, other improvisors join a split second later—or if lazy, a split second and a half later. There are a few ways to determine who joins.

Whoever initiates the scene may indicate who should join with a finger point, glance, or nod. But if the initiator takes the stage without such a signal and pauses, it may indicate they have no idea what comes next or they don't care who joins, at which point one or more improvisors step out from the back line to enter the unknown together. Sometimes no one joins. That's okay, things will work out. If being alone on stage sounds scary, the secret is to find the fun in engaging the scene on your own. You might even miss that alone time when others eventually join.

Improvisors can make assumptions about joining based on the progression of scenes or who else has taken the stage. They join to fulfill a pattern ("Hmmm, we've been switching between the home team and away team locker rooms. This must be the away team—I'm on that team!") or to obey their gut ("I think I'm needed," or "Damn, I haven't been out in a while . . .").

Solving the mystery of "who joins the scene" can be sloppy. The result may not be what anyone expected: too many people, too few, or the "wrong" ones. It's okay. After a beat, the result is burned into the indelible record of the staged reality. Take what you get. Your job is to mine it for brilliance.

Watch the initiator for clues of how to start.

Sometimes an improvisor initiates with a bold choice in dialogue, emotion, or spacework before anyone has a chance to join. This is a gift. Support their choice as you enter.

If the initiator is less quick or bold, but you still expect a strong initiation, start in neutral so you don't accidentally counter the initiator's intent: adopt mild emotion, no (or generic) spacework, and avoid dialogue. When their intent becomes clear, shift out of neutral and instantly support. Commit quickly, maybe even recklessly. The immediacy of support gives long form its life.

If there is a hesitation in delivering the first lines or actions, the intent is not clear, or the expectation is to not have strong initiations, those on stage know it's time to get busy with whatever is happening in that moment. This is more like the spirit of a spot scene. Connect with your scene partners with an attitude and spacework. Discover the scene together.

THE INSPIRE-EDIT-INITIATE PATH

With several improvisors simultaneously supporting and switching scenes, long form can move fast. To play fast you must trust your impulse to edit and initiate. The briefest delay can be the difference between a majestic move and an opportunity lost forever.

Long form presents some obstacles that hinder you from acting on impulse. Editing and initiating are high-visibility moves. It's easy to delay asserting yourself publicly to spend precious seconds debating whether your impulse is good enough, searching your mind for "something amazing," or worrying that you will not be supported. That is a lot of psychological debris on the path from inspiration to action.

You can clear that path with experience, finding a long form structure and style you like, and playing with the right people.

SIDELINE INERTIA

With several improvisors on stage, some can get more sunshine than others. It's just the way it unfolds sometimes. Each improvisor is responsible to involve themselves with edits, initiations, and support. If you stay on the sidelines too long, you can get cold. Don't resign to this fate. Make a move, even a small one. Do it for the piece. Do it for yourself. I bet you're worth it.

One improvisor does not need to caretake another, but it is wise to involve everyone. When you signal who joins a scene, do it with awareness of who has been on the sidelines. Consider it a professional courtesy that you may need one day. It also engages more minds, which lets us cover more ground, more thoroughly, more easily. But equally, the audience notices. If they sniff that someone is excluded, even by chance, it can stir their concern—fun is at risk. Don't risk fun!

Scenes Make More Than Scenes: Links and Threads

To make the many scenes of our long form feel like a single unified piece, each must share some content with an earlier one. This sharing makes them cohere. Every scene in a multiscene long form has a link to something prior.

Any element can link scenes, whether major or minor: a character, a location, the time, an object, a word, a concept, and so forth. An inspiration pulled from one scene to initiate another will automatically serve as a link between the two. It is discovered like any other discovery.

If we link multiple scenes by the same element we will perceive those scenes as related—they cohere as a thread. For instance, if a few scenes are about Gary who is digging a ditch in Spokane, and a few scenes are about Claire who is repairing a space station orbiting Mars, we have two threads.

Multiscene long forms can have several threads. To keep threads clear, the content of each must remain separate. Elements from Gary's thread should not mingle with Claire's, and vice versa, unless we consciously choose to combine them. For instance, if Gary severs a power line while digging his ditch, we can discover that the line powered the Mars Orbital Control Center of Spokane, affecting Claire's mission.

A multiscene long form structure has many scenes, those scenes link, and linked scenes may form one or more threads. Scenes, links, threads, and the patterns they form distinguish the many multiscene long form structures.

GENRES HELP LINKING

How scenes link can be grouped into genres. A genre helps an improvisor discover a link for the next scene, making the piece cohere. The genre of a piece may be decided before or emerge during the performance. Here are some types of genres:

- **Story.** Follow the impact of concepts and actions to characters and relationships. When Gary and Claire take an apple from a tree, we explore how that theft affects their relationship, their family, and their town.
- **World.** Follow the impact of concepts and actions across geographies, cultures, and time. When Gary and Claire take an apple from a tree, we see the ripple effects to the apple industry, international relations, food technology in a hundred years, and the thoughts of those in the Garden of Eden.
- **Premise.** Follow a premise applied to more extreme situations. Gary and Claire take an apple from a tree, and we explore in more extreme situations the idea of "if it's still attached to nature, it's not stealing." Perhaps we'll see Gary and Claire nip an umbilical cord or two.
- **Mechanic.** Use a designated element of the staged reality to inspire the next scene by rule, such as initiating a new scene with

the last line of dialogue of the previous scene, but with different characters, activities, and location. Gary and Claire end their scene with the line "Mmm, so tart!" Then that same line will be used to start the next scene, that will have nothing to do with food, apples, or those characters. Perhaps in the next scene Gary says in a randomly chosen friendly tone, "Mmm, so—tart?" And Claire responds, "Oh yeah, I'd call myself a tart, scads of lovers." And from there they discover the scene.

- **Montage.** Follow whatever is the most fun, blending any of the aforementioned. Usually we blend in bursts: we may follow story, then explore the world, and drill down on a premise here and there.

HELP!

You don't need a big idea for the next scene. If you can't see any possibilities for where to go next, leave the fog by taking one of these roads. (Those roads conveniently form the exciting acronym ROADS!)

- **Relationship.** Explore who is affected, which can be as simple as who witnesses: neighbor, friend, enemy, coworker, pet, housefly, God. . . .
- **Order.** Explore what comes before or after: cause/effect, first/last, past/future.
- **Analogy.** Explore the situation in the context of another domain: the animal kingdom, historical periods, action movies, other cultures, and so on.
- **Degree.** Explore what happens with more, less, or the opposite of something.
- **Space.** Explore impact on people and things in the environment: above/below, inside/outside, in front/behind, close/distant.
- **!** Isolate what caught your attention, no matter how small, and explore it.

General Multiscene Long Form Structure

Each type of long form structure carries its own expectations about scenes, links, threads, editing, and so on. It would be foolish to try and define a general structure that fits them all, let's try. A generalized long form structure looks like this:

- ❊ Suggestion
- ❊ Opening (or Preparation)
- ❊ Anchor scenes
- ❊ Progression scenes
- ❊ End scenes
- ❊ Epilogue

SUGGESTION

A long form structure begins with a suggestion solicited from the audience that serves as the inspiration for the piece. It is the first sharing that occurs and testifies to the piece's spontaneity, it is the origin of the work. Just as described in chapter 15 on spot scenes, a suggestion for long form is most useful when simple and avoiding story or premise.

And just as in spot scenes, a suggestion from the audience could be replaced with any inspiration that acts as the origin of the shared reality, of which the improvisors have no prior knowledge.

OPENING / PREPARATION

There is always some preparation before starting a long form structure. When that preparation is exposed for everyone to see it is commonly called an opening.

An opening is an observable process that uses the suggestion to generate potential content for the piece (characters, locations, ideas, dialogue, and so on). Openings produce many associations that can feed a longer structure. The opening primes everyone with potentials for what lies ahead, enabling faster play—the opening is a baseline from which we perceive the shared reality. Anything shared in an opening may appear in the ensuing piece, but not everything must. Unused elements are graciously forgotten.

An opening can be simple, such as an individual retelling a personal story inspired by the suggestion, or it can be complex, involving all the improvisors in a mosaic of sound and movement. There are many types of openings; they emerge, evolve, and fade daily.

Instead of a public opening, the improvisors may have a private and silent preparation in which they individually discover their associations with the suggestion. This primes them with information to start a scene and is the same as the preparation in our spot scene. The preparation occurs in a couple of seconds and is usually not perceived by the audience.

ANCHOR SCENES

Anchor scenes are most directly related to the suggestion and are based on the public opening or private preparation. A long form has at least one anchor scene, the first scene, but it can have more. We can trace any thread of a long form back to an anchor scene.

Anchors tend toward the preferences of our spot scenes. They require context, last longer, are more complete, and tend to be more grounded with simpler scene physics.

For long form with multiple threads, the anchor scenes should be far apart conceptually to reduce the risk of the threads being confused. For example, if our suggestion is "apple" and our long form structure has three anchor scenes, our characters could be picking apples in an orchard, polishing a candy apple red Camaro, and restoring a vintage Apple II computer.

An anchor may not link to subsequent scenes. A long form structure could exclusively anchor scenes, all relating back to the opening but not to each other. It is more common to find an independent anchor within a threaded structure, serving as a break from the threads and indicating progress, like marking acts of a play.

PROGRESSION SCENES

Progression scenes are what make up the bulk of a long form piece. They could be defined as "characters advancing, exploring, or illustrating elements that are created or implied in previous scenes."

This is how long form can propagate endlessly: a scene creates content that inspires a subsequent scene, which creates content that inspires a subsequent scene, and so on. A progression scene can take its inspiration from any prior content, not necessarily the most recent scene.

A progression scene may be brief or lengthy. Some last only long enough to capture a reaction, while others may be as complete as a spot scene. As we progress, shorter scenes are possible because we have a robust shared reality to provide context.

Each scene can increase or decrease energy, often rising toward the end of the structure. Just as the energy of a spot scene varies as it progresses through moments, so too the energy of a long form structure varies as it progresses through scenes.

Several tactics can add energy to the piece: faster edits, shorter scenes, more emotion, more action, more extreme situations, more entrances and exits, more characters on stage, and the ultimate tactic—collapsing threads. This last tactic is usually saved for the end.

END SCENES

Long form allows us to keep expanding and exploring the staged reality with more locations, characters, and ideas. But it can't expand forever. Whether the clock compels you or it happens naturally, at some point we must begin to contract. That point is the beginning of the end.

The end is where we seek closure. We complete patterns, answer questions, exhaust ramifications, and reach peak energy. Long form can take us on a meandering adventure, so finding closure can be challenging.

You can help achieve closure by reintroducing elements from throughout the piece (including elements from way back in the first scenes) into its later scenes. In this way, to find the end we look to the beginning. We can also incorporate elements from different threads into a single scene, collapsing those threads. Characters, ideas, events, and locations that appeared disparate are brought together, their coexistence makes them cohere—what was many is now one. Reintroducing and collapsing can get wacky or surreal, but the staged reality is about to disappear forever, so many figure "Why not? Let's blow this up."

Elegant closure is rare. Fortunately closure doesn't have to be elegant. Or really good. We just need a definitive button, a ribbon, a period.

EPILOGUES

Long form can continue after the end. We extend the piece to meet time requirements, tie-up loose ends, or have everyone share the final moments. In literature we call them epilogues; in music perhaps codas; in cuisine it's an after-dinner drink. They are typically simple and subdued: a group scene, characters reciting diary entries, behind-the-scenes interviews, a ride into the sunset, whatever you like. If it fits, why not? You earned it.

Visualizing Long Form

We can diagram a long form structure to see how suggestions, openings, anchor scenes, and progression scenes relate. We'll walk through an incrementally more detailed diagram for an imagined long form performance. All the diagrams shown here use the same key (see figure 11).

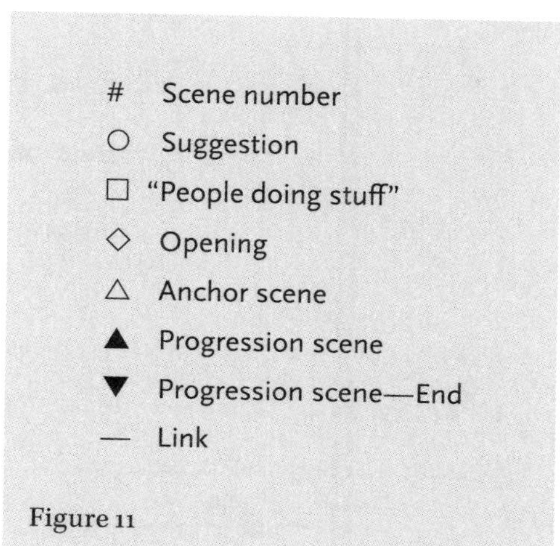

Figure 11

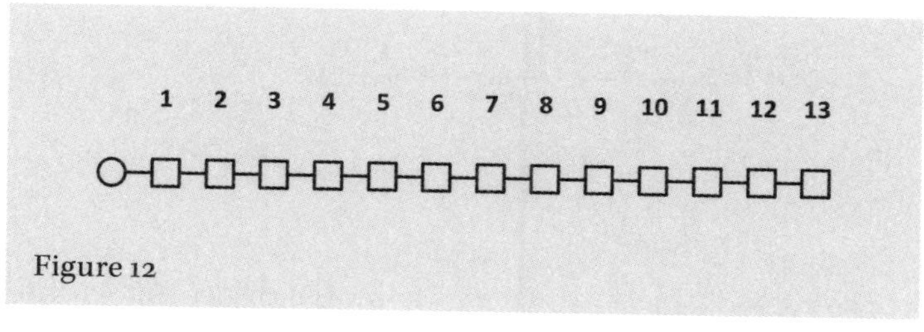

Figure 12

Someone new to improv would see our imagined performance but may not have our words to describe it. They might see its structure in a simple way (see figure 12). They would see a suggestion (circle) followed by thirteen scenes (squares) that were linked (represented by a line). They would use the word "scene" in a generic, nontechnical way to mean "people doing stuff." And although they may not say "linked scenes" they would recount "This girl did this, and then this guy did this thing, and it referred to this other thing, and I was like no way, and at the end it all came together, that Gary and Claire are cool!"

A more experienced viewer might enjoy the same performance with more clarity (see figure 13), recognizing the suggestion (circle), the opening (diamond), anchor scenes (light triangles), and progression scenes (black triangles). They would recognize how the scenes link and might say "It was

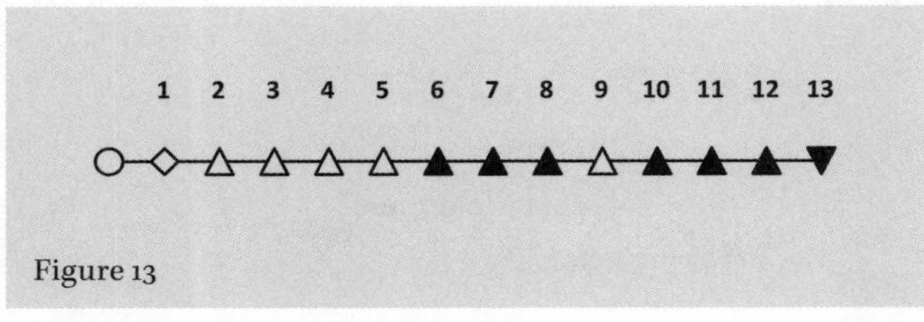

Figure 13

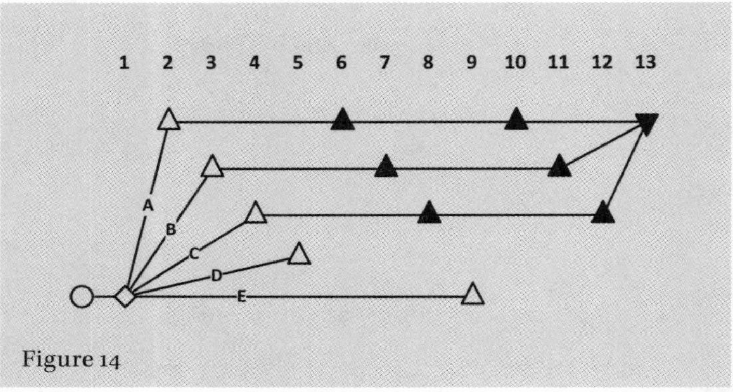

Figure 14

a cool opening and then three strong two-person scenes that kicked it off, then a scene where everybody was on stage, and then they followed those first three scenes wherever they went, tying it together at the end. That Gary and Claire really rocked it."

And an even savvier viewer might enjoy that same performance with more clarity (see figure 14), seeing the scenes not only in sequence but also clearly seeing the different threads, noting anchor scenes that were standalone, and how all the threads (A, B, C) collapsed at the end. They would recognize this familiar long form pattern and say "That was a tight Harold. We should build a statue to honor Gary and Claire."

Other long forms could be broken down similarly, even if they did not follow a well-known pattern, such as the one known as a Harold.

We could have a long form that uses a suggestion to launch three anchor scenes and three threads that collapse at the end, omitting an opening. We see that structure (see figure 15) first as the scenes would appear sequentially in time, and then separated into threads A, B, and C.

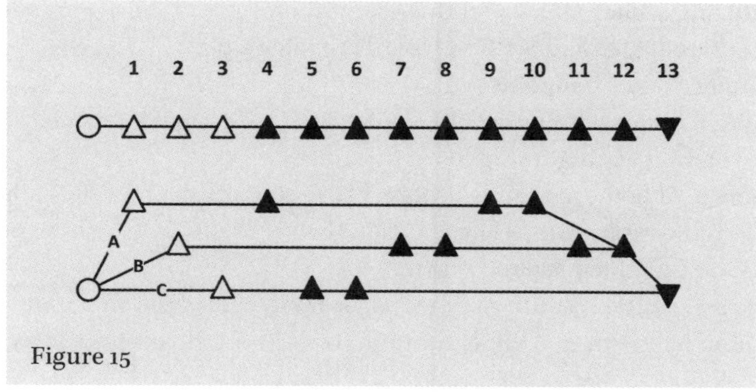

Figure 15

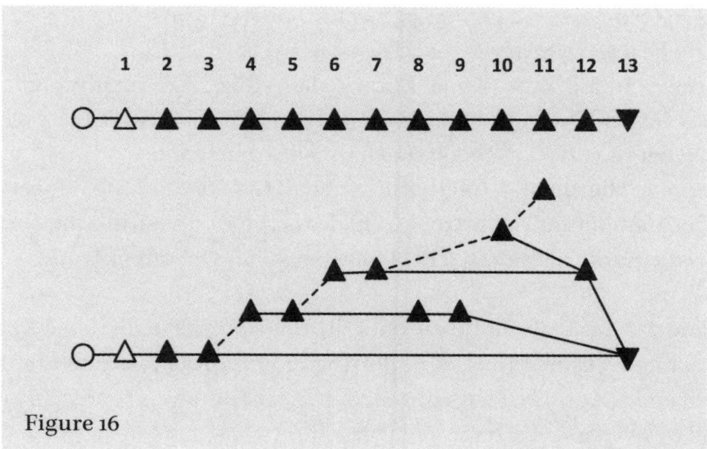

Figure 16

The following (see figure 16) is a long form that starts with a suggestion that inspires a single anchor with a single thread. However, inspirations for later scenes lead far enough away from the original thread to feel like a new thread (shown as a dotted line). The branch for scene 11 was never really tied to the rest of the piece at the end—that's fine. I bet Gary and Claire had a fun little diversion.

The following are some brief scene descriptions that fit such a long form pattern. Each description is numbered to correspond with a scene in the diagram (see figure 16). The content described doesn't matter as much as recognizing scenes, links, and threads. You may prefer more grounded or more outlandish examples. Feel free to provide your own!

The suggestion: ballpoint pen.

Scene 1. Claire signs a check at a restaurant with a ballpoint pen. Gary is her husband. They are trying to eat healthier.

Scene 2. At home in their bedroom, Claire realizes she kept the ballpoint pen from the restaurant. They question their morality and call the police. Claire and Gary have separate beds.

Scene 3. At the restaurant, a manager interrogates the waitstaff about a missing ballpoint pen while a radio plays a hosted soft-jazz show. The manager fires the waitstaff.

Scene 4. On a fishing boat, a father throws a microphone into the water, telling his red-headed daughter he lost the passion to host his soft-jazz show and will be a more involved dad. They catch one trout.

Scene 5. In a middle school library, the red-headed daughter gifts the contents of her backpack to schoolmates as a farewell, telling her peers she has lost her passion for school. One friend has a lunchbox.

Scene 6. The sinister International Book Consortium (IBC) meets in a luxurious mountaintop fortress to address the rampant talking that has replaced reading in middle school libraries. They run out of orange scones at their meeting.

Scene 7. An accountant confronts the IBC's president, Stephen King, to inform him that operating costs for the mountaintop fortress are out of control and the group must downsize. The accountant is repeatedly interrupted by telephone calls for "Kimber."

Scene 8. The father coaches his daughter's recreational baseball team in the only style he knows—like a soft-jazz radio host. A reporter from the middle school paper comments.

Scene 9. Ten years in the future, the father, now a professional Major League Baseball coach, argues in soft-jazz style with an umpire in the final game of the World Series while sports announcers comment.

Scene 10. The neighborhood Welcome Wagon brings a gift basket to a young couple and their dog who just moved into a mountaintop fortress, purchased at a rock-bottom price. The fortress is drafty.

Scene 11. Three goats on a neighboring mountaintop comment from afar, their "baa'ing" is translated into English by a goat interpreter who appears in a split-screen. A commercial airliner flies by.

Scene 12. The couple discovers Stephen King living in their fortress's wine cellar. All are trained in lethal combat, including the dog, resulting in a slow-motion tragic Shakespearean ending. The thermostat is set to sixty-five degrees Fahrenheit.

Scene 13. A red-headed girl gives a tour of the wine cellar of a mountaintop fortress to a group that includes unemployed servers. Sports announcers comment on the tour. The ghost of Stephen King rises to haunt the group but relents to their requests for an autograph. Gary and Claire run from the back to offer a ballpoint pen that they swear they are going to return to the restaurant.

My simplified descriptions eliminated the details of a real scene, which is why I added a few superfluous details. Those bits are to remind you that a scene contains a lot of information, any interesting element could have inspired totally different scenes. I hope those extra elements prompted some thoughts, such as: *How did the police respond to Gary and Claire? Who is Kimber? What did the trout do with the discarded microphone? Where is that commercial airliner going? What's in the lunchbox?* And so on.

Remember, you only need an inspiration to launch a scene; you don't need a "scene description" in your head. The scene will become what it must become, moment by moment.

All our diagrams had thirteen scenes just for comparison. That is neither a maximum nor minimum. A show that runs ninety minutes may have a hundred scenes (remember, long form scenes can be extremely short), while others could have much fewer.

For instance, the long form example shown (see figure 17) launches five scenes from the single suggestion of "an event," such as a Fourth of July barbecue. Although the scenes are viewed in sequence in the performance, they portray the same minutes in the staged reality with different characters at different locations. The scenes do not share elements except their relation to the suggested event, and in a sixth mega scene, we may see them all come together. There is little progress or story, but it paints a world and its characters like a mosaic.

Diagramming helps convey the general structure of a piece, but it can get complicated. Even in something as defined as our first example, the Harold, a scene I represent with a single triangle, could actually launch several quick bits or miniscenes closely related to that main scene. For simplicity I don't show them all, just the main scene. We could use the term "beat" to

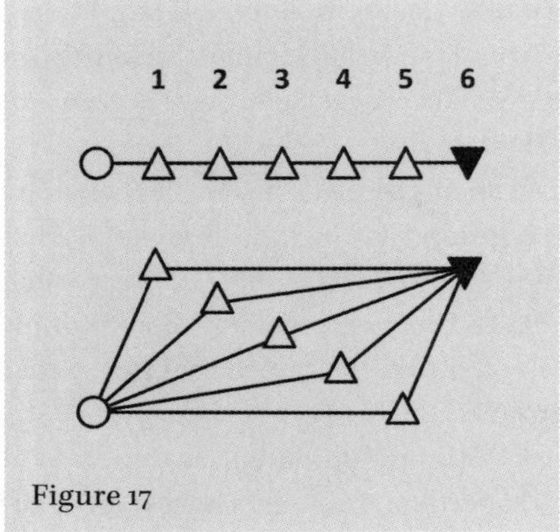

Figure 17

group the main scene and its closely related bits . . . one of the many flexible uses of the word "beat." What I labeled as scene 10 in the first example (see figure 14), could be called the third beat of the A thread, or A game.

Sloppy and Fun

Your long form adventures will both help and hurt your spot scene skills. Long form has great latitude compared to spot scenes, and sloppiness will be spun into gold by multiple improvisors over multiple scenes. But acclimating to sloppy play punishes you in spot scenes, which are exacting. At the same time, long form is the universe's training camp for fun. The indulgent and flexible minds we develop there help bring life to spot scenes. Long form and spot scenes are complimentary.

Beware of "Making a Story"

Long form is more capable of conveying a story than a spot scene, but story still holds risk. The goal of "making a story" puts us in our heads about what should happen. That is dangerous.

Think more in terms of exploring story elements (character, relations) that are fun or interesting, but do not get attached to the outcome. Start a scene in motion, then let it run. It will reveal what should be pursued next.

The piece will progress, expanding until we must contract and resolve in the end. By reincorporating elements from the entire piece toward the end, discovering connections instead of engineering them, you will achieve a feeling of completion. That is a good enough story.

After one long form performance, our coach asked what we thought the show was about. As we recounted the scenes and threads, he stopped us, "No, it was about aging, it was about how friendships change over time." I was surprised, he opened my eyes. By building moment to moment, by making connections between scenes, and by heightening, themes emerge. The improvisors may not even know it. Maybe our brains picked up on those themes. Maybe the show was an elaborate Rorschach test. Either way, it's how long form can work.

Try It Once

In long form improv the human mind is fully engaged to build, interrupt, and resume dozens of structures in a staged reality, in real time, with no rehearsals, using only our words and actions. A willing audience and competent improvisors can produce a cascade of yee-haw that distracts from the astonishing mental acrobatics that everyone effortlessly and simultaneously executes, oblivious to the wizardry they are performing.

Multiscene long form is open, adaptive, and entertaining. Almost anything conceived can be explored. Any impulse pursued. In that exploration you act as whatever you fancy: director, writer, actor, editor, engineer, pundit, composer, psychologist, anthropologist, historian, costumer, set designer, stuntman, critic, and so on. It may be the only activity that successfully assigns no one a specific responsibility but assigns everyone all specific responsibilities. And it works. Because everyone listens to and executes each other's intent. Willingly. Nay, excitedly.

It is like discovering a loose slot machine that pays out caffeine, dopamine, and love.

It is addictive.

I hope you become an addict.

Wrap It Up

Within the big world of long form we focused on multiscene long form. We called multiscene long form simply "long form" in most of this chapter for convenience. Long form scenes collectively achieve the goals of being efficient, contained, and complete. This collectivism allows us to play with a variety of scene types.

Long form can involve several improvisors. When not in the current scene, improvisors are part of the back line and are prepared to support the scene in an instant. The back line provides support through a side-call or walk-on.

Switching from scene to scene requires improvisors to edit the current scene and discover who initiates and who joins next. Each improvisor has authority to edit the current scene from the back line or from within the scene. Determining who initiates is nuanced, often indicated by how the edit is performed. Scene initiations are the first words and actions of the new scene, and the initiator can have strong or little intent behind them. Watch for signs from the initiator to indicate who should join but also follow your instinct. No matter anyone's intent, whatever the imperfect edit-initiate-join trifecta produces is good enough—take it and run hard.

The multiple scenes in our long form cohere into a single structure because they share content. Every scene in long form links to something that came before. Several scenes that link on the same content form a thread. The task of discovering a new scene is helped by knowing the genre (story, world, premise, mechanic, montage). When in a jam to find an inspiration for the next scene, follow one of the ROADS! (relationship, order, analogy, degree, space!). There is no one structure that represents all long form, but we looked at a general structure for multiscene long form.

- ❊ **Suggestion.** An audience provided inspiration from which the long form piece grows.
- ❊ **Opening / Preparation.** Generates associations with the inspiration that act a baseline for the piece.
- ❊ **Anchor scenes.** Scenes that most closely connect to the suggestion and serve as a starting point for threads.
- ❊ **Progression scenes.** Scenes that advance, explore, or illustrate an element of previous scenes, expanding the staged reality.
- ❊ **End scenes.** Scenes that contract the staged reality, building energy and achieving closure.
- ❊ **Epilogue.** An optional, relaxed concluding section of the long form.

You should try long form at least once; you might get hooked.

18

Short Form

Ancient Egyptians held an annual Gauntlet of Homes. Before the leaves fell off the trees in late October, each family would allow neighbors a three-minute opportunity to rush through their home and levy an unvarnished critique of it. Cats were not allowed to participate, as their words were too cutting even for the Gauntlet's critical spirit. Digging up your neighbor's backyard was encouraged, since analyzing what a family had hidden was not only considered healthy but a sign of neighborly care. Every critique ended with an embrace to affirm that although a neighbor may express disdain for your family's home, decor, and secrets, no harm was meant as these were simply the rules. Fun was the spirit of the Gauntlet of Homes, and invariably the outcome—regardless of what might be critiqued as a "success" or "failure."

The ancient Egyptians knew what made the Gauntlet of Homes entertaining, and their wisdom applies to short form improv today.

Short form improv includes structures with entertainment value that last a few minutes or less, the dynamics of which are assigned as "rules" before the piece begins. This contrasts to our spot scene or long form, where dynamics are discovered from within the piece. We build these structures one moment at a time, like any structure; however, the rules heavily influence how an improvisor is affected, discovers, shapes, and expresses.

The rules of each short form piece are designed to challenge improvisors in various ways and drive up the entertainment value. Like a sport, skills are tested within defined rules. This earns short form the alias "theatre games."

The existence of clear rules allows the numerous short form pieces to be codified in books and lists. We'll mention only a few to get an idea of their scope.

A short form piece can be a spot scene with a requirement such as "the first word of every line of dialogue must begin with the next letter of the alphabet." The first paragraph of this chapter not only describes the rules for the Gauntlet of Homes, but its sentences also follow a similar alphabetical rule: "Ancient Egyptians held . . ."; "Before the leaves . . ."; "Cats were not . . ."; "Digging in your . . ."; "Every critique ended . . ."; "Fun was the spirit . . ."

Rules for scenes can be more elaborate. The short form piece "Game Night" starts by asking a few audience members to describe their parents. One improvisor is assigned to portray each parent. Then the improvisors, portraying parents of audience members, pay off the assigned traits in a scene where all have gathered to play a board game, such as Parcheesi or Monopoly.

Short form pieces can also be simple and non-scenic. An example is "One Word Story," in which improvisors collectively tell a story by turns, but each improvisor only gets to add one word to the story at a time.

Other short form pieces, such as "Party Quirks," have "success" and "failure" outcomes. In this game several improvisors are assigned to be the guests at the party based on the suggestions of the audience (such as a woman shooting skeet, Abraham Lincoln, Aphrodite, and Captain Ahab). An improvisor who is not privy to these assignments is the party's host. The host begins on stage and the guests enter over the next few minutes. As they interact, the guests pay off their roles but never say who they are directly. At the end of the piece, the host guesses the identity of each.

The idea of success and failure can be leveraged for entertainment. Teams of improvisors can "compete" with each other in the performance of short form pieces, with judges assigning scores. Despite the appearance of competition, however, the scoring is irrelevant. It is only a way to dress up the improvisational challenges with the manufactured drama of winning.

Regardless of how elaborate games are—or if judged for success or failure—the key to short form is to embrace each structure with gusto. The audience wants to see players grapple with the challenges. Just like the Gauntlet of Homes, fun is the spirit—and usually the result.

The first time I ever saw improv was one of those competitions. It looked like fun, but also nerve racking—I couldn't see myself doing it. Who were these people? Later that evening over pints with friends, the conversation turned from "Who does that?" to "I bet I could do that." Expecting an argument, I instead got practical words from a practical friend: "Yes, I bet you could." She knew anyone could do it. It would be years before I got involved.

PART FOUR

Treachery

Our epic journey of improv has taken us around the world and through history; we've crisscrossed science, art, and technology. It has been fun.

My words have painted a rosy picture. Perhaps too rosy. For even the greatest Pollyanna knows deep down—beneath her happy bonnet, below her optimistic curls, at the center of her sugary-sweet brain stem—an epic journey is never rosy. Darkness exists.

You must learn to recognize treacherous behaviors lurking in others and in you. Treacherous behaviors serve no one; all in their sphere suffer.

These behaviors are friends until they strike with venom. And moments after they strike, you will be seduced again. Over and over and over, you'll tussle.

You cannot banish treacherous behaviors. You must work with them. You may even toy with them. But stay on guard to their true nature, for you are waltzing with the Devil on the edge of oblivion.

Watch your step.

19

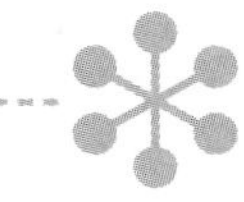

Treacherous Behaviors

Certain behaviors of improvisors have shown themselves to be particularly treacherous. These culprits appear in the many lists of improv "do not do's." But their betrayal isn't guaranteed. Forbidding them is extreme.

Instead let's get to know them. The following are some common treacherous behaviors. These are behaviors of the improvisor who plays a character, not the character. If you recognize yourself, don't fret. In examining each to see what makes it tick, we may get a glimpse into what makes you tick.

- Question!
- Do good!
- Be cool!
- Win!
- Be great!
- Hurry up!
- Be polite!
- Authorize it!
- Fix it!
- Protect yourself!
- Run!
- Dress Up!
- Entertain Us!

Question!

Why do they say don't ask questions in improv? Is there ever a good question? Am I unlovable if I ask a question? If those questions don't answer any questions, let's look at what a question is—a statement or gesture intended to elicit information via a reply. In our everyday reality, questions are the traditional method to avoid catastrophic mistakes.

In improv, however, question askers are treacherous bastards.

A question can be a subtle tool of control to slow things down, like installing speed bumps on a highway, or to restrict another's actions because we are conditioned to respond to a question. This control is wielded from a seemingly benign position of helplessness.

Even more treacherous, a question asker becomes passive, curiously deferring to others for information when no one has a monopoly on information. After all, this is fiction. We are creating everything as we go along. Gary can ask, "What time does Mom get home?" to which Claire might think *How the hell would I know, you just made Mom up.*

Some types of questions can be useful in improv, such as questions that provide information ("Did you ever think we'd be baking brownies with this toaster oven?"), clarify legitimate issues between improvisors ("What did you just say?"), or advance a dynamic ("Okay, let me try this again. Will you marry me?").

Do Good!

Society values do-gooders, those who go the extra mile, who plow snow from your driveway, who bring an extra six-pack to the party. When times are tough, we like these people because they impulsively raise their hand to shout, "I'll do it!"

In improv, however, do-gooders are treacherous bastards.

Doing more than your part disempowers others. This manifests as an improvisor taking continuous action while giving little opportunity for others to participate, often called "steamrolling." It also appears as a character who teaches, instructs, directs, or commands.

The do-gooder's instincts may be noble, trying to singlehandedly give order to a spontaneous endeavor. But doing more than your part, regardless of one's intention, prohibits others from doing their part. Don't mess with other people's parts!

Be Cool!

This paragraph is about being cool . . . whatever.

In improv, cool people are treacherous bastards.

It is pretty cool to be considered cool, but it's not cool to admit that. What defines cool is at the whim of others. The cool must focus on the image they project, contemplating whether it meets the expectations of others. This uproots an improvisor from their most essential resource—themself.

The traditional definition of cool, which includes independence and composure, can result in being emotionally unaffected. This strikes at our ability to make moments, which requires us to be affected. Totally not cool.

To some degree, we are always interested with how others perceive us. But keeping a cool image can prevent us from doing what we must to build the staged reality . . . or doing what is fun.

Win!

When people's goals cannot be achieved mutually, we have conflict. The world becomes one of win or lose. And with a planet covered with humans, we lionize or at least begrudgingly admire the winners who emerge from the fracas.

But in improv, winners are treacherous bastards.

Those who are "wired to win" are quick to abandon their goal as an improvisor to build a staged reality to pursue their goal as a person to win goodies. They can't help it; a winner is conditioned to win. They may call it "being the best" or "being right," but those righteous words only dress up the base desire to win.

Unfortunately for winners, improv is unwinnable. An improvisor creates moments that form a structure in a staged reality, that is it. It either survives with integrity, or it does not. You cannot "beat" those with whom you improvise. Improvisors have different skill levels and can be compared, but when improvising, everyone's skills combine to realize the same goal.

An improvisor's ego can also be suckered into winning within the staged reality. Someone who has never made toast in everyday life can become hell-bent on winning a chili cook-off in the staged reality. The improvisor's ego gets fooled into thinking the character's success is the improvisor's success.

There are no real dollars, no real bragging rights, no real happily ever afters. Nothing a character achieves in the staged reality is available to the improvisor in everyday reality. This may ruin your retirement plan, but it's true.

In addition to that tragedy, winners never experience the fun of playing the non-winner.

The staged reality provides many scenarios to bait your inner winner: arguments, contests, rivalries, and one-upmanship. Here are some signs your inner winner has taken the bait:

- ❊ **Antagonizing.** Manufacturing conflict regardless of its relevance to the staged reality.
- ❊ **Attacking.** Criticizing another's point of view without offering an alternate.
- ❊ **Dodging.** Ignoring information that puts your character at a disadvantage.
- ❊ **Steamrolling.** Dominating by not allowing others to express (like the steamrolling done by those do-gooder bastards).

Characters in a staged reality can have endless conflict, arguments galore, and contests of contests, but the improvisors beneath are not in competition, they are in cahoots. They know their characters are competing, but their job is to collaboratively build the staged reality without attachment to the outcome.

To note, there are questionable improv competitions called "cage matches" where teams of improvisors perform for an audience who votes on which team was "the best." Under its veneer of competition, it's a tactic to generate an audience for the theatre because, not surprisingly, the team that rallies the most supporters usually wins. Don't let cage matches bait your inner winner, but do get out the vote.

Be Great!

Rarely is there an improvisor who doesn't want to be great. Someone who reads a book on improv clearly wants to be great, as much as the person who wrote that book. Who doesn't want to be respected? Appreciated? Admired? Damn. Being great sounds great!

In improv, however, the great are treacherous bastards.

Greatness is more treacherous than winning, because the pursuit is endless: if you somehow claim greatness over those who live, that goal is superseded with proving greatness over those who no longer live, which is superseded by dominion over those yet to live, superseded by achieving perfection, then constant perfection, then low-calorie constant perfection . . . and so on. It's a never-ending train of comparisons to ill-conceived and ill-defined standards, a fantasy scale by which every experience will be found lacking.

Even more problematic, greatness is an evaluation that requires one to contemplate an experience, which precludes participating in it. The desire for greatness does not help form a moment, especially those that eventually may be considered great.

Greatness may rent cars under the names Perfection, the Right Way, or Strictly by the Rules.

The desire to be great motivates us to invest, leading to deeper understanding, skill, and opportunity, which increases the chance of having an experience that feels "great." In the moment, however, the desire for greatness is treacherous.

Hurry Up!

- ❊ Time is short.
- ❊ Hurriers r treacherous bast'ds.
- ❊ Hurrying prioritizes speed over contnt & meang.
- ❊ Hryng leaves no rm.

Be Polite!

I hope you don't mind me saying that I don't feel society—by which I mean my society because I would never claim to know someone else's society—compels people to be polite. Speaking for myself (and I could be wrong and wouldn't mind one whit if you corrected me in a strongly worded letter—in fact I'd be flattered by your attention), I feel we choose to be polite because we want to be liked, avoid conflict, show respect, or it's just how we've been trained. Of course, if you disagree, I will gladly change my position. I just want to be polite.

However, in improv, the polite are treacherous bastards. Polite is often practiced as putting others' needs ahead of your own or pretending you don't have needs at all. This can appear as deferring to others whenever a decision is made, or guessing what the other would prefer, or just waiting . . . for . . . someone . . . to . . . do . . . something. Politeness can be an excuse to hide yourself, a high crime in improv since your participation is vital.

As a polite person, you may find it difficult to assert yourself because your body thinks it must offer guilt, embarrassment, and judgment as payment to the universe for being heard. Don't bother paying. The universe is filthy rich. Have you seen its yard?

Politeness can also appear as minimizing your contributions. It's the old I-can't-take-a-compliment syndrome. Graciously own your amazingness, especially if someone points it out . . . who knows when it will happen again.

Politeness travels under a few aliases that include Being Nice, Taking Care of Others, I Don't Want to Be Pushy, and I Don't Want to Rock the Boat. If you see any of those, tell them to piss off.

Authorize It!

We've been taught to claim our work. Even if our work is just urinating in the snow—we sign it. Postmodernism celebrates the artist who conceives of a piece but never touches it, leaving the production to staff. The credit goes to one because "they done thunk it up."

In improv, however, authors are treacherous bastards.

In improv you are the author of your moment, but that's where it ends. Pursuing personal ideas that span moments requires the improvisor to spend time in their head and then to control others to enact their personal vision. It is referred to as "planning" or "writing." It is weapons-grade trouble for a collaborative creation.

There are many pursuits where one can author a product to fulfill a personal vision, but improv is not one. Even a one-person improvised show requires input from at least one other (e.g., "Can I have a suggestion please?").

Fix It!

Most jobs are about fixing problems, but some of us can't stop. When we exhaust fixing toilets, relationships, or hockey games we move on to people, especially their emotions. If you are sad, the fixer cheers you up. If you are proud, the fixer brings you back to Earth. If you are enraged, the fixer calms you down. Some call those actions kind; others call them controlling. In everyday reality you decide their value.

In improv, however, fixers are treacherous bastards.

When a character encounters a challenge in the staged reality, it can be an automatic behavior to fix that character's emotions or immediately solve the problem.

When we fix emotions, we invalidate them. We might do it actively with words and actions or passively by ignoring their existence. In doing so we dismiss the character's point of view, effectively dismissing the character.

When we fix a more tangible issue, like a leaky faucet or zombie attack, we eliminate any challenges the character must go through. We never see who they are.

In the extreme, fixing annihilates the staged reality. Let's say we discover that zombies are approaching our treehouse and we have no bullets. A fixer can invent more bullets to avoid dealing with the challenge of no bullets. But if we avoid that challenge, why have any challenge? Why not make the zombies unable to climb ladders? Why not have the zombies die of boredom? Why fear becoming a zombie? Why have zombies at all?

The issue lies in what we consider a problem. In the staged reality where the stakes are fictional, nothing is a problem to an improvisor. There is no preferred state. Zombie or non-zombie, birth or death, joy or despair, success or failure—all are conditions worthy to explore, not necessarily fix.

The world needs fixers, but treachery flourishes when we fix automatically in the staged reality.

Protect Yourself!

We protect things with fences, passwords, and vaults. We invented those devices because we don't want people, sometimes ourselves, fiddling with our valuable bits.

In improv, however, protectors are treacherous bastards.

Protecting is the desire to keep the product from being "ruined" and to keep ourselves from experiencing undesired emotions.

If we have a wonderful staged reality, made from wonderful moments, we can become attached to our wonderful product. As the tower of wonderfulness grows higher, we worry that a misstep will bring all that wonderfulness tumbling down. And it is hard to act when all you are thinking is *Do not ruin this wonderfulness. DO NOT RUIN THIS WONDERFULNESS.* To protect ourselves from the possible pain of ruining wonderfulness, we freeze.

We also protect ourselves when the staged reality feels distinctly not-wonderful, when it feels like we are tanking. Whether such an assessment is accurate doesn't matter—in the moment we do not like what is happening and want out. We can't escape physically so we distance from the staged reality while still in it. It's ingenious really.

We can distance by dropping commitment intellectually, physically, or emotionally. This is called "bailing." We can also distance by making an observation about the staged reality as if we are not part of it, perhaps with a whiff of judgment. This is called "commenting."

Remember that moments—wonderful and not-so-wonderful—are complete. They have been glued into the universe's scrapbook. There is no way to change the past and no way to escape the present. You only can make the current moment with all the skill you can muster.

Run!

Life makes us deal with things when we don't want to deal with them. Your garbage can smells when Life says so; Life lays you off when it wants to; your baby is born when it's convenient for Life, not you. Life is a hard-ass.

To squeeze some control from our powerless predicament, we learn how to avoid Life's challenges. We can avoid for a loooong time. So strong is our desire to avoid the issues of Life, that we invented Death.

However, in improv, avoiders are treacherous bastards.

Improv does not have Life's iron fist to make us deal with events. Our habit of avoiding becomes hyper-effective in a staged reality. It can have the devastating effect of giving us what we want—boredom. Signs of avoidance include:

- ❋ **It's not us.** We focus on those who aren't present to avoid those who are.
- ❋ **It's not here**. We focus on being someplace else to avoid the place we are currently.
- ❋ **It's not now**. We focus on events of the future or past to avoid what is happening now.
- ❋ **It's not this**. We focus on words or activities but avoid what they mean.

We run to the safe space where "nothing matters right now," and after arriving we are uncomfortable because "nothing matters right now."

Running frequently shows up in spot scenes, and invariably leads to scenes in which characters go through minutes that do *not* matter to them.

Dress Up!

So many people wear clothes that I feel clothing has become fashionable. It makes sense: clothes are a practical means of comfort, protection, hygiene, and communication.

In improv, however, people who wear clothes are treacherous bastards.

Clothes cue expectations. We must be careful what we cue in others and ourselves.

If you dress as a sexy beast, your sexy cues are going to shine through and take precedence in any staged reality. Because, frankly, sex is more enticing than improv. And if not more enticing, sexy is distracting, as are flashy, hip, quirky, formal, or slovenly. If clothing deviates too far from expectations it becomes the focus, pulling the audience out of the staged reality.

More dangerously, you restrict yourself. If you dress sexy, it will be difficult to be anything but sexy to fulfill expectations, even if they are only your own. We restrict ourselves when we dress too far from "meh." Clothing also has practical limitations: a top hat and high heels limit what you can do.

Most theatres have dress codes that establish "normal." Watch the locals to see it in action. Expectations around clothing differ by geography, institution, and group. A code takes the power out of clothes. If everyone dresses in the same range, clothing effectively disappears. Not in the sexy way, but in the we-can-imagine-anything-we-want way.

Entertain Us!

Improv is a form of entertainment. That means if you improvise you enter the ranks of entertainers, which includes icons like Buffalo Bill, Oprah, and Lassie.

Unfortunately in improv, entertainers are treacherous bastards.

"Entertainment" is a catch-all term for any activity that holds attention and gives pleasure. It encompasses everything from burning ants with a magnifying glass to a Hollywood action film about burning ants with a magnifying glass.

We have formed expectations about what it means to entertain, all of which we silently bring to our improv. Those expectations probably include qualities like original, smart, interesting, funny, and creative.

Those expectations don't help create moments. If you possess one of those lovely qualities, there is nothing special you need to do—no extra effort is required for you to be you. If you lack one of those qualities, you cannot spontaneously possess it. Someone who is not smart cannot instantly become smart through an act of will. Smart people have told me it doesn't work that way.

To flaunt a specific quality or skill—to force a display—damages the shared reality. It feels needy. Often this dysfunction appears as being wacky, crazy, going blue (being unjustifiably sexual, scatological, or otherwise crude), or . . . oddly, making a joke.

Whoa, wait, making a joke? Isn't improv funny? Often it is, but when someone gets a note that they are "making a joke" (aka "reaching for it" or "trying too hard") it refers to trying to elicit a response by doing something that does not fit the staged reality. The improvisor no longer acts as a character, but as an individual hustling a laugh. The staged reality is damaged, and a price is paid. It may be worth the price if the bit is really good, but if it's not . . . brrrr, it turns cold very fast.

Your qualities will be evident when you improvise. Which qualities shine and whether they are entertaining (spoiler: they probably are) are worries that do not help make moments.

Wrap It Up

We are all treacherous bastards. Treacherous behaviors are part of being human. But we can recognize them and understand when they cross the line from benign to betrayal. We examine that next.

20

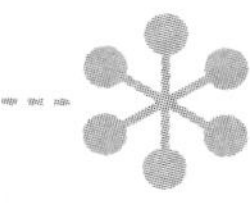

Treacherous Systems

Treacherous behaviors are part of a system orchestrated by a single leader with a single goal. Unfortunately, for an improvisor that goal isn't improvising.

That is why treacherous behaviors feel out of our control in improv. We may not even realize we are doing them until someone tells us. The more we try to suppress them, the more they appear.

If we look at the treacherous system, we have a chance to defuse it.

The Discomfort

Treacherous behaviors arise to address a discomfort. We'll call that discomfort "fear." It is not boot-shaking, quivering, headless horseman type of fear, but a small flash that predicts an unwanted experience is about to happen, or a wanted experience is about to be denied.

In the afterglow of that flash, you can catch what is pulling the levers and pushing the buttons, orchestrating the treacherous behaviors. It's okay to look. It wants you to catch it. It wants you to stop it. It wants you to control it. Because that is what it is, control.

We work with control daily: we follow a schedule, stay safe, and hold our urine until urinating time. But control also works without our knowledge—that is when problems begin.

Control instinctively gets your needs met as it has been trained to do. From innumerable repetitions or a few impactful events, these behaviors are not just habits, but an enduring, self-reinforcing survival system. Every day cements them as "the way shit works." This system is on high alert in an unusual or stressful situation, and improv can be a county fair–winning recipe for unusual and stressful.

At the slightest hint of fear, control and your treacherous behaviors try to help you improvise which, for them, means returning to the security of the familiar, even if the familiar is unneeded, unwanted, or harmful. It is what they know.

Control steers to familiar roles. The word familiar comes from the Latin *familiaris*, "of one's household," describing families, friends, and servants (aka coworkers). These are relationships in which we learn how to get needs met. That's where we found it best to navigate life as something smart, funny, helpful, helpless, chaotic, invisible, logical, emotional, authoritative, problematic, or whatever.

Control also steers to familiar structures. It wants to produce fuzzy copies of what we have seen before, even if we just saw it moments ago. We get stuck in cliché or creative ruts. But even while forging fresh work, improvisors may find themselves inexplicably repeating beats of the very scene they are making, effectively "treading water."

When we automatically control to achieve the familiar, we cross into betrayal—of you and everyone else.

Crossing the Line of Betrayal

Performers have needs; that's why they perform. The audience has needs; that's why they audience. Everyone participates with expectations about what they will give and what they will get. It's an unspoken agreement. When needs are met within the expectations held about the art form, happiness abounds.

But when an improvisor tries to fulfill an inappropriate need, one outside of expectations, the line is crossed. The unspoken agreement has been broken. This can give rise to the blunt note from the instructor: "it's needy."

To pursue an inappropriate need, an improvisor betrays needs that are legitimate to the setting. They betray their creative needs, the needs of the piece, the staged reality, and the necessary conditions. They betray their fellow improvisors and the audience by using them without consent. To reclaim a familiar role, others must play a complimentary role; they too must be a specific thing. That is one big mess of betrayal. Bring a mop.

The aftermath of all this betrayal feels like a disorienting frothy wake, in which the improvisor isn't sure what went wrong but knows the experience did not feel right—it felt hollow, or sour, or filthy.

If that sounds dramatic, it's because it is. Those dramatic feelings are perplexing when they occur in improv because they seem so out of place and it's not immediately clear what prompted them. Thus, an improvisor quickly ignores them, or thinks it's a sign they are no good, or that those feelings are caused by something external (the class, the audience, they day of the week, and so on).

Sorry, Mr. Trash Can

I deal with those same dynamics as an instructor, and sometimes they manifest more dramatically. In an early teaching experience, I had a flash of frustration so powerful that, while leaning back in a chair, I kicked a trash can and sent it sailing across the room to hit the far wall, scattering debris everywhere. It was the greatest athletic feat of my life. It was also a poor choice. One worth examining.

At the time, I thought my anger was because students were failing to execute an exercise—but that's part of being a student. In truth, their struggle had provoked a fear in me, a fear that I was a failure and a fraud, or worse, that I would be seen that way. My body pumped adrenaline to act, and the thing I acted on was the trash can. Sorry, Mr. Trash Can. Fortunately, most improvisors see the humor in being human. After picking up the mess, we were back on track.

Don't underestimate flashes of fear. When they occur in improv you don't have a trash can to kick, so your treacherous behaviors act instead.

Rewiring

Your automatic controlling behavior has served you; I would never say abandon it. But for improv, we need to rewire. For improv we want to modify our fear response and controlling behaviors to prioritize serving creative needs and the needs of the piece, instead of reflexively seeking the familiar.

Fortunately, improv workshops are made for rewiring. A class run by a competent instructor at a respectable institution with a critical mass of sincere participants produces an environment that your psychiatrist or pastor would endorse: it involves others, it is supportive, it is honest, it is corrective, and it is fun. But don't burn your psychiatrist's number. Improv is not therapy. In such an environment you can experiment in real time with how you respond to and take feedback. The stakes are lower than in your everyday reality, although they may feel high. The environment is almost therapeutic. But it's not. Improv is not therapy.

If you can take small risks in such an environment, repeatedly, you can reshape your model of you and the world. Different ways of being will become available to you in the staged reality and just might transfer to everyday reality. But there is no promise. Improv is not therapy.

To help you rewire, an instructor will give notes on your improv. But why rely on that slacker? Help rewire yourself with these tricks, most suited for spot scenes and long form.

- ✻ **Isolate.** When a treacherous behavior occurs, isolate it. If you realize you are instructing, simply say, "Oh my gosh, I'm instructing you." Then see what happens.
- ✻ **Correct**. When a treacherous behavior occurs, address it. If you ask too many questions, start answering your own questions. "What is in the oven? Wait, I can smell it, potatoes au gratin!"
- ✻ **Oppose.** Challenge yourself to oppose a behavior: if you must win, commit to losing; if you must be sexy, be disgusting; if you must be polite, be a loudmouth. Fair warning: you may never go back to your old way.

Time and Repetition

Rewiring takes time and repetition. It's frustrating to have treacherous behaviors come up again and again. This can lead to self-criticism. But criticism, even the anticipation of criticism, often activates the controlling behavior that needs to be relaxed. When changing how one responds to stressful situations it does not help to generate more stress.

No doubt, sometimes we require a stern talking-to. Sometimes we need someone to shout at us. Sometimes we need a big emotion to puncture a thick defense. Sometimes we need one fear to propel us through a different fear. Sometimes.

For the rest of the time remember that your behaviors have been your buddies, even the self-critical bit. They are trying to help, even if now they are a bit clumsy and out of place. Be a pal when they act up. Thank them and let them know they can take a rest—they've earned it.

Wrap It Up

Behind our treacherous behaviors is control. We cross into betrayal when we use control to meet an inappropriate need, one that is outside the expectations of a relationship and setting.

In a supportive environment, such as improv, we can rewire to develop different automatic responses. This takes time and repetition.

21

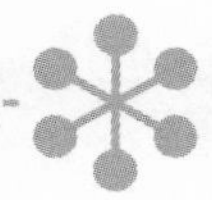

On the Superiority of Dogs

Dogs were the first animal domesticated by humans, somewhere around 36,000 to 13,000 B.C. It was 3 thousand years before anyone tried to find a better companion. That attempt was a shambles: unable to catch a frisbee and cursed with devil's eyes, the domestic goat was cancelled on August 12, 10,000 B.C.

In conclusion, 7 thousand years ago we morphed the African Bobcat into the 2nd most popular domestic animal, *Felis Catus*—the moderne cat. Whilst beautiful, 'twas a monster: narcissistic, devoid of language skills, and unable to divine the meaning Of a pointing finger. Cat apologists soon popularized the phrase "I love my cat. She's just like a dog!"

The next most popular domesticated animal appeared in 300 B.C. as the goldfish so lagging dogs and even cats no one dares whisper you'd like my fish it is just like a dog that person would be shamed even by a goldfish the only being loyal enough to defend such a heretic would ironically be a dog

!god eht—dradnats dlog s'ytinamuh ot derapmoc ,eb syawla lliw dna ,si pihsnoinapmoc rieht ,srekaterac namuh rieht morf evol devresed dna seitilauq elbarimda rieht etipseD .srehto fo edaclavac a dna ,spmihc ,sregit ,star ,sterref ,sgip ylleb top fo ynapmoc eht kees ew sa yadot seunitnoc hcraes elituf ruO.

Woof. What the Hell Was That?

I hope that essay on dogs was unexpected in a book on improv. And I hope you found unexpected facts written in unexpected ways (seemingly error riddled) that lead to some unexpected reactions. Because this chapter is about the invisible highways that silently guide our minds, sometimes helping and sometimes hindering our ability to improvise: expectations.

Your expectations and those held by others affect every topic in improv. Expectations influence the making of a moment, a structure, a reality, and what we find fun or funny. Perhaps more importantly you hold expectations about improv, what it will provide you, and what your progress should look like. These will largely determine whether your experience is positive or negative. We must respect the power of expectations.

BENEFITS OF EXPECTATIONS

An expectation is a belief of how things will or should be. We "hold" expectations because they provide value, regardless of whether they prove accurate. Like a child's favorite blanket, it is the act of holding that provides benefits. The following are those benefits.

- **Security**. We feel secure when we think we understand how the world works and what the future holds. Even if we expect discomfort, it is the knowing that gives comfort.
- **Satisfaction**. We evaluate experiences relative to our expectations, and that determines what is "good" or "bad." Expectations also tell us what to pursue, with the belief that the pursued will deliver satisfaction.
- **Simplicity**. Expectations elevate one possibility above infinite other possibilities. This lets our complex brains handle complex problems in a complex universe. It's simple.
- **Sanity.** Expectations help form and validate our reality. We interpret information to be in accordance with expectations and, if it deviates, we are moved to update our model of reality.

With all those benefits it's no wonder we cling to what we think should happen, especially under the stress of improvising, even though we have no idea where our expectations came from.

FORMING

We form some expectations consciously, such as when a significant other says, "Hey, we need to talk." The bulk of our expectations, however, are formed with little awareness. This is concerning. Where do these powerful beliefs come from?

We form expectations from our direct experience. From our interactions we expect rocks to be hard, water to be wet, and the sun to be bright. This is also true for intangibles. If you frequently experience success, you may come to expect success. Unfortunately it also applies to non-success.

We form expectations based on a perceived authority. How we decide someone is an authority is murky, but it is clear we allow others to meddle with our expectations—whether a brother, boss, or beer commercial.

We form expectations through an agreement, whether inked on paper or whispered to the wind. We may never tell the other party about the agreement. Our brain has no problem unilaterally forming expectations with a person, a border collie, or God.

We form expectations from our imagination. If you pursue a goal you have never achieved before, your pursuit is based on what you imagine that goal will provide. As King Midas said, "Dreams are tricky, let's shake on it."

Your response to the opening essay on dogs was influenced by expectations set through all those means: your lifetime of reading; authorities who taught you proper English; unspoken agreements between reader and author; and what you imagined this chapter would be about.

An example of setting expectations consciously in improv occurs during the introduction of a show when a figure of authority, such as a host, tells the audience what improv is, the structure they are about to see, that they should respond when asked for suggestions, and that they will not be asked to do anything embarrassing. Audience expectations are also set unconsciously by the demeanor of the host and every experience surrounding the show—from parking the car to finding a seat. When expectations have been set well, the audience is primed to enjoy the event.

We form oodles and oodles of expectations. Most putter about their business in our minds without notice. The first hint we hold one may be when it is violated.

DEVIATING

We have a visceral response when our experience deviates from our expectation. Words that may substitute for deviate are "defeat," "foil," or "defy." It sounds like something we prefer to avoid. But if all our expectations were met all the time life would, ironically, not live up to expectations—that existence is D-U-L-L. Deviations provide variety, excitement, and novelty (sometimes we call these "twists" or "punchlines"). We crave them.

Our response to a deviation is considered positive (heart flutters and laughter) just as frequently as negative (disappointment and fist banging), although the deviation itself is neutral. It is merely the difference between "what is" and "what is in your head." You can bias people toward the positive with an environment that is fun and safe, which sounds suspiciously like improv.

"Give us what we expect, but not the way we expect it," is not the worst tattoo an improvisor could get. We have expectations for what a scene is but want them to be satisfied in an unexpected way. We form expectations about a character, but we want that character to surprise us with how they live up to them. It's the same as when you go to a scary movie: you expect to be scared, but those scares must be unexpected.

If our response to a deviation is too minor, life rolls on uninterrupted. If too intense, our big emotions overwhelm us and we forget the underlying expectation we hold, how it was set, and if it is useful. But if our response is between those extremes and we are in a positive mood, we reset expectations—the deviation becomes the new normal. "The dog is on the bed?! Okay, just this once."

This resetting of expectations creates the appetite for heightening: we need greater deviations to experience the same feeling. In improv you may hear the comment "That's a lateral move," which means you are repeating (perhaps with superficial changes) what was previously fun but to which everyone has since reset expectations. You need to outdo what came before to elicit the same response.

There is a limit. A deviation can be so great from an expectation that the experience becomes unrecognizable. We may not be able to name, much less interpret it.

The essay on dogs at the beginning of this chapter deviated from your expectations. The deviations started small and grew until the final one was so large the text may have been unrecognizable, being written opposite of the left-to-right and top-to-bottom expectation for English. During that cavalcade of deviations, you had many responses, and some may have been negative (especially if you love English or cats). You may have recognized the essay for the game it was and reset your expectations as it went along. To account for your new expectations, each paragraph had to deviate further from competent writing to elicit some response—each paragraph had to heighten.

CUEING

If you can conceive of something, you can develop an expectation about it. That is a lot of expectations. A cue helps you figure out which expectations to hold for a particular situation.

Almost anything can be a cue—a kitchen, an angry voice, a corporate logo, the smell of bleach. An internal state can be a cue. Fear may activate expectations of either catastrophe or fun. Even existence can cue expectations, popular ones being "everything will be horrible" and "everything will be wonderful."

Cues are all around us, but we forget that they are cues. A common cue is a paragraph break. It is a cue to expect the introduction of a new idea. Let's see if it works. . . .

Designers, writers, cat trainers, and just about everybody establishes cues to influence themselves and others, whether they realize it or not. The time, the room you're in, even the clothes you wear to a recurring improv workshop can become cues. You might feel "off" doing that same activity at a different time and place without those cues. The context of a spot scene (relationship, location, activity) will cue expectations for the scene. We need those expectations so we know when and how the staged reality deviates from our everyday reality. Without them, we can't have surprises, we can't have fun.

GROUP EXPECTATIONS

Expectations may be declared by a bossy person called a "dictator" or written by a bossy group called a "congress" or enforced by a bossy club called the "cool kids," but when referring to the expectations of group, it's called a "guess." Expectations only exist in the head and heart of an individual.

Therefore the expectations of a group, such as an audience, are really a guess at expectations commonly valued by each person in that group. No two members have the same expectations. No individual knows all the expectations they hold, much less held by another in their group, and even much less those held by anyone else.

A work can delight some and enrage others. If you hit the sweet spot, enough common expectations will be met, everyone will say "that was great," a few hidden expectations will have been revealed, and some might even get redefined along the way.

You might want to discuss expectations before playing. When one long form show reached the perfect ending point, I stood up on stage, pointed to the tech booth, and shouted "Lights!" But the stage lights didn't go off. I continued to stand and point. Other improvisors looked at me. The audience looked at me. Several painfully long seconds later, the lights went dark. I was coming from a place where improvisors called endings from within the show. Clearly that's not what they expected at that venue. I'm confident the booth knew what I was signaling for, but I suspect they were pointedly setting my expectations for who calls the end of a show. Well played, booth.

CREATIVE INDIFFERENCE

Improv lets us reveal and play with expectations. We choose which to set, defeat, or honor. To do this, an improvisor must become aware of expectations but not be beholden to them.

We can call this a state of "creative indifference," where we recognize and selectively detach from our beliefs about how things should be, including our product and ourselves. We still hold expectations, but we hold many of them loosely.

The word "indifference" sounds alarming. Its top definitions include ideas such as uncaring, unfeeling, and uninterested. That *is* alarming! Fortunately we focus on the latter definitions that include impartial, unbiased, and neutral. We could call it creative impartiality, but I fall asleep just typing that.

Creative indifference expands your options. You carry little preference for what character or situation you will explore. You are willing to go in any direction. The staged reality can become whatever it demands, and you can become whatever is demanded.

Creative indifference does not mean we improvise without standards. For any collaborative effort some basic expectations must be met so people participate. Schools, theatres, and teams have unique expectations that are the admission to be in that group.

THE DOWNSIDES

It's easier to give something up when we know it has a funky smell. To loosen your grip on expectations, here are some downsides.

Expectations simplify the world, but the world is not simple. Expectations prevent you from accepting "what is" when it does not match "what is in your head."

Expectations and cues work automatically. Operating on autopilot prevents us from making moments purposefully. Holding tightly to expectations locks us and others into a narrow band of behaviors. There is little freedom. It's also exhausting.

Expectations can be unreasonable. Chronic dissatisfaction can plague an improvisor if their expectations about their abilities or what improv will provide them are set too high.

Wrap It Up

Expectations affect how we create a moment, a structure, a reality, and what we find fun or funny. Our expectations also influence whether our time improvising feels positive or negative.

PART FIVE

Character

Character serves us several ways: it is an element of the staged reality; a tool to discover, shape, and express; and a device that allows one improvisor to play multiple roles. It would be swell to own this Swiss army knife of improv. Luckily, you do. You are a character. With understanding, we can hack your existing character to unleash its limitless improvisational power.

To do so, we must travel back to England on the evening of March 25, 1859, at 8:59 P.M. The minute three characters changed history . . .

It's a damp London night. A horse-drawn carriage rumbles across the cobblestone of Albemarle Street. Beyond a wrought-iron fence and behind the white classical façade of Number 50, two gentlemen wait inside a gaslit parlor room.

One man slouches on a wooden bench. Pinned to his tattered topcoat is a nametag printed with "Hello, I am . . ." and scrawled underneath in pencil is "Charles." He clutches a worn leather satchel under one arm. As the grandfather clock ticks, his knobby fingers fumble about his beard, aimlessly twisting and untwisting its coarse white hair. He wheezes through an open mouth while staring intently at his feet, as if his focus serves greater purpose than its true function of avoiding eye contact. He wonders if it would be odd to excuse himself to the restroom, yet again.

An English setter is curled at his feet, wearing a collar from which hangs a tag that says "Hench." On the wall above Charles, hangs a mirror.

Staring into the mirror is Mr. Smiles, who towers in the center of the room: feet wide, chin high, hands clasped behind his back. His top hat glints the dim light. On his lapel is a sterling silver pin depicting a pint half full. His name tag is inked boldly with three smiley faces and an exclamation point. He grins at his reflection, admiring his grooming decision: his dramatically swept forward mutton chops make it appear like he is always in a wind. *A man of action*, he thinks, *even when standing still!* He sways gently in place. The polished leather of his riding boots creak under his shifting mass.

On the far wall are double doors, each affixed with a brass plaque. The plaque on the left is engraved with "JOHN MURRAY PUBLISHING, EST 1768," the other reads "DO NOT DISTURB." The gap beneath the doors leaks flickering light and murmuring voices from the room beyond.

John Murray Publishing administers the "Alright Already All Write!" competition, an annual contest to discover who will be Britannia's next superstar author. Any citizen may submit their book and themselves to the grueling eleven-month contest of endless notes, revisions, and promotional events in the hopes of winning the grand prize—a publishing contract. The contest is followed passionately, even by illiterate hooligans. It is a true national sensation.

The competition has reached its final month, final minute of the final hour of the final day. These two men are the final finalists.

The minute hand of the grandfather clock creeps to upright. It is 9 P.M.

Donnnnng! the clock chimes.

Footfalls sound from the room afar. The clock chimes again—*donnnnng*! Charles and Smiles and Hench the dog look at the doors. *Donnnnng*! The doors swing open to reveal a thin figure in tailcoat casting a shadow into the parlor. *Donnnnng*! In the distance of the newly revealed room, two gentlemen sit by a fireplace eating chicken drumsticks, while looking back into the parlor. *Donnnnng*! Charles stands and drops his satchel, spilling medicinal pills across the floor. *Donnnnng*! The figure in the doorway extends his hand, palm up, while Charles scrambles on all fours to pick up each pill. *Donnnnng*! Smiles steps over Charles and offers his hand to the figure in the doorway.

Donnnnng!

Smiles and the figure engage in a vigorous handshake, which becomes a vigorous two-handed handshake.

"Mr. Smiles!" says the figure, voice wobbling from the handshaking.

"Mr. Murray!" responds Smiles with a wobbling voice.

"Mr. Smiles," says the figure, "I am very, terribly, profoundly sorry."

Donnnnng!

Charles, on his knees, picking up pills, looks up. His face catches the light of the fireplace. Mr. Murray offers his open hand.

"Congratulations, Mr. Darwin."

Clarity

The word "character" has many meanings. We must first distinguish which relate to our work. We care about character as:

- ❊ A role in a story (Gary played the character of Zombie #4).
- ❊ A quality (Gary's cotton sheets had a silky character).
- ❊ An unusual or notable person (Gary was so goofy at the party—what a character!).

In an improvised staged reality, we are a character, as in a role. As we act, through chance or choice, we express that role's character, as in qualities. Those qualities may be unusual or notable enough to stand out as a character, as in a person distinct from most.

Differing Views

Darwin and Smiles not only are diametrically opposed characters but are diametrically opposed on the nature of character, as reflected in their writing.

In his book *On the Origin of Species* (published by John Murray), Darwin continued the efforts of naturalists as far back as Aristotle, who struggled to find a way to classify every living thing on the planet. Most relied on physical traits: if it has a pouch, it's a kangaroo; if it has a long nose, it's an elephant . . . or something like that. Darwin's work transformed all previous efforts, as he evidenced that the physical structures of different species were, in fact, related by an evolutionary link. He also described the mechanism of this invisible link. In his watershed description of natural selection, Darwin credited both biology and fate for distinguishing an organism.

So esteemed was this and his other works that upon his death, Darwin was one of the select commoners to be buried in Westminster Abbey, resting in the abbey's nave, sharing geography with scientific titans like Sir Isaac Newton. Not bad for a guy who dropped out of medical school.

By contrast, in his book *Self-Help* (fittingly self-published), Samuel Smiles never considers physical characteristics. Where Darwin made exhausting studies of biology, Smiles made exhausting studies of biographies. His book is a parade of stories that describe men rising from humble beginnings to achieve notability in art, science, industry, and politics. To Smiles, the randomness of one's origin or talents has little influence on what one can achieve. No fan of fate, Smiles contends that every person can achieve distinction if one masters the qualities of perseverance, patience, industriousness, courage, energy, and resourcefulness.

His book was an instant success, making Smiles a celebrity guru and defining the self-help genre. Smiles continued to write, and was a political and social activist, and rumor has it he was offered knighthood, which he modestly refused. Not bad for a guy who dropped out of medical school.

Darwin studied physical characteristics, acknowledging the power of nature over a being. Smiles studied personality, promoting one's choice over one's lot.

For our work, we must be both Darwin and Smiles. We deal with qualities predestined by nature and qualities we account to free will. Then we must go where Darwin and Smiles dared not. We will relate the qualities of biology, fate, and choice to become an integrated whole. If you travel this road, knighthood is certain, burial next to Isaac Newton is probable, and dropping out of med school is recommended.

The Big Parts

We can deconstruct character based on the work of Darwin and Smiles, focusing on choice, biology, and fate. We will use different words to avoid lawsuits from either. Character is an aggregate of the following.

- Point of view
- Physical traits
- Backstory

We will examine each in isolation, how they cohere to form a whole, what distinguishes characters, and, finally, we will peek at the awesome and frustrating raw material you have to work with: the character of you.

Put on some coffee. It's gonna be a late night.

This is character.

22

Point of View

Mr. Darwin, Mr. Smiles, and Mr. Murray knew the final night of the "Alright Already All Write!" competition was filled with importance, but not for the reasons they thought.

As a carriage rambles outside 50 Albemarle Street, keen ears can hear it brush against the branches of an English elm. That tree is home to five of London's most dastardly squirrels, who ignore all reasonable commands to vacate. With this pack of humans in the parlor, this could be the night those vile squirrels are annihilated! THE SQUIRRELS ARE IMPORTANT.

In the room where two men eat chicken, the scent of a dessert (pear Charlotte topped with . . . vanilla custard) wafts from underneath a cake cover—a devilishly impenetrable device. The strategy is to nudge the cover from the side so the food falls on the floor—where food belongs! THE DESSERT IS IMPORTANT.

The men shake each other's hands, but under the bench in the room is a wool sock. Nothing beats a sock for a tug of war. Nothing! THE SOCK IS IMPORTANT.

The squirrels, the food, and the sock are more important than *On the Origin of Species*, *Self-Help*, or the book competition—at least to Hench the English setter.

Hench is perhaps the only living body in that gas-lit parlor room who is aware of those three items. His size and senses allow him to perceive the world differently than the gentlemen who tower over him. Hench's thinking and emotions, shaped by his dog brain and dog status, lead him to assign these items great value. We must admit THEY ARE IMPORTANT, from his point of view.

In a previous section we mentioned point of view as it related to a physical location. What can you see from where you are standing—like Hench and the sock under the bench. However, a character's point of view is more than spatial. It is how one perceives the world, both the tangible and intangible.

How a character perceives reality is how a character creates reality. What we say and do hold creative dominance in an improvised staged reality, and a point of view drives what we say and do. Of the three components of character, point of view is the most central to an improvisor's work.

A point of view helps a person navigate life. Once proven viable, there is little incentive to suffer the time, effort, and discomfort needed to modify a point of view. It is a defining feature. Persuading Hench that squirrels are not important would be near futile.

A point of view is the most memorable part of a character. We may recall a few details of someone's past or what they look like, but how we interact with that character has the greatest impact—how points of view collide. Its persistence is what makes a character recognizable over time, despite bodily changes ("Oh Gary, you haven't changed a bit!"). Too bad for you, Gary.

A point of view gives a character portability. It liberates a character from a specific backstory. We can set a character down any place, in any time, with any resources, and have an idea of how that person will manage.

The ability to hold different points of view helps the improvisor build a shared reality with integrity. An improvisor must interpret the staged reality not only through their own point of view, but through that of a character and an audience member.

We automatically compare a character's point of view with our own to learn about ourselves, the character, and the shared reality. It turns out all three are amusing.

Words that substitute for point of view are "personality," "personality traits," "perspective," or "attitude," along with phrases like "the lens through" which a character sees the world or the "voice" created by what a character expresses and how it is expressed.

The ABCs of POV

A point of view is defined by what one feels, does, and thinks about an element in the shared reality. We will use the words affect, behavior, and cognition instead of feel, do, and think. These words are fancier and more accurate, and who can pass up the mnemonic allure of A-B-C? No one.

- ✻ **Affect.** Affect is how one feels toward things, which includes values, opinions, evaluations, and emotions. Words like "good/bad," "attractive/ugly," "happy/sad," "better/worse," "love/hate" are expressions of affect. Those words are relative; they point to a position on a personal scale. You may hate squirrels, but hate is your evaluation. It better describes you than it does squirrels. (Note: this is different than the word "affect" used as a verb, as in "Gary was affected by the pepper spray.")
- ✻ **Behavior.** How one acts toward things; what one does and how they do it.
- ✻ **Cognition.** What one believes about things, whether considered fact, assumption, or superstition. Reasoning is also part of cognition. It is a cognition that nudging a cake cover off a plate will topple the contents onto the floor, making them easier to eat if you have paws.

TARGETS

You hold a point of view about a target, a "thing" in the world. Affects, cognitions, and behaviors are aimed at targets. The world is filled with targets.

What is your opinion of a brownie, a self-help book, or an ancient space alien? How about intangibles like love, Greek history, evolution, or improv? Why limit ourselves to what exists? Our hopes, dreams, and fears reflect our point of view about the yet to exist. We can even hold a point of view about our own thoughts, feelings, and behaviors. What is your point of view about your own point of view?

A point of view is best communicated when everyone has experience with the target, it is a common reference. If I prefer my pear charlotte cold, someone else must have eaten that dessert for them to relate to my point of view. This means everyday objects and activities are perfect to reveal point of view. No need to get fancy.

A simple formula to start a unique point of view is to pair any affect with a mind-numbingly common target. State a self-evident fact to a friend with a clear emotion such as seductively whispering "a steering wheel is round." We may not understand that point of view, but it draws interest—is the allure about steering, the wheel, roundness? And why? This is the start of uncovering a point of view.

When we have similar affects, cognitions, and behaviors toward a target, we share the same point of view. When Gary and Claire are disgusted with each other, they share the same affect but hold it toward different targets. They do not share the same point of view. When Claire is disgusted with Gary and Gary is disgusted with himself, they share the same point of view: Gary is a steaming mess.

EVIDENCE

To learn about someone's point of view, nothing is better than an intimate dinner for two. But don't get seduced by conversation. Words are only part of the evidence. A decision reflects a point of view, whether the decision is big or small, mundane or exotic. The words we say, when we say them, and how we say them are clearly choices, but so are scores of other elements of the dinner's food, setting, and attire.

An object and its details reflect a point of view. An object is the physical evidence of decisions related to its creation, acquisition, and use. Any physical feature can represent a series of decisions driven by a point of view. Is the dinner table adorned with a slender candle in a silver candelabra, or is it stumpy and bubblegum scented, or is it a Zippo lighter taped to an empty bottle of gin?

How we execute activities of everyday life reflects our point of view: the order you choose to eat food at dinner; the pattern in which you vacuum the floor; how you pack a suitcase; how you answer the phone . . . if you answer the phone. Our everyday mundane acts testify just as much as our flashier choices—how we dress, where we live, whom we socialize with, how we spend our spare time.

A life is littered with the evidence of a point of view. Words are only a tiny portion. A confession of "I believe . . ." is one element floating in a sea of objects, actions, and emotions that equally testify to the character's point of view. This supports the reliable advice "Show, don't tell."

AGENCY

A character must have agency for an object or action to reflect a point of view. Agency is the capacity to exercise power over one's self and circumstance. Most simply, it is the ability and opportunity to make a choice.

Point of view is not evidenced by things over which we are powerless. What the world imposes on a character may shape that character's point of view. It may be a target about which a character can express a point of view. But what the world imposes does not articulate a character's point of view—unless that character is "the world."

It is more difficult to reveal point of view when a character has less agency, but rarely impossible. As agency fades, we approach oppression and helplessness. But even if oppressed, a point of view can bloom from the small choices that survive, even if the sole choice is how one complies with an oppressor. And when helpless, we can at least express how we feel about our plight. If this is unclear, rent a baby for a day.

Agency makes a staged reality safe for observers to enjoy. Decent folk are more comfortable being amused by a character who exercises their agency, no matter how small. Otherwise we risk evoking pity. It's also more comfortable because agency lets us believe we can choose to be, or not to be, like a character.

We diminish a character's agency when they act to elicit a desired response from authority, whether to placate, please, or anger. No matter the goal, when navigating by an authority's point of view, a character must suppress their own. They may survive, they may advance, but they are never fully known.

That authority can be any entity, whether they have formal power or not (e.g., the government, a crush, an employer, an improv instructor). Competitions can also be an authority, as they involve submitting to standards.

Beware of the "big boss trap," in which an improvisor invents an authority to justify their character's actions instead of discovering the point of view that propels those actions. If you paint your office lavender because the boss told you to, we miss finding out why you want to paint, what color you choose, how you hope your life will change by painting.

Authorities can be a valid part of the staged reality, just avoid the big boss trap.

Where It Begins

In everyday reality our point of view starts forming before we can walk and talk, and probably consolidates around the age of reason. Aristotle agreed when he wrote, "Give me a child until he is seven, and I will show you the man." You can't argue with a dead philosopher.

A character has a fully formed point of view the moment they appear in a staged reality. They have used it to navigate life before the audience's time with them; their world reflects their point of view. However, the improvisor has no knowledge of that world or point of view when they begin. Nevertheless, they must forge ahead to discover both. Two tactics to help this discovery follow.

In the first tactic, an improvisor begins by connecting to some general point of view. The inspiration for this may be based on a suggestion from the audience or perhaps a type of character the improvisor likes. This could be as simple as starting with a strong attitude. The improvisor uses the general point of view to discover specific elements of the staged reality. A character who has the general trait of "reserved" at a bar may order a gin and tonic—"No ice, hold the gin, lime on the side." That character also pays with cash, since "I don't like bragging that I have a credit card."

In the second tactic, an improvisor uses specific elements of the staged reality to infer a general point of view. Making bold assumptions from the unassuming is brash, but it is our job. Specifics help discover a generality, which then drives more specifics. For instance, an improvisor could start with a specific drink order and infer the personality of their character. They could even use the same drink as our previous example (gin and tonic, no ice, hold the gin, lime on the side) to infer one of many fitting traits such as meticulous, demanding, or plain.

Any element of the staged reality can serve as evidence of, or a target to express, a character's point of view, whether the element was created with intent or by accident. The staged reality brims with opportunities.

REASONABLENESS

A character's point of view does not have to be profound or even reasonable to be functional. In improv, as in our everyday lives, we don't have to craft anything brilliant. We must only discover a point of view and explore its ramifications.

Committing to an unreasonable point of view is a challenge for many improvisors. Our everyday reasonableness prevents us from making the leap. Let's call this the "reasonableness trap," which is discussed further in chapter 26 on distinguishing. To escape the trap, an improvisor needs an "edge," a willingness to carve a point of view sharply from their own.

BASKET VS. SINGULAR

If you identify with a singular point of view in your life, it was created lazily: deduced from curated memories, adopted from a social group, or chosen because it sounds badass. It probably reflects a relationship with something big—ourselves, our parents, our universe, or our god.

For everyday life, an all-season point of view is intellectually alluring but comically impractical. A person who claims fierce independence probably enjoys collective evils like fire departments and golf courses. A person sworn to collectivism indulges selfish sins like nicknames and bathroom doors. In practice, our point of view is really a basket of numerous points of view regarding many targets and isn't necessarily consistent to a single concept. This is a sometimes cool, sometimes annoying, rarely fatal perk of being human.

For a staged reality, however, a character can have fidelity to a singular point of view. They can be less complex and more consistent than a real human. We can afford this because it's a fictional world where the cost to explore is zero. We need this because improvised pieces usually are short; simplicity allows us to see in a limited time where a point of view leads. We enjoy this because a singular point of view is horribly flawed when taken absolutely. Entertainment is built in.

Two singular points of view that are well known are the optimist and pessimist. These opposing perspectives give you a way to exercise improvisational muscle in your everyday life. For any development in your day, state how it would be viewed by the optimist and then by the pessimist. If you can do that for a week, you might learn your life is much better than you thought. Or much, much worse.

Throughout this chapter, the phrase "point of view" may refer to a character's singular point of view toward everything or one point of view toward a specific target.

MULTIPLE TRAITS

We can be tempted to make a character interesting by adding multiple personality traits, as in "This character is courageously shy and antagonistically innocent in a charmingly rude way like the frantically melancholic girl next door." It is difficult to connect to a layered point of view quickly, and it often puts you in your head to figure out how to express all facets. It also is harder for an audience to decipher what this character is about in a short time when the point of view is muddied. Embrace limited personality traits; the bumps and hiccups of the process will impart complexity.

NAMING IT

We often reduce a character point of view to a word because words are what we use when we write and speak. Searching for a word to describe a point of view is a useful exercise that requires us to reflect, connect with our experience, and evaluate subtleties. It's a surprising challenge to identify the *exact* word to describe a person's attitude.

However, in practice we don't slavishly live a word. Even simplified characters in improv are richer than a single word. A word helps us connect to a specific point of view that exists inside us. Think of a word as an address in a neighborhood, and you want to live in that neighborhood, not necessarily be locked up at that address. Or consider it like the name of a color. You may wear a red dress for your portrait, but the painter knows there is variety around that red—it is more than a pure color from a single tube of paint. Slavish adherence to a single word causes problems.

Words take us into the intellect, which makes it harder to viscerally connect to the persona described by the word. If we mislabel a character, we will distort what occurred to match the label. Holding tightly to a word makes us bypass fun and variety, often prompting the comment we are being "one-note." The impulse to throw a cigarette out a car window may seem out of character for a caring person, until they reveal "I'm giving birds material to build their nests." Variety lets us fulfill expectations for the character in unexpected ways.

Improvising from a single word point of view also risks violating the acting advice "Do not act an adjective." The more complete advice is "Do not act an adjective that is not justified." We get some form of justification by linking feelings, thoughts, and behaviors so the character is as full as possible. This is the self-propagating A-B-C triad, described next.

A word can clarify our observations or sharpen our play, but we do not rely on a word to react. In the moment these things are felt.

Self-propagation

A point of view interprets the world to reinforce itself. In other words, it self-propagates. How we view the world defines how we construct our world, which determines how we view our world, and so on. We sustain the same paradigms even if the results aren't constructive. Don't blame your point of view. It's continuing a perfect record of keeping you alive. Darwin gives two knobby thumbs up.

For example, the optimist is happy to have a losing lottery ticket. They get the excitement of playing again tomorrow. The pessimist is unhappy to have a winning ticket. It's a hassle to pay all those taxes. The point of view sustains itself regardless of the event.

The point of view keeps the A-B-C triad in harmony. What I feel about a target aligns with how I behave about the target, which aligns with what I believe about a target. The affects, behaviors, and cognitions remain related. In practice, the model is not absolute, but it is serviceable.

Marketers are notorious for exploiting self-propagation: a commercial elicits emotion to change our affect; a coupon motivates us to change our behavior; a news article gives information to change our beliefs. They know if one leg of the A-B-C triad shifts, the others are likely to follow. Soon we are proud our clothes have whiter whites because we tried washing with the advanced technology of Oxi-Eco-Sani Plus, now with extra Plus! By changing affect, behavior, or cognition, our point of view about the product changes and will self-propagate. We then sell ourselves. Clever? Yes! Evil? Maybe!

Improvisors similarly exploit self-propagation to uncover more of a character's point of view from the little that is defined. If we know any of the three, we can infer more.

- ❊ From an affect about a target, we can infer behaviors and cognitions.
- ❊ From a behavior toward a target, we can infer affect and cognition.
- ❊ From a cognition about a target, we can infer affect and behavior.

It doesn't matter where we begin on the A-B-C triad. We must only be bold enough to define something clearly. The character must state a belief, have a reaction, or take an action. Only after that can we discover more. Affects, behaviors, and cognitions are linked; all will be revealed.

In everyday reality, inferring from scant evidence can be wildly inaccurate and rude, but for improv we don't mind. An improvisor knows what is asserted will be accepted as valid. This is how you uncover a novel point of view.

To make a bold move before understanding its logic or impact can be intimidating—do it anyway. It is closer to the way humans work than we would like to admit. In everyday reality we react instantly and only afterward do we ponder our beliefs, or if tired, rationalize.

To embolden you, know that almost any action can be justified through any point of view. Point of view drives us, but it also is how we interpret what we have done—especially if we are blind to our true motivations. In those situations, our brains work overtime to keep our view of self consistent. Love can justify acts that others consider cruel, just as nefarious motivations can propel generous acts ("A free towel if I join the gym today? How generous of you!").

MOVING AROUND THE A-B-C TRIAD

We must keep moving around the A-B-C triad, using one component to discover another. It's easy to get stuck on one leg. Let's get unstuck.

The statement, "I like my girlfriend—she is great!" is tautological. It expresses two nearly identical affects about the same thing, "I like her because I like her!" It does not differentiate the speaker from other characters who like their significant other. We have yet to move around the A-B-C triad with specifics to find a point of view. We are stuck.

"I like my girlfriend, her hair is gorgeous!" is better, but we still use one affect to justify another: "I like what I think is gorgeous." We have no common reference for gorgeous. But at least this statement has a touch of specificity that we can crack open to reveal point of view. We could infer the character values superficial features like gorgeous hair. Now we are getting unstuck.

"I like my girlfriend; our children will inherit her thick hair and we won't need to buy winter hats." From the affect of "liking my girlfriend's hair," we can infer a belief and behavior, or in this instance a future behavior. The specificity of thick hair, which is still subjective but less so, leads to the idea of warmth and a hat (at least for me). This statement reveals more of this character's point of view that we can then explore.

Challenging Personalities

Some personality traits challenge the productive behaviors of an improvisor. Many of them depend on other characters to "play along." Without such helpers, the character is rudderless. Here are some ideas to work with them.

A trait such as "angry" can lead to constant arguments. You can avoid that by ensuring the two characters have the same target for their anger: washing the car, Mother Nature, socks. Even if someone gets mad at Gary, Gary can be mad at himself, then the two characters have nothing to argue about.

"Belligerent" compels a character to fight, but more options are available if we find adjacent words like "assertive," "protective," or "loud"—or probe beneath belligerent to find "insecure," "self-destructive," "cavalier," or "feral."

A trait like "admired" is about how others view the character. We can find adjacent ideas, such as "confident" or "arrogant," or we can find words that describe what is admired ("courage," "kindness," "intelligence," or whatever you may personally admire).

A description like "gets taken advantage of" is backstory pretending to be a personality trait. It requires a duplicitous other to take advantage of the character. We can substitute near traits such as "naïve," "innocent," or "simple," which are more enabling to the improvisor and no one is compelled to hoodwink the character.

Traits such as invulnerable, dishonest, confused, helpless, or disbelieving are more difficult to manage. They strike at the heart of building a staged reality, especially a spot scene. The best advice is to have the characters go through minutes that matter to them and exercise whatever agency they have. This may require them to struggle with their own traits.

NEGATIVE NINNIES

Characters who are critical, whiny, or cynical are especially challenging, and deserve extra attention since they threaten the very act of creating a staged reality.

Just as an improvisor learns to build a staged reality by asserting what exists rather than what does not exist, a character must have preferences for what exists. Stating what you do not prefer is a valid part of point of view ("I do not wash my hands before dinner"). But to be fully functional for improv we need to know the affirmative belief behind that ("I believe germs deserve to eat too"). This leads to the wisdom, "A no is just a yes in disguise."

A character who dislikes all things reveals little of themselves. They are a pain, not only because they are a terminal downer, but because they take forever to order a beer—they can only list the beers they don't want. We must see what they prefer, not what they do *not* prefer, in order to see their character.

Similarly, a character who chronically attacks other points of view hides who they are. We never get to know them. It is fine if they disagree with others, but we must hear what they believe. Even if they believe in nothing, that is something we can explore. A dislike is a starting point, but we must eventually find what the character prefers. This is how differing points of view can clash and continue to fuel a scene. We keep advancing both points of view, building each instead of whacking away at one. We keep discovering.

No doubt it is fun to trash everything. But it is thin ice that must be skated on purposefully and occasionally.

DRUNK IDIOT CHILDREN

Characters that are drunks, idiots, children, or otherwise reduced in capacity have less agency. They have suspect information, which confuses the staged reality. If a drunk idiot child is needed, grant that character some agency, reliable information, and a point of view. Then have a good time with that idiot.

Recasting for Agency

Improvisors often focus on physicality or backstory, mistaking them for the more central point of view. This most commonly occurs with accents, afflictions, and accidents. An improvisor embraces one (or more) and is then confused why that trait doesn't help navigate in the staged reality. A hunchback-with-a-Texas-drawl-who-was-struck-by-lightning-as-a-child most definitely has a point of view, but those traits are not their point of view.

We can take a physicality or backstory that involves no agency and recast it to reveal point of view. This is done by either expressing an opinion about the condition (and its ramifications) or giving the character agency over the creation of the condition.

❊ **Accent.** An accent is not a point of view. Speakers of every region represent a wide range of personalities. Put more bluntly: assholes exist everywhere.

An accent is usually bestowed through geographic and cultural fate, not choice. If you have an Australian accent because you were raised in Perth, you had no choice in the matter, it reveals little about you. However, if you chose an Australian accent because you believe it makes your stories sound more exciting, that reveals point of view.

- **Affliction.** A character with an affliction, such as a wart, had little to do with the creation of their wart. A wart may influence a point of view or be a target about which the character expresses a point of view, but the wart is not a point of view. For our purposes the word "affliction" can mean any physical or mental condition over which one has little control, such as speaking with a lisp, having blue eyes, or suffering from the bubonic plague.

  If you have obsessive-compulsive disorder, you are at the mercy of your condition. You can give agency if you back off a clinical diagnosis; you can be fastidious, detailed, or meticulous. This allows us to explore the affects and cognitions that drive the fastidious behavior.

  Trauma responses and phobias are also afflictions. You may be terrified of clowns because of an industrial clown accident in your youth, but you have a point of view beyond clown phobia.

- **Accident.** Accidents may influence the development of a point of view, they may provide opportunity to express a point of view, but they do not substitute for a point of view. An accident is an unforeseen event. You are a victim unless we discover how you had agency in the situation.

  If you had your arm bitten off by a shark, it reflects the shark's nature more than yours. However, if you add "It's true, sharks don't like to snuggle," we learn about your choices. By having agency in the creation of your physical condition, your point of view is revealed.

Wrap It Up

A point of view is central to how a character navigates the world. A point of view is the self-reinforcing affects, behaviors, and cognitions—the ABCs of point of view—held toward a target. A point of view is evidenced by choices, from the mundane to exotic. This requires a character to exercise the agency they have.

In a staged reality, the character has a point of view before the improvisor understands it. We can simplify a character to a loosely held singular point of view, which we can use to infer the specifics of the staged reality, or we can take the specifics and infer a loosely held singular point of view. We may think of personality traits as a singular word, but in practice they have variety in and around one named trait.

Some traits make improvising a challenge but can be functional with modifications. We can interpret other parts of character (backstory and physicality) to reflect a point of view.

23

Physicality

On New Year's morning, three months before they would meet at 50 Albemarle Street, Samuel Smiles and Charles Darwin each lay in their respective beds, in their respective homes, staring at their respective ceilings, and spoke these same words—"I need to get in shape." Their vanity worried about the promotional portraits for the "Alright Already All Write!" competition, knowing a painter's judicious hand was being replaced by the unforgiving camera lens that "adds two stone." That day they both joined the same local gym and, coincidentally, signed up for the same Saturday morning kickboxing class. They would never meet.

Darwin never set foot in the gym, despite paying for a full year in advance and buying a monogrammed sweatsuit. He could not overcome his belief that biology and fate had ultimate power over his physical traits, and that six-pack abs were an impossibility for him. He was informed not only by his studies but by his constant struggle with mysterious ailments throughout his life. He could not bear another defeat by his own body. He also hated public showers.

Smiles would jog shirtless the three miles between home and the gym. Within six months he won his first kickboxing match by TKO, later admitting sportsmanship made him withhold his signature roundhouse kick. He was the picture of Victorian vigor, strutting nude about the locker room to everyone's discomfort. Smiles believed we choose the condition of the body we've been given. Fat or skinny, graceful or awkward, fast or slow are not to be left to nature. We make our selves. What we can't change alone we hire another to do for us, be it in the salon or surgery.

Darwin and Smiles both have valid points. Both inform how an improvisor's body, with its opportunities and issues, is the gateway to vastly different physicalities.

Physicality describes attributes that can be seen or heard, the tangible landmarks by which we recognize a person. It encompasses how you hold your body, how you move through space, and the morphologic differences we observe in humanity every day (stout/slender, soft/hard, smooth/rough, and so on). Physicality refers to the qualities of your voice (high/low, quiet/loud, smooth/raspy, and so on) and how you speak (articulation, resonance, tempo, accent, inflection, and so on). Your voice is an extension of your body.

A physical trait is not a point of view. Your age, weight, or height is not your point of view, although traits may influence or evidence a point of view.

Physical Range

You have developed a unique physicality dictated by your genetics, environment, and lifestyle. Whether you fancy the result or not, improv does not care. Any body can work.

In a staged reality, an improvisor can be a character who has physical traits that differ from their own. If Gary is a slouch and the character is an athlete, then how does a sloth play a gazelle?

An improvisor's everyday physical characteristics are accepted as they appear but are held loosely. They remain a potential or nonessential part of the staged reality until labeled. Thus, a person is accepted like any other object in the staged reality such as a chair.

A chair in improv is often painted black to mute its distinctive features so it can be more easily imagined with different qualities or as a completely different object. Similarly, an improvisor wears unassuming clothes to facilitate a few tricks they have to overcome the limits of their everyday physicality.

To play characters with physicalities that differ from our own, we have three approaches that, in practice, we blend.

1. **Simulate.** You accurately represent traits with your existing body such as posture, gait, accent, or tone. No imagination is required; what we see is what we get. Think of how you sound and look when irritated and exhausted after a long week, it is you but you look different than typical you (hopefully).

2. **Indicate.** You suggest traits your body cannot accurately represent. It's a type of symbol. We lose some informational integrity since what is portrayed cannot be taken at face value, but it'll do. For instance, a petite person cannot instantly change their mass but can indicate obesity by how they hold themselves (e.g., the curvature of the spine, a laboring of breath, the position of resting arms). Similarly, a rotund person can embrace their "petiteness" to change their stature, movement, and voice. Darwin may say, "Nature has made you short," but Smiles says, "Tall is how you stand."
3. **Label.** If we cannot simulate or indicate a trait, we rely entirely on a label. If you are blond but your character is brunette, there is little we can do but label and put the onus on people's imaginations. It's good to accompany the label with some change in physicality to cue the labeled trait in the audience's mind ("Oh, she's slouching again, she must be the brunette now").

In general, simulation is preferable to indication. A viewer's imagination must do heavy lifting when you portray a grandfather clock, but the burden is lowered when you simulate a grandfather clock as closely as possible with how your body stands, moves, and makes sounds. It will always require effort by the viewer, but the more simulation the better.

Some theatres and schools may limit you to only playing human characters, but you should try being an inanimate object at some point. It's good exercise. Samuel Smiles once played a grandfather clock for twenty-two consecutive days in the London Library. He only ended his performance when Londoners, curious to learn how this clock kept such perfect time, tried to dismantle him. The crowd was shocked as he leapt to life, shouting words that are now etched above the library's main stairs, "Behold! Clock is merely how I stand!"

Believable Range

Your body has a physical range of expression, which includes your voice. But your entire range is not considered believable human expression. You can make your voice sound as if you sucked helium, but that is not a believable everyday voice.

Within your physical range lies a believable range. When believable, your body and voice may be unusual, but we think a person such as this could exist with minimal imagination.

A character outside this range asks more of the audience's imagination. The character doesn't look or sound real, but we "get it." Not everyone is able or willing to lend that imagination.

Terms that describe when we are outside our believable range include big, broad, caricature, cartoonish, or absurd. This also points to another definition of "bad acting"—a portrayal that requires more imagination than an observer is willing to give.

A physicality outside the believable range is palatable if it falls within expectations. Some people only value an amazingly realistic human simulation, while others enjoy the portrayal of a caricature, or a squirrel, or a grandfather clock. Each theatre, show, and performance have their own expectations.

Don't underestimate your physical skills. In one long form show a fellow improvisor took the stage as an ape investigating the appearance of a vending machine. She moved with surprisingly accurate ape-ness, which inspired two more improvisors to join from the back line, committing fiercely to their ape-ness. And then three more joined. The stage filled with apes, mirroring the opening scene of *2001: A Space Odyssey,* complete with soundtrack provided by the back line, and as action climaxed the apes simultaneously shifted their mayhem into slow motion. Perfect ape simulation? No. Impressively memorable? Yes. Even real apes would agree.

Your Distinct Traits

Typically our everyday physical traits are accepted as unnoteworthy in the staged reality. They are assumed to be part of the world, but not defining to a character or structure. If we frequently call attention to a trait, such as Gary's big nose, it limits how people can be imagined, dooms us to repetition, and calls all the features of everyday reality into question—what is part of the staged reality and what is not? It applies to common qualities, such as skin color, height, weight, age, and attractiveness, as well as for less common traits such as stutter or prosthesis.

If your everyday trait is drawn into the staged reality by accident or intent, you have been granted license to ride it hard. Go for it. Your unusual feature can be a ticket to awesomeness. This means we must be willing to examine all our traits publicly, with the expectation it never becomes malicious. Gary's big nose can become the star, solving crimes, seducing others, or providing shelter.

This doesn't give us license to call out traits willy-nilly (unless that turns out to be what drives the piece), they should be relevant. Letting a person call out their own trait is a wise strategy. Set your sensitivity to ultra-turbo overdrive before you purposefully call out someone else's trait.

Your unique physicality may grant you unique opportunities. Any novel feature can be called into the staged reality and made available for play. Any feature can be redefined. A wheelchair can be a throne. A cast can be a gauntlet. A prosthetic leg can be a flamethrower. Or they can simply be what they are.

Your features make your work unique. Two people trying to portray the same physical traits will present as different characters simply because their bodies are different.

If you want to portray a different gender, go for it, knowing you will be indicating. With no costumes or props, when you play a gender that differs from what you present to the world you rely on indication and labeling, courting their drawbacks. The audience will be asked to use more of their imagination, and your portrayal is taken as a symbol more than at face value.

Consider that you can play qualities you associate with the opposite gender without portraying that gender. If you are a woman and want to play a guy, play exactly as you think a guy would, but remain a woman. We will take your character at face value—a woman with unique, perhaps guy-like traits. You aren't compelled to gender bend to explore the traits you associate with the opposite gender.

Some institutions prefer simulation, and the expectation is to play the gender you present. That's dandy. However, if you are labeled a different gender, then that is what you are, regardless of expectations. Support the integrity of the staged reality.

Mannerisms

Individuals have movements and utterances that appear to serve little purpose. These are called mannerisms. Once upon a time these may have served a purpose, but now are just part of you. Maybe you rub your nose with the palm of your hand, maybe you close your eyes when you start talking, perhaps you stand with your legs crossed. Everyone has a few.

Mannerisms are like spice—some are mild, some are strong, and sometimes a little goes a long way. We can bestow or discover a character's mannerisms without any justification, just as they require no justification in everyday life.

Mannerisms are most impactful when they are not continuous. Nodding your head continuously reads as a general way of being and is soon ignored as the background. But nodding periodically, or varying the intensity of the nod, gives the appearance of specificity. It suggests a curious meaning, even if it initially has none. By playing with it, you may discover its underlying logic—perhaps you nod when others look at you to keep their attention, like bobbing a fishing lure.

Restricted Zones

Areas of play that people will not entertain are restricted zones. We can accept an improvisor as almost anything—a different species, an inanimate object, even an abstract concept. But that same improvisor may not be accepted as something much closer to themselves. Such as being different ages, ethnicities, speaking with certain accents, or whatever. These zones usually have little to do with the performer but depend on two factors that reside in others.

The first factor is the willingness to extend imagination, if there is any left to extend. A fictional reality requires an investment by all the participants, which includes the audience's mental energy. At a certain point they may have no gas left in the tank or they resent donating it to sloppy improv.

The second factor is expectations that are based on ever-shifting social norms. You can rail against the matriarchy, patriarchy, oligarchy, monarchy, or any other archy you feel dictates the norms, but your improv may not benefit. Building a shared reality requires awareness of restricted zones. It is the perpetually changing social terrain that must be navigated. And remember, in the right environment, expectations can be reset. You are part of the social terrain.

Wrap It Up

Physicality is the attributes of a character that can be seen and heard. In the staged reality, improvisors change their bodies and voices to accurately represent or symbolically indicate the physical traits of different characters. The everyday physical traits of an improvisor are not brought into the staged reality unless germane. Everything you can do with your body defines its physical range, and within that lies a believable range—what we accept as a plausible human without too much imagination. People have different expectations about how believable they want characters to be.

Whether you achieve a physicality that you envision is largely irrelevant. No one knows what is in your head. We only see what comes out. The goal is to adopt a physicality that differs from your everyday self, so if your body doesn't behave as you prefer, use what it gives you, it's just as brilliant. Never doubt it. Play on!

24

Backstory

"The environment causes variations in an organism which allow them and their progeny to survive and thrive. Thus, backstory makes the person, like a baker makes a sweet, sweet brownie."—Charles Darwin, sailing journal, *HMS Beagle,* 1835

"Backstory is the manure from which the vine of your life grows. Everyone has shit. Who cares?"—Samuel Smiles, dinner toast, Hogmanay, 1837

Backstory describes a character's past. This includes what a character has done and what has been done to the character. Relevance to a character is what separates backstory from the broad subject of world history or, if you will, the world's backstory.

Like any story, backstory can be of different lengths and detail. It can be a meandering retelling of all wrongs suffered and triumphs earned. Just as equally it can be short ("I had a pet pig named Piper").

Much of the information we associate to a character is technically backstory. It is rooted in the past. It can be dramatic, but most is not. How you organize your shower, what you ate for lunch, and where you bought those boots are all valid bits of backstory.

Darwin and Smiles both recognized the existence of backstory but viewed its impact on character differently. Darwin focused on how an organism's environment affected its fate; Smiles focused on how an organism's choices affected its fate. If those gentlemen disagree, we should take warning: backstory can be the key to great fun, but also great sorrow. Let's take a look.

Benefits

Backstory reveals a point of view through the character's past. Specifics from a character's off-stage life are evidence of the point of view lived on stage. We discover a past that serves the present. Lives are littered with evidence of a point of view, and thus so is backstory. After all, the past was once the present.

We develop familiarity, even intimacy, when details of a life are shared. We perceive the character to be more complete, existing beyond the staged reality. Through details, our minds transform a character from a symbol of a human into a human. This works in the staged reality as it does in everyday reality.

We relate to three areas of backstory that are common to all characters: home, work, and play. These not only reflect a character's interests and values but tell of their areas of expertise. A soldier of fortune and a puppeteer have sharpened different skills from their work, and each would approach baking brownies—or any activity—differently.

- **Home** is family, romance, health, spirituality.
- **Work** relates to coworkers, jobs, survival, money, food, achievement.
- **Play** is about friends, hobbies, pleasure, recreation.

Backstory is fun. The specifics of a character's history are not tethered tightly to the current moment, which gives us great freedom. We color the present with fragments of the past. Sometimes they are pulled from the improvisor's personal backstory, and sometimes they are completely fabricated.

Some backstory is essential and unavoidable. Something as basic as a character's name has a hint of backstory. It reflects a decision made in the past that lives in the present. Or a simple label like "our kitchen" indicates a backstory of relationship and ownership.

Different Disciplines, Different Uses

Writers and actors often explore a character's backstory before they make the character come alive. An artist may spend hours in research and imagination, understanding the character's experience to develop authenticity and nuance, even if that backstory never appears directly in the final piece. In such an approach, the backstory comes before the character is realized.

Improvisors must take a different approach: they must be the character before a backstory can exist. In improv, a character rarely has a known history prior to appearing in the staged reality. Nevertheless, an improvisor must immediately begin with thoughts, feelings, behaviors, and physicality. In everyday life you lived a past that made you who you are. As an improvised character, you live who you are to reveal a past that made you.

Risks

Backstory is the past, which is not the focus of many improvised structures. There are structures that allow us to explore backstory—we can time-jump to live events of the past in the current moment of the staged reality. In structures where we cannot travel to the backstory, the only thing of the past we can experience is a description of it in the present. That works for some structures, but not for most. If indulged too much, backstory has the following drawbacks.

Backstory can create a death spiral. We become seduced by backstory, spinning stories of the past, yet failing to connect it to our affect, behavior, and cognition in the current. Without a point of view to guide us in the present, we panic and double down on this losing backstory strategy. In the end, we get a bucket of vomited history, but never experience the character navigating the present.

Backstory wanders and can easily become unrelated to the situation of the staged reality. We are in trouble when backstory includes characters we cannot experience, it monopolizes time, or does not reveal a point of view.

Backstory is not bound tightly to the current moment and tempts us to pursue our singular vision of history instead of collaboratively building a shared reality. If not careful, the improvisor's creative needs start to dominate the needs of the piece.

Backstory is confused for a point of view. What happened to a character may influence a point of view, but it does not express a point of view. What a character did in the past may reflect their point of view in the past, not necessarily now. Neither what a character has done or what was done to a character can substitute for the expression of a point of view in the current moment. The most accurate meter of personality is how one deals with the here and now.

Backstory is not portable. Portability is a concern for those who improvise with the same character in different pieces. When backstory is the interesting part of a character, trouble is a-brewing. You can't rely on a fixed backstory to make sense in every scenario, and if it does, you can't rely on it being germane to that staged reality. Gary's amazing story about living in a minivan will not fit a staged reality set in 1776. Gary's amazing story about his kids will not fit if his character is labeled as childless. None of Gary's amazing stories will fit if his character is labeled "not amazing." Point of view is highly portable, backstory is not. Not to mention, a fixed backstory is repetitive and preplanned—it is holding you back!

Wrap It Up

Backstory is the personal history of a character, both what they have done and what has been done to them. It is beneficial because it reveals point of view from the past, builds intimacy with the character, exposes relatable areas of information, indulges fun, and it can't be totally escaped. Backstory can be risky because it focuses on the past, lures you into a backstory death spiral, easily wanders off topic, tempts the mind to be greedy, is ruinously conflated with point of view, and is not portable.

25

Inspiration

A passerby looking through a window into the parlor at 50 Albemarle Street would see three men engaged in rousing conversation and inhaling each other's secondhand cigar smoke in a celebratory hullabaloo. It would be reasonable to assume these men were longtime friends, perhaps even childhood chums.

But these vastly different men were strangers moments ago. Their instant fellowship was inspired by the "Alright Already All Write!" book competition. It was an inspirational force that shaped each man, brought them together, and made them appear inseparable.

Mix and Match

Just as you find inspiration for a scene or long form, so you can find inspiration for a character.

We've looked at the big parts of character separately and, like a children's mix-n-match book, you could throw any point of view, physicality, and backstory into one sack of skin. With enough exposure, your mind would organize those into a character. Simply existing together does the work for us. But like our three gentlemen at 50 Albemarle, an inspiration makes things "go together" instantly.

For our work, it is useful and easier to connect to an inspiration and let it inform the parts of character. Connecting with an inspiration allows you to take on a physicality and general point of view instantly. Details will be discovered with time. An inspiration also helps make the big parts of character "go together" and not feel like random things in a sack of skin.

For our purposes, the word "connect" means to grasp something in a nonintellectual way. The intellect may help identify an inspiration, but the gut says, "Yeah, I get that." Starting our spot scene with an attitude is a kind of inspiration, one that should be relatively easy to connect to.

We can find an inspiration anywhere. Some are universal, some cultural, and some personal. We might choose it ourselves, or it might be drawn from an audience suggestion. It may happen in an instant, such as in the preparation for a spot scene, or we can take a long time to ponder what character would be fun to explore and bring that to an improvised piece.

Let's look at a few categories of character inspirations.

- **Humans.** You share more than 99 percent of your DNA with Neanderthals, ancient Egyptians, and Victorian Londoners. They, and all other humans, can inspire a character. Humans are convenient inspirations because they have done all our work. They spent a life developing a point of view, physicality, and backstory. Our job is to steal what we find interesting.

  The most potent inspirations are people with which we have direct experience, such as family, friends, enemies, schoolmates, and coworkers. Random memorable people we meet also work, as do people we "know" through our shared reality: stereotypes, celebrities, politicians, fictional characters, job roles. You may wonder if we are celebrating these inspirations, mocking them, or using them. I wonder that too.
- **Animals.** We share 84 percent of our DNA with dogs, 73 percent with zebrafish, and 45 percent with honeybees. It makes sense we can be inspired by other living creatures since we are also living creatures. While we can't understand their minds, we can emulate what we perceive as their attitudes, movements, and sounds.

  When you portray an animal, your job is to simulate as best you can. You may have to endow them with human traits, however, to help them in the staged reality (e.g., perhaps your dolphin must speak because she is a patent lawyer).

  More common, and believable, is portraying a human that has the essence of an animal. A dolphin can inspire your movement, voice, and point of view—although you remain plausibly human. You are not a dolphin that is human, but a human that is dolphin-like.

- **Snippets.** Sometimes just a snippet of character is enough to inspire a change in you. A snippet is a glimpse of a character. It could be an action, a facial expression, a sound, a phrase, a photo, a magazine, a hairstyle, a postcard, a T-shirt graphic, or a brief description ("They are the type of person who brings beer to church"). A snippet is a lure used to fish for a character lurking inside us.
- **Objects.** Our objects are like friends. We spend a lot of time with them, and they seem to have their own personalities. The appearance and function of an object can inspire a character. Who can look at a manual can opener without feeling its desire to walk awkwardly, its pride in its unique skill, and its excitement when called to action. Those same qualities would make a fine human.

  You may be called upon to physically simulate an object. You can give it additional traits as necessary (e.g., the coffee table you portray can be endowed with the ability to speak if it must say "Please use a coaster"). When you connect with the imagined life of an object, you will find a point of view about its existence and relationships with other objects. It's startling to discover how a pepper grinder views a salt shaker. It's complicated.

  More common and believable is to portray a human character inspired by an object. The more evocative the object, the better—such as a meat grinder, a straight razor, or a dollop of warm shaving cream. Using an object as inspiration may sound odd, but try it; don't be a stick in the mud.
- **Abstracts**. As we progress from people to animals to snippets to objects, we become more and more abstract until we are only left with abstracts. To find inspiration we can connect with an idea—attitudes, emotions, textures, shapes, places, words, paintings, music, energy—many of these can be a launch point. Even the sound of a word, rather than its meaning, can be an inspiration—though you may shillyshally whether this is piffle or futtock.

Poking About

Sometimes you may be unable to connect to an inspiration. To help, poke around for related concepts that are more evocative. Usually that means moving up or down the abstract-concrete spectrum.

You can deconstruct an inspiration to find a constituent that is more helpful, often an abstraction. If a can opener does nothing for you, deconstruct it to find what you connect with, such as shiny, utilitarian, or hingey. You could further deconstruct utilitarian into boring, efficient, or terse.

Making an abstract inspiration more concrete can be useful. Perhaps the word "elegant" does nothing for you, but you can connect with concrete examples of elegance, such as a champagne flute, a gazelle, or Grace Kelly. You may have never been messy in your life, but you can connect with a lump of chewed bubblegum glistening with saliva.

When using a human as inspiration we often subconsciously limit ourselves to people that match our gender. Don't worry about that. If you are a man and find inspiration from your Aunt Claire, go for it. You don't have to play a woman. We will accept your Aunt Claire–inspired character in the context of your gender. You can 100 percent think of yourself as Aunt Claire and we never need to know what's going on in your head. Your head is your business.

Disposability

You are not beholden to your inspiration. The inspiration is to help you find something different than everyday you. Whatever comes out, if committed, will define the character. For instance, if you are inspired by your Uncle Gary, but as you hear yourself you don't sound exactly like Uncle Gary—don't fret. Comparing yourself to Uncle Gary only keeps you from connecting to what you are discovering. No one knows or cares about Uncle Gary. (Sorry, Uncle Gary.)

You can dispose of an inspiration after you are connected to a character. Keep it if it serves you; otherwise let it go. Inspirations are like tissue paper; they were made to be used and tossed. They don't mind.

Out of a hat I had drawn the role of Scrooge for an improvised loose retelling of the classic story *A Christmas Carol*. Improvising Scrooge intimidated me. He's on stage nearly the entire event and, since it's created on the spot, whatever Scrooge you discover in the first few moments is the Scrooge you must be for the next two hours. Based on the feedback after the show, I consider it some of my strongest work. But I can't be sure. I don't remember much of what, to me, seemed like five minutes. I credit that experience to playing with seasoned improvisors and looking at my clenched hands on an imagined Victorian desk in those opening moments to find a Scrooge that wanted to work for a while.

Subverting

Everyone has their wheelhouse, physicalities and points of view they are comfortable inhabiting. When trying to find new characters, your brain has tricks to subvert the inspiration and end up back at the familiar. Stories and clever ideas that intercede between you and the inspiration are telltale signs.

For instance, with an inspiration like hardcore techno music, an improvisor may play a meek character—an energy that is familiar to them. That can be a legitimate choice, but it is worth probing how it came about. An improvisor's mind often hides the truth with a clever justification such as "I was inspired by someone who would *not* listen to that kind of music." Such an "interesting" choice is really a familiar choice. Instead of working directly with the inspiration, the mind has intellectualized a path to the familiar. That approach is actually avoiding a connection to the inspiration. The antidote is to take the inspiration "on the chin." Don't noodle with it. Be a human with the essence of hardcore techno music.

One exercise in workshops is to play a friend or family member. Frequently afterward, as the improvisor describes the relative who inspired their character, they will spontaneously portray that relative with a novel voice and physicality. It is effortless. But when they play that person in the exercise, the portrayal is much tamer. I can only guess that in preparation for the exercise they had analyzed and practiced their family member, giving the brain opportunity to twist traits for its comfort. But when speaking casually, their brain is not on guard and connects directly to the inspiration.

Cliché

Clichés can work as inspiration, but they carry risk when the improvisor relies on the cliché and fails to discover specific information. They hammer the generic features of the cliché but never find how the character is distinguished from similar characters. Fulfilling the cliché damns the improvisor to the expected.

Ideological clichés, such as a conspiracy theorist, political junkie, or bigot, are particularly vexing. These characters usually focus on people and events outside of the time, space, and relationships of the staged reality; their nature is to *not* contain a spot scene. They mainly spew thoughts about other people doing other stuff some other place. Yawn.

Clichés also are ripe for fusing traits. Fusion is when two or more traits are so strongly associated that it is difficult to access one without invoking the other. Accents and personality traits are a common fusion. For instance, at even the whisper of the word "sophisticated," pinkies extend and British accents arise. Rarely do we see a jolly conspiracy theorist, an empathetic political extremist, or a sweet bigot.

Like all clichés, ideologies inspire a character, but they do not define the character. Vastly different personalities have subscribed to the same ideologies for different reasons and live those ideologies different ways.

Clichés can inspire, but the improvisor must discover the specifics that distinguish their character, fulfilling expectations of the cliché in unexpected ways.

Wrap It Up

We can get inspiration for character from anywhere, including:

- Humans
- Animals
- Snippets
- Objects
- Abstracts

If we cannot connect to a given inspiration, we can poke around for a related one with which we can. The inspiration launches us in a direction, after which we are not beholden to it. Our brain may subvert an inspiration to wind up with a familiar character. Clichés are valid inspirations, but they do not define the character. The character must be specific.

26

Distinguishing

We like characters to be distinguished not only from each other but from our everyday selves. But you can go too far. Being distinguished holds reward, but also peril. Something the gentlemen at 50 Albemarle Street knew all too well.

The naturalist Charles Darwin, the motivational writer Samuel Smiles, and the publisher John Murray were distinguished. So too were the two gentlemen eating chicken drumsticks by the fireplace, one of whom was Bryan Waller Procter, a solicitor who moonlighted as a poet, publishing under the pseudonym Barry Cornwall. His literary gifts may not have distinguished him, but his position as a member of the ominously named Lunacy Commission did.

As a commissioner he was joined by eleven other distinguished politicians, doctors, and legal professionals who had the privilege of distinguishing who could leave the lunatic asylums dotting the British countryside.

Appealing to the Lunacy Commission was your only ticket out if you were institutionalized in error. The legal system was of no help, since the mentally ill were distinguished as patients instead of criminals, per the Lunacy Act of 1845. That well-intentioned act increased the number of mental health facilities in the United Kingdom. But those newly funded beds needed to be filled. The hunt for lunatics was on.

This led to the Lunacy Panic, the public's fear of a person being distinguished as a lunatic and institutionalized involuntarily. It was a sane fear, since mental illness was poorly defined, and there was limited recourse to escape once diagnosed.

Not everyone liked how lunacy was being distinguished. The other gentleman sharing chicken with Bryan Waller Procter that evening was the distinguished literary great Charles Dickens. Dickens had recently founded his weekly literary magazine *All the Year Round,* which later published the article "Of Right Mind," giving voice to reason:

> If there be [a man in Europe with an absolutely healthy mind] rely upon it he stands at the head of the class of social bores. For he must have, to be healthy, that abomination of desolation, a well-balanced mind, in which, because there is everything in equal proportion, there is nothing in agreeable excess. Anything like exclusive regard for a particular idea upsets the balance; and so it is that the men whose minds are not whole, round, and perfect, we owe all the progress of the world.

The gentlemen at 50 Albemarle Street, including Hench the English setter, were distinguished from each other by their unique physicality, backstory, and point of view. They were also distinguished from millions of fellow citizens, so much so that they are known more than 150 years after their respective passings. They were unusual, yet none of them were condemned to the lunatic asylum.

This is the line you must skate, even in the staged reality—how to distinguish your character but avoid lunacy. To begin, we have two choices to distinguish characters: harmonize or contrast.

Harmonize

You can distinguish characters by harmonizing with others—sharing elements of a point of view, physicality, or backstory. When characters share enough similarities, especially regarding points of view, they "clump" or "blend" together, alternately referred to as mirroring, matching, or being peas in a pod. Repetition creates impact, similar to stacks of Campbell's soup cans or a flock of birds.

Harmonizing allows multiple people to discover a single point of view. Not only does it ease the discovery process, but it predisposes everyone to accept the result since they are of the same mind.

Harmonizing allows us to observe our own character. Mirroring activates special wiring in our brains. When we reflect what another is reflecting to us, we mix up who is who. What we observe in others becomes what we know of ourselves. I don't realize I smack my lips, but if you reflect my lip smacking to me, I can then see it.

Harmonizing can create character on its own. When each person reflects the other, we create a positive feedback loop, evolving what exists. Your lip smacking makes me do it more consciously, which changes my lip smacking slightly, which you see and reflect to me, which I see and reflect back to you. Traits evolve and amplify on their own. No thought is needed, just mindless harmonizing.

Harmonizing reduces the number of points of view. If there are eight characters, a structure may not allow exploration of eight points of view. Instead, characters clump into fewer. Clumps also provide opportunities for characters to form or change alliances, altering dynamics.

The perception of a group point of view is created when characters harmonize. The group's perceived (or loudest) point of view dominates, although a group always has variety within it. This becomes *the* point of view. Simplicity beats complexity again!

Contrast

You can distinguish a character by contrasting with others, having notable differences in point of view, physicality, and backstory. A simple strategy at the beginning of an improvised piece, such as a spot scene, is to immediately contrast the most apparent traits such as physicality and attitude. You may hear this comment from an instructor as "choose a different energy." Different points of view and backstories will develop as the piece progresses.

Contrasting puts the responsibility for a character entirely on you. You are the only one who can discover what your character is about if you aren't harmonizing with another.

Contrasting distinguishes the multiple characters an improvisor may play in one piece. Differences in physicality are the immediate cues as to whether one appears as Gary or Gary Junior. A little difference helps a lot. Without it, we court confusion.

Using physicalities to distinguish characters helps the improvisor in addition to the audience. With time jumps, entrances and exits, location changes, and multiple threads it is easy to forget who the hell you are. A physicality cues you just as it does the audience. Be a pal and help everybody out.

DIRECTION AND DEGREE

Points of view contrast when we hold different affects about the same target. If you love chicken drumsticks, I can hate chicken drumsticks. Love and hate seem like they point in opposite directions, but other directions are just as handy for contrasting. I could be fascinated by chicken drumsticks, or fear them, or respect them.

Points of view contrast when we hold the same affect about a target, but in different degrees. We both love chicken drumsticks, but my love exceeds yours: I named my dog Drumstick, modified my van to look like a drumstick, and when flying I buy an extra ticket so my drumstick is never far away.

Similarly, physicality and backstory can contrast by direction and degree. Follow a stranger and mimic how they walk, then exaggerate how they walk, then walk the opposite way they walk. How do you walk the opposite of someone? Who knows, but whatever your solution, it will contrast.

SPECIFICITY

You distinguish yourself by the specificity of your points of view. The details of a point of view offer limitless opportunities to differentiate a character, even if points of view seem to blend at first glance.

We both love chicken drumsticks. You prefer them because they require no utensils to eat. I prefer them because without changing my grip I can eat the drumstick or use it as a weapon.

Sometimes you contrast without having a big plan. In one improvised scene, five of us were on the bridge of a spaceship. I busied myself at an imagined control panel, manipulating knobs and dials and levers. As the other four drove the scene brilliantly, I never found a reason to speak. So I focused on figuring out what I was doing with the controls. But being the only person on the stage not speaking drew attention to my character. As the scene progressed, I felt tremendous pressure—if I spoke, it would have to be amazing. As the others heightened their emotions and the crisis escalated, I remained steadfast in my button and lever work, hoping I would never have to open my mouth. But the captain finally prompted me—"Don't you have anything to say?!" As feared, I had nothing amazing to offer, so I offered the truth—"I'm just trying to figure out what these buttons do." The audience approved; the truth turned out to be amazing enough.

Related to Everyday

We distinguish characters relative to our everyday reality, what is familiar. A character harmonizes or contrasts with three groups: the crazy, the reasonable, and the unusual. Recognize into which group a character falls, whether by choice or chance.

THE CRAZY

Psychiatrists say the term "crazy" is not professional and perhaps offensive. Improvisors are a different type of professional. In a fictional staged reality where anything can happen, we have a duty to build a staged reality that has integrity. Crazy is the enemy of that. Crazy is a constant threat. Crazy must be identified for what it is—crazy.

Crazy is a point of view to which the average person cannot relate. It occurs when a point of view is consistently inconsistent ("I want to be a zombie . . . I don't want to be a zombie . . . but I do want to be a zombie . . ."); unintelligible ("Please folder carousel cloud grgzkst . . ."); defies the established staged reality ("We are the same height, but it's too bad we are not the same height . . ."); or contains no common references ("I love fresh Aphoxia in the fifth season on planet Garygary . . ."). A physicality or backstory can be crazy, if similarly implausible. Almost any piece of information can be incorporated into the staged reality, but if a character generates enough crazy, they earn the label of lunatic.

Crazy characters threaten the shared reality because, by definition, they do not share a reality. It may be possible to portray a babbling idiot in an entertaining way, but the entertainment lies in the babbling. As an improvisor you are screwed. Plenty of crazy occurs naturally that we must justify. We need not manufacture koo-koo bananas.

THE VOICE OF REASON

The voice of reason is the point of view that falls within the norms of the majority. The norms are those of the participants in everyday reality, not the characters in the staged reality. The voice of reason is a proxy for when a point of view harmonizes with that of the participants. In this sense, the voice is akin to a ruler; it is a standard against which another point of view can be compared.

The voice of reason speaks for the audience's point of view, but with flexibility. This flexibility allows fictional characters to exist and affords room to explore their unusual points of view.

If the voice of reason is inflexible, it can break the staged reality or unusual points of view. At its simplest, an inflexible voice of reason could say "I am not a character, and you are not a character, this is a stage, we are making this up." Ugh. Who invited that guy? The voice of reason can challenge other characters, but exists to help reveal their unusual points of view—not to dismantle them.

An inflexible voice of reason will prematurely use the label "crazy." Calling something crazy in the staged reality dismisses its importance. It is slang for "I don't have the capacity to make sense of this." It is the opposite of your job as an improvisor. But there is a limit.

When things go hopelessly off the rails and get bat-shit crazy in the staged reality, it is a relief when a voice of reason tells it like it is ("This is bat-shit crazy."). Labeling true craziness restores sanity. We perceive the same thing. We agree on what is crazy. We are again building a shared reality.

Although the unusual or crazy character often gets the attention, a character who sincerely represents the audience is appreciated. When the voice of reason expresses what the audience thinks and feels, a favorable response is likely.

The voice of reason is not necessarily "correct." The voice of reason, for us, represents the point of view of the participants. It does not have a monopoly truth, which is often revealed by the unusual and occasionally by the crazy. Sometimes the craziness of the voice of reason is revealed—and no one has to buy a jester's hat.

THE UNUSUAL

The unusual character is the one who expresses something that is outside of normal but does not venture into crazy. It is unusual but understandable. Observers are interested in exploring how and why that person is different, and the ramifications of that point of view.

Laughter can signal when you have uncovered something that is unusual but not crazy. One theory holds that laughter originated as a not-so-nice way for the group to identify what is different. Baring teeth and gums was a measured threat. The more people laughing at you, the greater the incentive to get back in line. If you survived grade school, you understand.

Unusual can appear crazy at first. In improv we cannot dismiss any affect, behavior, or cognition outright. For instance, someone who eats their arm for a snack would be judged "crazy" in everyday reality, but an improvisor must look for the sense of such an action: one could argue the most effective way to lose weight is to eat one's own arm. The voice of reason may disagree with the values of this unusual point of view, but it cannot assail its logic.

EARNING CRAZY

As we explore an unusual point of view, its ramifications become more extreme. This often propels the staged reality into areas that would be deemed "crazy" to someone who has not witnessed them develop. But for those who have witnessed the staged reality unfold, everything is understandable. The evolution is clear. The crazy has been earned. The crazy makes sense.

INTERNALIZED VOICE OF REASON

Even if there is no character representing the voice of reason, the unusual character must address its concerns. The improvisor must sustain an internal voice of reason to recognize unusualness and answer the how's and why's of the staged reality through the voice of their unusual character. This will address the questions the audience is thinking.

An internalized voice is crucial when characters are "peas in a pod." These characters have the same point of view and can lose touch with what the voice of reason would want to understand. In everyday reality when a group lacks an internalized voice of reason, we call it "group think."

Without an internal voice of reason things get crazy, fast. It creates a perplexing world in which an unusual proposition like "Let's open an umbrella up my bum," is heartily pursued but never justified.

THE REASONABLENESS TRAP

Your everyday reasonableness can hinder discovering an unusual point of view. This happens when an improvisor automatically uses their own reasonable point of view to generate information, instead of generating information and then reasoning a point of view from it.

This often shows up in the start of a spot scene. If we begin a scene with a random emotion and action, the improvisor instinctively searches for a reasonable justification for that combination. However, when the situation and reaction are reasonable, the character is normal, it is drama. With no unique point of view to explore, an improvisor forces some dynamic to progress in an "interesting" way.

For example, a curiously common scene start involves the action of digging sadly. This combination is often justified as burying a pet. That discovery is reasonable. Sadness is a reaction most pet owners would have in this situation. The point of view is common; we have sympathy.

However, we may discover details from our own experience with digging that could be the reason for sadness. My first association with digging is the pristine condition of a new shovel. I have no grand plan behind that tidbit, and in five minutes my association may be different.

If I combine sadness and digging with a new shovel, I might infer this character is a perfectionist, devastated that they must sully an unblemished shovel; or this is when the honeymoon of home ownership is shattered and the work begins; or it means the shovel cannot be returned, marking a life now shackled to the domestic. Are those brilliant? Maybe. Their brilliance will be determined by what we do with them. But they are unusual points of view that we can comprehend and explore.

The "reasonableness trap" is only a trap when the voice of reason has an unshakeable grip on us.

It Is Relative

Almost one hundred years after the Lunacy Panic, the American Psychiatric Association published the first *Diagnostic and Statistical Manual of Mental Disorders* (DSM). In the United States, the DSM is the mental health professional's big book of lists, profiling all the known mental disorders and by omission, normalcy. Over the decades it has renamed, added, and removed lots of disorders.

In later editions, the DSM recommended that "abnormal" must be interpreted in the context of culture. If I am a Wall Street broker who gets advice from house plants, my psychiatrist should be concerned. But if I lived in an arboreal village, having conversations with plants may not only be normal, but prudent—why ignore good advice?

As improvisors, we are psychiatrists without the fancy DSM, fancy schooling, or fancy billable rate. We know that what is "normal," "unusual," and "crazy" is relative to the participants.

THE WORLD IS A SPECIAL CHARACTER

The world is a character that has a point of view. By "world" I mean any system larger than an individual in which that individual must exist. It could be a family, a company, a country, or a planet.

A staged reality implicitly has a world. That world serves as the background against which characters exist. Harmonizing or contrasting with it determines how a character is viewed in that world—as normal, unusual, or crazy.

By default, the world in the staged reality is assumed to be normal. It has a point of view like our everyday reality. However, the world in the staged reality can be the unusual character, in which case we want to explore its point of view.

The world can't express its point of view directly (unless we allow "the world" to speak). But its point of view is expressed by any character who is considered "normal" in that world. It also leaves evidence such as institutions, art, law, architecture, family dinners, game shows, and proms. The world's point of view in a staged reality can be consistent and simple, just as we allow any other character's point of view to be.

To explore a character who is unusual it is best to keep the world normal, relative to our everyday reality. This allows the character to contrast with what we are most familiar. The character is foregrounded. When both the world and its characters are unusual, it's harder (but not impossible) to explore either. There is less contrast. It's hard to see a drawing if the ink and paper are the same color.

Wrap It Up

A character is distinguished by harmonizing or contrasting with another's point of view, physicality, or backstory.

Harmonizing aggregates characters into groups, and a group has greater presence. A group also has more minds uncovering one point of view.

Contrasting differentiates characters by direction, degree, and specificity. When contrasting, the improvisor must uncover the character's point of view alone. Characters are evaluated as either crazy, reasonable, or unusual per the standards of the participants. A voice of reason, representing the view of the participants, must always be present in the staged reality either externalized in a character or internalized by the improvisor who plays an unusual character. The voice of reason is a proxy for the audience and helps to explore the unusual point of view—the how's and why's of its existence.

We can pursue the unusual into what would formerly be considered crazy if the evolution is clear and incremental.

27

Here's to You's

"Congratulations, Mr. Darwin!" The words were still bouncing around Charles's head minutes after they had been spoken to him. At least he thought it was minutes ago.

Charles was standing with two men in a gaslit parlor room exchanging congratulations and thank you's and compliments. He recognized the gentlemen. One was Mr. Murray, the esteemed publisher, and the other Mr. Samuel Smiles, an author. Mr. Smiles wore cologne, *too much cologne* thought Charles.

Charles was speaking. He wasn't sure where the words were coming from, but Mr. Murray and Mr. Smiles seemed to enjoy them. In his hand Charles held a cigar. Odd, he never smoked. Nonetheless he puffed away.

Mr. Smiles held a flask high, and in a voice louder than necessary said, "To the better author, and perhaps the better man—to Mr. Darwin!" Mr. Smiles closed his eyes and savored a long draw from the flask. He smacked his lips and, with eyes still closed, held it out to no one in particular. Charles seized the flask and brought it to his lips.

To Mr. Darwin, thought Charles. To which Charles Darwin was he referring? Was it the sickly Darwin who feared socializing so much he pretended to be away when friends called, occasionally hiding in the pantry? Was it the fearless Darwin who hazarded a two-year ocean voyage a quarter-century earlier, studying flora and fauna around the world? Was it the Darwin who was an attentive husband, who fathered ten children over whom he doted? Was it the Darwin who sought the company of papers and specimens over humans, working himself to near death on occasion? Was it the little Charles who sought nature, if only to escape the tyranny of his childhood home? Or was it the Darwin in this parlor chumming and smoking, about to drink whatever was in this flask?

I don't care which of us this perfumed wag means, thought Charles, *we are going to change the world.*

Charles threw his head back. The flask's contents spilled over his lips, into his mouth, and down his gullet. He gagged. He was not expecting the smooth warmth of Earl Grey tea.

"Alcohol is weakness!" shouted Smiles. "Tea is strength!" His heavy grip landed on Charles's shoulder. The three gentlemen laughed.

As the banter ebbed and flowed, the words of Mr. Smiles and Mr. Murray slowly drifted away, until Charles heard only the sound of his breathing and the ticking of the grandfather clock.

His focus wandered from the two gentlemen, down to his scuffed leather shoes, along the patterns in the Turkish rug to the rug's knotted fringe, onto two paws, and floated up until meeting the patient gaze of Hench, the English setter. There the two lingered. The air was warm and heavy.

All was understood.

It's All You

We like to think of ourselves as having a single, tidy personality, but that thought hardly holds up to scrutiny. Just like Darwin, we wear different personas for a traffic stop, a lazy Sunday morning, or a squirrel fight. Some theorize we have various personalities, each called upon to address a situation to which it is best adapted—a devilishly Darwinian view of personality indeed.

An improvisor may play different characters, but each is that improvisor. We say we are playing a character, but it is more accurate to say we are playing a part of ourselves. It is all you.

Of the personalities inside us, one tends to dominate. This personality elbows to the front of the pack, jumping into action time and time again to handle life's heavy lifting. This is "the habit."

The Habit

The habit is our conditioned way of being. Just as a character has a point of view, so does your habit. Just as a character creates a reality from a point of view, so does your habit. Just as that character propagates a point of view, so does your habit. Your habit is a character you play very well.

Not only does the habit dominate our other parts, but it is hard to recognize when the habit is in charge. Fortunately, in improv you get feedback on the habit's behavior when building a shared reality. The feedback may come from an instructor but most reliably comes from your experience—what works and what goes awry.

When improvising, the goal is not to suppress the habit as much as relieve it from its duties. When we allow the habit to relax, other parts can rise. We say we "play a character," or we could say we "play a part of us," or we could say "we relax some parts of us to allow other parts to emerge."

The habit is a workaholic. They may promise to take a day off but whenever we look, they are toiling at their desk. Here are ploys the habit uses to sneak back to work when they should be lounging by the pool.

- **Character traits that mask dysfunction.** We often play a character who is a version of our habit: a personal struggle to discover information is camouflaged by a character who is clueless, a fear of making choices is embraced by a character who is meek, a discomfort with emotion hides behind a character who is invulnerable. Dysfunctions do not become functional by calling them character traits.
- **Repeating the same character, perhaps disguised with superficial differences.** We may tweak one part of character but find our point of view, physicality, or backstory is the same. We play with similar energies. We feel we are taking a risk, but the observed result is nearly the same.
- **Distorting an inspiration.** If you are labeled a wild rock star, backstage at a wild rock concert, wildly rocking out, and choose to be refined and demure—there is a good chance that refined and demure is what your habit prefers. It may be defended as an interesting choice, but that is typically just mental acrobatics to arrive at the familiar. Chapter 25 on inspiration refers to this as subverting the character inspiration.
- **Being unreasonably reasonable.** The habit's need to be reasonable interferes with the pursuit of a unique point of view. One can't present as reasonable and unusual at the same time. The habit sets the "reasonableness trap" we talked about in chapter 26 on distinguishing.

Help Yourself

We can force the habit to take the day off by putting someone else at their desk. We can delegate any character to counter the habit's most cumbersome behaviors. For example, if you ask too many questions, play a brainiac; if you are timid, play a reckless mess; if you are emotionally calcified, play a drama queen; if you struggle with stage fright, play a badass. This way the habit is forced to crack open a soda and kick back, at least for a bit.

This experiment is sometimes awkward and sometimes brilliant. Regardless, with practice the habit becomes comfortable taking a break, thereby allowing us to gain easier access to different skills. In chapter 20 on treacherous systems, we talked about this as opposing certain behaviors.

The habit prefers the familiar and uses control to achieve it but when you are dead set on trying something new, the habit will try to distance you from the results.

Distancing

When we distance, we treat a character as something foreign. We refuse to connect. We deny a relationship. Distancing is a response to discomfort with a character. Congratulations, you just uncovered the point of view of the habit. Distancing shows up several ways:

- **Dropping commitment.** We are the character one moment and regular old us the next. We can only tolerate connecting in brief bursts, so we part ways.
- **Thinking *What would a character like this do?*** This denies that we are the character. This question is useful to help initiate a connection if we are totally adrift, but it is an occasional tool not a principal one.
- **Judging.** If we dislike the character, our disdain is hard to hide. We play them insincerely and perhaps even mockingly. It happens often with characters that hold a political, religious, or other ideology that the habit finds contemptuous.
- **Making indefinite-you statements.** The indefinite-you refers to an unspecified individual. It is a casual version of "one" such as "One must floss before brushing." When a character speaks

indefinitely, they might say "You want to make everyone happy," instead of "I want to make everyone happy." The indefinite you is a statement about a concept or advice to another, rather than ownership of a personal belief.

- ❊ **Overly focused on another.** We ignore our character by focusing on another.

I once experienced a peculiar case of reverse distancing—when a character didn't prefer me. It was during a "character interview" in which an improvisor is peppered with random questions that must be answered without breaking character. When the inquiry veered to the economy, my character, an arrogant lunkhead, answered with a statement about federal reserve policy and foreign exchange rates. It was very insightful, and very out of character. My brain couldn't resist being smart and thought everyone would adore the cleverness of a randomly smart lunkhead. They didn't. I didn't. The lunkhead didn't. After an uncomfortable pause, the lunkhead distanced himself from my answer by confessing, "That's what my dad says." He was right, those weren't his words. We were back in business. Thanks, lunkhead!

Coaching

Characters don't fully comprehend improv. You are the only one who can understand the process, juggle multiple realities, recognize structures, know expectations, and prioritize needs. You must coach characters while they help you improvise. Here's a few coaching tips.

- ❊ **Advocate.** Steadfastly support a character with all your resources. The character is your responsibility. Without you, the character dies. Always support a character's point of view to the height of your abilities.
- ❊ **Guide.** The improvisor has final authority over what a character does or does not do and can help with a vexing problem. Don't forget who has ultimate responsibility.
- ❊ **Empower.** Let the character do their thing, even if you aren't sure where it will go. As long as an action supports the shared reality, trust its logic. A character's wisdom may only be apparent after action.

The Improvisor's Stages

People seem to go through common stages as they develop improv skills.

- **You play your everyday self.** We observe the everyday person, the habit, trying to build and exist in the staged reality with their everyday behaviors. They are figuring things out. It's like watching someone build a toilet while using it.
- **You split and alternate between improvisor and character.** We observe the improvisor making a structure in the staged reality, and we observe the character live in that reality. These parts alternate depending on difficulty and task. Sometimes we see the improvisor working; sometimes we see the character living. The former appears workmanlike, while the latter appears natural.
- **You primarily present as a character.** The character is more persistent, with shorter appearances by the improvisor. The improvisor has been internalized and is able to coach the character to create the staged reality. The range of characters portrayed is limited; the improvisor's comfort zone is small and close to the everyday person.
- **You primarily present as a character with a range further from your everyday self.** It becomes harder to see evidence of the improvisor, and the characters we observe have physicalities and points of view further from that of the everyday person.

The Wild Beast

When the habit relaxes and we explore new characters, we reveal more of ourselves. It's like a dusty mirror. In the center of the mirror is a clean spot in which we can see our everyday self. When we explore characters we clear the dust from around that center spot. The further we explore, the more of the mirror we clean.

If we could clear away all the dust, looking back we would see a wild beast. The beast is everything we can access within us. The beast is the source of impulses and fun (and probably plenty of not-so-fun issues in life—but we're not concerned with that now). The wild beast wants to do whatever it wants to do. That's why it's a wild beast.

The habit has figured out what of the wild beast can be revealed. The habit is the original clean spot at the center of the mirror. This explains the habit's reluctance for change—this is what works. However, the improvisor can take responsibility—let the habit relax, and help other characters reveal more of the beast.

As we clean the dust from the mirror, we find it is much bigger than expected. No matter how hard we work, we can't seem to uncover it all. That's okay. We only need to clear what we like. How much is up to us. Even a little is enough. The wild beast is happy to be seen.

You's

We hold a bunch of parts in us. Some of them show up as characters in improv, some show up in everyday life. We've been fostering one that is an improvisor. We named a dominant one "the habit." And we have the party animal called "the wild beast" that seems to be propelling it all. From these different parts we identify with a special one called "me," which is aware of and separate from the others. All those parts reside in one body, which is different from the body of several years ago as cells die and are replaced in its daily mission to build imperfect copies of itself. That all seems quite whacky.

And it prompts the question: Who the hell are you?

Wrap It Up

Every character you play comes from you. Different characters can emerge when we relax our everyday personality, which we call "the habit." This feels risky, so your habit has some common tricks to stay in charge. You can help your habit take a break by choosing traits that counter its nature.

We must avoid creating distance from our characters, and it's our job to coach them when we improvise. The improvisor always has authority over what will and will not be done.

As improvisors, we go through multiple stages as we figure out how to work with the various parts of ourselves to build and live in a staged reality.

Charles Darwin was a wild beast, and so are you.

PART SIX

Your Role in History

Experience is the ultimate teacher for an improvisor. You must go do. How you get experience is up to you, but it is imperative that you arm yourself with a minimum of improv history to see where you fit in.

In the beginning . . .

"It looks like snow!" she said, as white flakes floated in the night sky above the cobbled street they walked along. But Thales of Miletus, the renowned Greek naturalist, knew it does not snow on a Mediterranean coastal city in June 595 B.C. or any other year.

He let go of his girlfriend's hand and squinted, following the white flecks back to their source. His stomach dropped. Down the street, in the third-floor window of his apartment, he locked eyes with his cat sitting on the sill, around whom spewed plumes of shredded parchment into the night. Shredded bits of his life's work.

Earlier that night, Thales had headlined at the Acropolis where he received a standing ovation and demand for two encores—unusual for a speech. He had read his thirty-two scrolls describing the mechanics of improv in unrivaled detail, accuracy, and beauty. It represented a lifetime of work, impossible to replicate—even by Thales. His words were later heralded as the most important performance of the century, changing the trajectory of art and science. It had been a good night.

But there on the street, he regretted one choice: not putting the scrolls in the bureau before he, his girlfriend, and his dog went out for celebratory gelato. He recalled his naïve words, "Why would the cat shred the scrolls? I just bought her a new scratching post."

As Thales watched the summer winds waft his life's work into the sky to catch the jet stream and disperse across the globe, he had no idea what would transpire in the centuries that followed.

The Planetwide Improv Community mobilized. Teams of scholars, generation after generation, scoured the planet hunting for these bits of parchment, trying to reassemble the original perfect text. But despite a common passion for improv, their different backgrounds fueled conflict over what the words on each shred meant, much less the best way to combine them. From this world war of words, teams retreated to interpret their shreds in peace.

Their newly minted beliefs needed protection, from cats and other threats, so each team chiseled them into a slab of granite, covered the slab with a wooden platform, and surrounded the platform with a fortress complete with air conditioning, a concession stand, and untidy bathrooms.

But no matter where each fortress was built, or what team built it, each served the same purpose—to be a place where scholars protected, repeated, explained, and tried to live the words that were chiseled in a granite slab hidden beneath a platform of black, words translated from a portion of the shredded remains of the perfectly articulated thoughts in the thirty-two scrolls of Thales of Miletus.

You can visit these fortresses today. We call them "theatres" and "schools."

Your Role

You choose where you go. You will likely get involved with one or more theatres and schools in your improv travels. In one way, the choice of where you go is very important. It defines your experience. In another way, the choice is very unimportant. If you apply yourself wherever you go, you can make the same discoveries as Thales of Miletus.

No one has a monopoly on insight. The history of improv illustrates that many people and many events intercede between you and the knowledge of the original thirty-two scrolls. While you may never see a slab of granite, one lies at the heart of every institution. That slab is only one of many.

Regardless of where you go, you are a member of the Planetwide Improv Community. It's big. It has a membership that stretches back in time. You have the same status as every other member. You are a scholar hunting, collecting, and studying tiny pieces of parchment that have words on them.

You are to discover what those words mean and jam that meaning into your body.

You determine the meanings. This is your job. The job can be frustrating, and not just because it doesn't pay.

Local Language

Each school or theatre has interpreted their shreds of paper based on their backgrounds. That interpretation is reflected in and differentiates how each institution operates, including the words and phrases they use. Those words may be memorialized on a slab of granite, or handouts, or books, or lectures, but all will include their buzzwords.

A buzzword is a symbol like any other word, but it has a supercharged meaning not easily explained. You may only be able to understand the buzzword after you associate it to an insightful experience. You may chase some insights for a long time through class, performance, and even teaching. But once you have that insight, that buzzword succinctly communicates with someone else who has had a similar insight. That's an upside. But there is a downside.

If you have not had the necessary experience, a buzzword is hollow—it offers little help. The word may be repeated, or explained, or shouted at you only to result in stress. It's not fun not getting what others appear to get. It can be even more confusing since others can feign understanding.

In addition to buzzwords there are pesky lists of do's, nagging lists of do-not-do's, and endless notes from a parade of coaches, friends, and strangers. Consider each as a shred of parchment to be examined and deciphered. Each is part of a whole.

As Time Goes By

If you feel success at the institution you choose, congrats! Keep on going. If you do not feel success at the place you choose, congrats! You have discovered words and values that do not work with your brain. You can change your brain or change your place. Either is fine. You might return to that place one day and hear their words differently.

You may, after time, leave the safety of your success at one institution to investigate another. How impressive! You will hear different words and values about the subject you already know. With two or more approaches you will see similarities and differences, overlaps and gaps. This is how you detect the dark matter of the subject. You will triangulate your own understanding. Thales of Miletus would give you two thumbs up—one thumb up to show he likes your haircut, the other thumb to say "good luck" because you have a challenging path.

It is hard to play one venue and be appreciated, then play somewhere else only to be less appreciated based on different values. The discomfort may tempt you to reject the words and values of the new place, even though they are the very things you seek. Your fellow students or your instructor may not relate to the path you are travelling. Thus, you may be on your own . . . but who else do you want tinkering with your brain?

Also, as you assess if an institution is a good match, note that any instructor or student can have a non-good day. But if you find an institution with many people who have non-good days and you start having non-good days, thereby influencing others to have non-good days, then it's a sign to move on.

Your Crew

While schools and theatres are persistent institutions, the Planetwide Improv Community is home to a multitude of smaller groups. These groups, typically from two to ten people, self-organize to practice or perform. They may hire instructors (aka coaches) to help pursue their improv goals.

Usually, these groups are formed by people who meet while taking formal classes at a theatre or school. Groups might exist for weeks or years or decades. Think of it like musicians. Some play with one band, others play around; some bands last a lifetime, others are experiments.

If you are affiliated with a theatre or school, your group can perform by being selected as a "house team," or as an individual you can earn a spot on an existing house team or get added to the roster of a standing show. If your group strikes out on its own, playing wherever it can, you are an indie group.

Schools or theatres may also host drop-in jams. Like going to a park for a pickup game, you play with whoever else shows up and act as an audience for each other. A jam may have entrance requirements like "you must be taking classes," but some are open to any random body who walks through the door. As you can guess, it can get interesting.

If you find yourself desperately calling a friend on a Wednesday night saying, "If we hurry, we can hit the jam across town at 11:30," then you are addicted. Be a good addict, only settle for a low-quality fix when you're desperate. Go top shelf whenever possible.

Like any skill, improv requires repetition. It's up to you to get those reps by whatever means necessary.

Concerns

You may not want to be a member of the Planetwide Improv Community, but it's too late. If you are reading this book—you already are. Still, you may be reluctant to get involved. Many current members felt that way once. Here are some concerns that now-experienced improvisors had before taking a workshop.

- What if I'm not funny?
- What if other people aren't funny?
- What if can't make all the classes?
- Why take a class, don't you just make it up?
- What kind of person is the instructor?
- What will the instructor make me do?
- I've never acted.
- I can't act without a script.
- My anxiety will kill me.
- What if I don't know what to say?
- What if I say something stupid?
- What if I offend somebody?
- What if I'm put in an embarrassing situation?
- I'm not good on my feet.
- I'm afraid to talk in front of people.
- No one will be talented.
- Everyone will be talented.

Despite their concerns, these improvisors forged ahead and now say they are happy with their choices. But that could be the brainwashing talking. It's hard to tell the difference.

If you are wondering whether or not improv is for you, so did I. I grew up never wanting anything to do with performance, nor did I have any idea what improv was. I saw one improvised show as an adult after which I though "I bet I could do that," but I didn't think about it again for years.

When I found myself living in Los Angeles, I remembered the murder of comedian Phil Hartman and how, before his industry success, he had performed at a little theatre called the Groundlings. I told a friend I wanted to take classes there. My friend did, I didn't. Only after I got jealous of his experience did I start. It was fun, but as I continued it was also uncomfortable. These weren't my strengths. I wasn't sure it was for me. I was ready to move on to a new interest.

I pondered quitting as I watched the lights go up on the first long form improv show I had ever seen, *The Crazy Uncle Joe Show*. By the end I wanted a part of what those people were doing, and I would go anywhere to get it. That is when I really started.

Your involvement with the Planetwide Improv Community can be a final destination, a curious visit, or one stop in a larger journey. If comedy is your interest, know that improv, sketch, and stand-up form the comedy trifecta. The three inform each other. Starting with one often leads to the next. Some programs even require you to take improv before you write, because they develop sketches through an improvisational process.

Wrap It Up

You are part of an historic and global network of scholars trying to piece together the original thirty-two scrolls on which Thales of Miletus described a single subject with unrivalled elegance. As you navigate the people and institutions on your journey, remember that every authentic scholar in the Planetwide Improv Community shares the same mission: we are all just trying to figure things out . . . and have a good time doing it.

Remember the mission.

28

The Gray

An improvisor must live in a reality before it is fully defined, one filled with potentials and fuzzy elements that float in a haze of not-knowing. This is "the gray."

The gray is most common when the staged reality is first being established but occurs whenever you hold experiences that have yet to form a meaningful whole: whether components of a moment, moments of a scene, scenes of a long form, or chapters of a book.

The unpleasantness of the gray provokes treacherous behaviors or, worse, it seems like a lovely time to panic. Hang on. Like wrestling a waterlogged sail in a lake, wandering through a sandstorm looking for your pyramid home, or figuring out which Charles Darwin you are, you find a way out of the gray one moment at a time.

Recognizing the two paths out of the gray will make your time there less unpleasant, treacherous, and panicky—perhaps even turn it into a curiously fun ride.

The Easy Way

The easy way out feels direct, as if you are on rails—it's so effortless that you suspect you are cheating. Each discovery clarifies in a linear fashion, suggesting the whole. The world is continuously revealed. The feeling "we are making progress" gives confidence.

This path is like a simple sentence. There is increasing security about the reality being made with each word, such as: The black cat with a bell around its neck runs across a thatched roof at dusk.

In a more theatric sense, this path is like revealing a room by pulling back a curtain. As the curtain retreats, we might see a pole with red and white helical stripes, a straight razor, and a barber's chair. Each discovery reflects a larger idea of "barber shop."

The Uneasy Way

The uneasy way feels slow and circling, it can make you think *Am doing something wrong?* We make discoveries, but they don't seem to fit—until they do in a flash. Until that flash, the feeling "I'm screwed" causes doubt.

Words of a sentence can behave similarly; we need to contemplate nearly all of them before a picture emerges, such as: They dance upward, gaseous spheres, to their freedom from this brackish world, their liberating behemoth unaware that his comfortable exhale, while nestled deep in the sediment of a pond, through his hippo-nose grants the escape of these young bubbles.

That's a long way to say: The hippo in a pond blew bubbles out his nose. But discoveries combine like that sometimes, especially when multiple people are expressing them.

In a more theatric sense this path is like a darkened room you illuminate by turning on narrow spotlights, one by one, to reveal disjointed content: a hairbrush, a biohazard bag, a radio. It's not clear how these fit until we see an embalming table. With that, all pieces make sense as elements of a funeral home.

To travel this path, your brain needs time. In some instances, time allows you to keep making discoveries and, like revealing tiles of a mosaic one by one, the meaning will eventually jump out. However, time is also necessary to let meaning emerge from what already exists. The existing information feels sufficient, but your brain hasn't put it together.

Something Other

You have probably heard the sloppy adage "The whole is greater than the sum of the parts," but a tidier adage is "The whole is *other* than the sum of the parts." What emerges can be entirely different than what any individual element suggests. This is not incremental progress to a new state. It is a quantum leap.

In text form—a semicolon and a parenthesis each have their own meaning, but together they create something other than their sum. It can't be explained better than that ;).

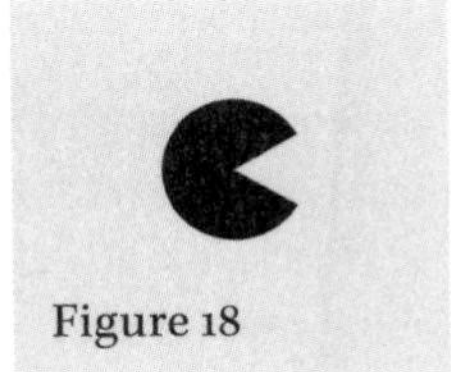

Figure 18

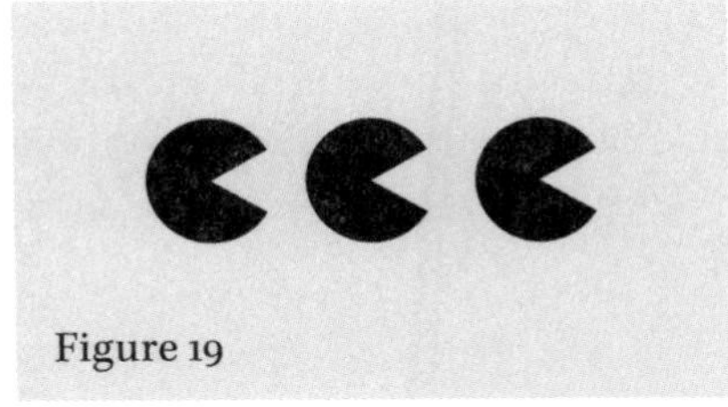

Figure 19

Figure 20

In more graphic form, we can see a Pac-Man walking alone (see figure 18).

And we can see when he is joined by his Pac-Man buddies for a hike (see figure 19).

But when those three Pac-Men turn to argue about where they are, we get something other (see figure 20).

Moments and elements of the staged reality behave similarly, and the relationships between them radically alter what we perceive. An example related to our Pac-Men: if Gary and Claire scream horrible names at each other while sitting on a couch in front of the television, it means one thing; if they scream horrible names at the television while sitting on a couch, it means something else.

(Note: no Pac-Men were harmed in the making of this book.)

Wrap It Up

The gray is living in a reality before it has definition and meaning. Its discomfort can prompt dysfunctional behaviors or panic. An improvisor advances through the fog until clarity is found. Whether your journey through the gray is a quick jaunt or elongated stroll, try to relish the trip—it is the trip you get.

If your time in the gray grows longer than you like, remind yourself you may be on the uneasy path, the adventurous path, the path that demands more time. Keep making your moments with attention and patience, believing that something will emerge, believing that something *must* emerge. And emerge it must.

Never give up.

29

So Long

Charles Darwin stares down into a bowl, empty save for a few Cheerios floating in a shallow pool of milk. He chases them, smiling as they dodge his spoon again and again. *Clever little oats,* he thinks.

He sits at a table in a brightly lit cafeteria. A wall of windows reveals, by day, a rolling lawn bordered in the distance by trees that veil a bay beyond. But on this night the windows are dark. The sky is dark. The campus is dark. The building is dark. Everyone has settled at tables in the center of the cafeteria in this last oasis of light. This is an ending.

Conversations and quips fly. There is the table of aliens, the table of Egyptians, of lumberjacks, of Londoners, of French physicists, of Greek lovers, of dogs, and of cats. Occasionally a soul ventures from their table to make a new friend, greet an old one, or get some frozen yogurt before that magical machine also goes dark.

A sailing instructor wearing a rope belt ambles through the tables stirring his soda with his fingers. In front of the black windows, he finger-combs his hair, approvingly nods to his reflection, and brings the straw to his lips.

He looks past his reflection, into the deep darkness outside. Condensation runs down his cup. With straw clinging to his chapped lips he wonders aloud, "Bud, what happens to us now?" Through the straw he blows bubbles, then takes a sip.

On its upward journey, his beverage stops. He stares out the window, catching a glimpse of—something. *What was that? A light? A spark? Out in the dark? Deep in the black?* His eyes stay fixed on that one spot, waiting.

A dish crashes and the cafeteria erupts in laughter. The clatter of plates and silverware mingles with the shuffling of personal belongings. It is time to go.

His body turns to join the group, but his eyes remain on that spot in the darkness. He lingers and lingers, and lingers, until it is time to go.

Through the window, from outside in the evening, he can be seen breaking his gaze, hurrying to his friends as they make their way to the exit. Soon the cafeteria is empty. Light spills out the windows onto the lawn, stretching to touch ever more distant blades of grass until the light is no more.

Watching from out in the dark, deep in the black, at the edge of the sprawling lawn, in the trees that border it, on a small hill, sitting on a log, is a fox who puffs on a freshly lit pipe.

It is time to go.

Acknowledgments

Science cannot say if there is a heaven, but I am lobbying for some to have preferred seating if there is. These people willingly gave substantial time, thought, and skill during the development of this work, for no other reason than to help. Their interest not only positively affected the book, but positively affected me. I am lucky to know them, and each has my thanks, gratitude, and admiration: Simone Stevens, Joe Rowley, Chase Winton, Kerby Joe Grubb, Brian Palermo, Guy Yosub, Vince De Franco, Chris Doyle, Michael Berry Jr., and Bryan Moses.

A special thanks goes to Jennifer Coolidge for her enthusiasm and commitment to writing the book's foreword during what I know was a very hectic time. I feel fortunate not only for her generosity and honesty, but for the entertaining chats we have had along the way.